The Sixties

Liz –
I thought this might
bring back some
happy memories
of "the good old
days"

Best wishes,
Bev & Peter

Eoin Cameron was born in Mt Gambier, South Australia, in 1951, the second eldest of ten children. He worked in a cheese factory, then as a farm labourer and roustabout in shearing teams in Western Australia's Great Southern, did a stint in a salmon fishing team at Parry's Inlet, and tried (unsuccessfully) to sell used cars in Albany.

At eighteen, he jagged a job as an announcer at Radio 6VA in Albany, where he met his wife Wendy. Eoin and his new family moved to Perth in the seventies, then Melbourne, then Perth again, to pursue his broadcasting career. In the nineties Eoin was elected the Federal Member for Stirling and served two terms in Canberra.

Eoin is still married to Wendy and has three children and four grandchildren. He is currently breakfast presenter on ABC Local Radio in Perth.

In 2003 he published his first book, the highly acclaimed and bestselling *Rolling into the World: Memoirs of a Ratbag Child*.

irreverent
GUIDE

The
Sixties

EOIN CAMERON

Fremantle Arts Centre Press

Australia's finest small publisher

This book is for Miss Wendy Parker,
whom I met just before the sixties were over
and who is now Mrs Wendy Cameron,
and for the three souls who, in the sixties,
weren't even a twinkle in their father's eye,
but soon thereafter graced our lives:
Jane, Ryan and Jacinta.

CONTENTS

Intro The Sixties   11

THE SOUNDTRACK TO THE SIXTIES   19
  Birth of the Backbeat   20
  Heard it on the Radiogram   27
  And the Hits Just Keep on Coming   33
  Just Waving   37
  The Beatles Take No Prisoners   40
  Aural Sex — Elvis in the Sixties   44
  The Brits Blitz the Known World   48
  Love and Understanding, and Other Weird Vibes 54
  1968 — The Summer of Lurv   62
  Where Did You Go to, My Lovely?
    The End of the Era   65
  Woodstock — Three Days of Music, Marijuana
    and Mush   69
  Out of the Garage and into Battle   71
  Lurid-vision Song Contest   75
  The Cream of Brill   77
  Diamond in the Smooth   80
  The Meaningful Moaner   81

GLUED TO THE BOX   83
    When the World Was Black and White   84
    All Set   87
    Tune In, Veg Out, Tuck In   89
    The Big Pull (As Seen on ABC TV)   90
    We Interrupt This Program to Bring You an Ad   95
    Is It Aussie, Is It, Lizzie?   99
    Lip Sync   103
    For Older Groovers   105
    Kartoon Kapers   109

AT THE FLICKS   111
    The LOOK   112
    The Horror of Hammer   114
    No. 007, with a Bullet   117
    Getting Down and Getting Dirty   121
    Smutty Carry On   123
    The Big and Most Gross   125
    The Drives   127
    Jaffas in the Stalls   131

ON THE HOME FRONT   133
    Décor Is Not a Dirty Word   134
    We Have Contact … and Vinyl   136
    In the Engine Room   140
    Mounting and Stuffing with Sophistication   144
    Aussie Barbie (and Ken) — in Apron and Thongs   149
    On Top of Spaghetti   152
    Plonk   154
    Goin' out for Some Fancy Grub   156
    What's Up, Doc?   158

WETTING OURSELVES   161
   Let's Baste Again Like We Did Last Summer   162
   Beach Clobber   165
   Yo Man, Yo   166
   Out of the Way, Dick Dragger, I'm Hangin' Ten   167
   Wet Celluloid   169

IN WITH THE IN CROWD   171
   The Whole Kit and Caboodle   172
   La Springfield   175
   Bodgies and Widgies   176
   'Before I Get Old'   178
   It *Is* Me, Babe   180
   Op In   182
   Hippie, Hippie Fakes   185
   'Girls Will Be Boys and Boys Will Be Girls'   187
   Stop Your Jiving, Babe   189
   Getting into It   192
   Slipping Between the Sheets   194
   Sixties Speak   197

NICE SET OF WHEELS   203
   The People Get Wheels   204
   Accessories after the Fact   211
   Wheels Wheels   214
   Pommy Bricks   217
   Rooty-toots   220
   Yankee Bulldogs   222
   True Blues   224
   They also Ran, Mostly   229

MEATY BEATY BIG AND BOUNCY   235
  The Sport of Kings and Spivs   236
  Revheads   238
  Faster than the Roadrunner   242
  The Adoration of the Boot   244
  Running, Jumping and Everything
      but Standing Still   246
  Flannelled Fools   251
  Biffo   255
  Whacking Balls   258
  (Mostly) Unsung   260

'STOP, HEY, WHAT'S THAT SOUND? EVERYBODY
LOOK WHAT'S GOIN' DOWN'   263
  What a Wonderful World!   264
  Hot and Cold Running Wars — The Sixties
      in a Flash   266
  Nashos and 'Nam   282
  Not Having a Bra of It   285
  Blue Peril   287
  A Change of Note(s)   290
  Icon Sails in Choppy Water   293

THE HITS AND MISSES OF THE SIXTIES   295
  My Top 40 Hit Songs   296
  My Worst 20 Hit Songs   308
  My Top 30 Flicks   313
  My Worst 10 Flicks   318

EPILOGUE AND CLOSE   321
  Born to Run, Babe   322
  The Dearly Departing   330

INTRO THE SIXTIES

US psychologist and all-round weirdo Dr Timothy Leary was reported to have said, 'If you remember the sixties, then you weren't really there.' I remember the sixties very well, and I'm pretty damn sure I was there. When that most interesting decade began I was eight but, to be entirely accurate, I turned nine just four days later, on 4 January 1960, and by New Year's Eve 1969 I was hurtling towards nineteen — it was quite a ride.

Most nine-year-old kids are optimistic, and when I turned nine in the new decade I thought life was pretty good. Second eldest in what was to become a family of ten kids, and with stacks of relatives, there was never any shortage of kids to muck around with, and the times being what they were we were pretty much 'free-range', with the biggest concern of the day being home at mealtimes.

We lived in the south-east of South Australia, in an area mostly concerned in those days with timber milling and farming. It seemed there were pine forests as far as the eye could see — in fact they stretched to, and well across, the Victorian border. Scattered through the forest were areas of farming land, mostly dairy and sheep.

In the sixties 'amalgamation' was not a word often heard, so there were cheese factories scattered throughout the district.

The biggest regional town was Mt Gambier, so at least there were some of the attractions of the big smoke, even if, in reality, the 'Mount' was pretty 'small smoke'.

Little did we know that we were lucky enough to be growing up in the best decade in history. Everyone in our area seemed to know everyone else, and if they didn't they knew someone who did. There was no such thing as wagging school because the local cops knew who you were, and after they'd given you a clip under the ear, they'd deliver you home to cop something more substantial.

The sixties were not without problems, but compared to what went before, and what has come since, they were ten magical years. Ten years which changed the world forever.

In the years before nearly everyone had a TV set, news was gleaned from the radio. And news was the parents' domain.

Seven o'clock at night was 'shush' time. Kids old enough to still be out of bed didn't dare make a squeak as the folks listened to the ABC news — as soon as the 'Majestic Fanfare' theme of the ABC bulletin started, it was shut-up time. The fifteen-minute bulletin seemed interminable.

Translating the news was the grown-ups' responsibility, so naturally enough, in a good Catholic family, there was a definite anti-communist slant, which was reinforced constantly with dark warnings about what would become of us all should the communists take over Australia. The way the grown-ups spoke, that was a very real threat. The reds would soon be actually in our beds.

Increasingly the news was dominated by stories about oppressed people behind the Iron Curtain, stories given even more credence by the fact there were so many migrants working in the mills around our area, migrants who had fled

Europe following the Second World War and, more recently, people who were lucky enough to have escaped from the communist regimes in Eastern Europe. In our street there were people from Hungary who had terrible tales to tell about how people were persecuted, how food was scarce and how everyone was frightened of the brutal regime in their homeland.

As well as the Hungarian family, there were people from Poland, Latvia, Germany, Holland, England, Ireland, France, Greece, Lebanon, Kenya and Fiji whose kids attended our school. It was a mini United Nations, and was a great way to learn about different cultures.

By far the largest single group of migrants in our area was the Italians. During the Second World War there had been a very large prisoner-of-war camp north of Mount Gambier, and this had housed mainly Italian POWs. Apparently they were pretty good prisoners because their hearts hadn't been in the war anyway, and we were told stories of how they would carry the heavy old 303 rifles for the guards who were supposedly guarding them. The prisoners worked in the pine forests of the district, and at war's end, after having been repatriated to Italy, they couldn't get back to Australia fast enough, which for us was a darn good thing.

Since the 1800s, Australia had implemented the so-called White Australia Policy. The policy originated from the goldminers' resentment of hardworking Chinese 'diggers'. The governments of the colonies of New South Wales and Victoria placed restrictions on Chinese immigration, and in Queensland restrictions were subsequently applied to cane field workers brought in from the Pacific Islands, the Kanaka people. When the Queensland authorities thought they may be excluded from the proposed Federation of the colonies, the Kanaka trade ceased. The governing bodies in Victoria and New South Wales warned there would be no place for 'Asiatics' or 'coloureds' in the Australia of the future.

With Federation in 1901, the government passed an act ending the employment of Pacific Islanders. In future any prospective migrants would have to pass a dictation test on arrival, including a written passage of fifty words in a European language chosen at the whim of the authorities. The White Australia Policy was hugely popular with most Australians of the day and in 1919 Prime Minister Billy Hughes described the policy as 'the greatest thing we have achieved.'

During the Second World War, many 'coloured' refugees came to Australia, some of them marrying Australians and, naturally enough, wanting to settle. When the war ended the immigration minister, Arthur Calwell, wanted to deport non-whites, creating something of a kerfuffle. The first crack in the policy began to appear when the then minister, Harold Holt, decided, in 1949, to allow more than eight hundred non-European refugees to stay, and for Japanese war brides to be allowed in. In 1957, non-Europeans who had lived in Australia for fifteen years or more were allowed to become citizens.

The White Australia Policy explained why the overwhelming majority of migrants to Australia immediately following the Second World War were from Europe.

Because of the numbers of Italian immigrants in our area, their influence was soon felt in virtually every aspect of daily life. As well as working in the mills, they established small businesses, restaurants (cafes would be a more accurate description) and market gardens, where they grew vegetables which were sometimes totally alien to born-and-bred Australians.

Through the sixties the Australian diet changed rapidly because of these European, and specifically Italian, influences. Capsicums became common (mostly still just the green variety), eggplants abounded, different varieties of tomatoes were introduced, we started to buy olive oil in two-gallon tins, and the waft of garlic was in the air. Shelves of the corner grocery stores and the first supermarkets stocked pasta, even though we still called it either 'spaghetti' for the long thin stuff, or 'macaroni' for any other shape.

At school we'd swap lunch money with the 'dago' (as any new Australian was called) kids, so that they could buy pies and sauce, while we hoed into their homemade lunch of crunchy bread with salami and tasty cheese. It was a very satisfying trade.

The prime minister, Robert Menzies, who had been prime minister since two years before I was born, was spoken of in respectful tones, and he was the man who knew full well what an evil lot they were in the various communist regimes, with the Russians at the top of the list of bad guys, closely followed by the Chinese. Then came any other country behind the Iron Curtain, with Cuba thrown in for good measure.

My first real recollection of sitting up and taking notice of what Mum and Dad were talking about was the face-off in 1962 between President John F. Kennedy of the United States and Premier Nikita Kruschev of the USSR over the Cuban missile crisis.

I didn't particularly understand what it was all about, but from what I could pick up from grown-up conversation, the Americans had discovered that the Russians were positioning ballistic missiles in Cuba, within easy striking distance of highly populated American centres, and President Kennedy had told them to cut it out. Because President Kennedy was a Catholic, he must have been a good fellow — at least in our house. Mr Kruschev told him to mind his own business, and sent a fleet of ships to take more supplies of a sinister nature to Cuba. President Kennedy said, 'If you don't turn back, we're going to attack the fleet.' This is when we learned that both leaders had their fingers poised 'on the button'. The button, we understood was the one which would start the third world war if pressed, and if there was a third world war, we were all buggered.

Naturally, for a while in October 1962, ours was not the only household in the world a bit on edge. The Russians had proved how advanced they were technologically by their superiority in the so-called 'space race'.

In October 1957 they'd put the first satellite, Sputnik I, into space and, what's more, virtually everyone on earth at the time got to see it by staring skywards at night. Then just a month later, they sent a dog called Laika into space aboard Sputnik II.

When the Russians then completed the trifecta by sending Yuri Gagarin in Vostok I into space in 1961, it was clear they were well ahead of anyone else in terms of rocket development. This fact was not lost on anyone who didn't much fancy the idea of an atomic bomb lobbing into their backyard.

The fact that the south-east of South Australia, and Mount Gambia in particular, was probably not at the top of the list of Soviet strategic targets was a point lost on me at the time.

At the beginning of the sixties, the confusion of the popular music scene of the previous decade had yet to coalesce into something with enough identifiable form and style to get billed 'the Swinging Sixties'. What popular music charts there were consisted of a mishmash of ballads, saccharine romance, light jazz, swing that was pretty much swung out, hillbilly country and a peculiarly sanitised form of rock-and-roll that owed everything to it's black rhythm and blues roots, but lacked the confidence to 'let it all hang out'. Come to think of it, that's a phrase which hadn't existed before the sixties.

The clearest way imaginable to check out how popular music changed so dramatically in so few years is to trawl through the list of best-selling records from 1956 to 1959, when Australia first started publishing music charts. Although, no teenager from the sixties had to check out those charts, all they had to do was look in the record bins of their folks' radiogram. Among the 'treasures' there within they'd be sure to find at least some, if not all of the following: 'The Yellow Rose of Texas' by Mitch Miller and the Singalong Gang, 'Whatever Will Be Will Be' by Doris Day, 'Hot Diggity' (Dog Diggity Boom) by Perry Como, 'A White Sport Coat' (and a Pink Carnation) by Marty Robbins, 'Love Letters in the Sand' by Pat Boone, 'Young Love' by Tab Hunter, 'Wonderful, Wonderful' by Johnny Mathis, 'Memories Are Made of This' by Dean Martin, 'The Great Pretender' by the Platters, 'He's Got the Whole World in His Hands' by Laurie London, (Now and Then There's) 'A Fool Such As I' by Elvis Presley and 'A Pub with No Beer' by Slim Dusty. Apart from the fact all these songs were popular in the late fifties, they *all* reached number one on the Top 40.

The movies of the sixties were at least a constant. They were as eclectic as movies had always been, and we were enthralled as the studios churned out a seemingly endless stream of B-grade westerns, contemporary dramas, biblical extravaganzas, lavish musicals and the occasional blockbuster James Bond and copycat spy movies — not to mention the twenty-seven films that Elvis made in that decade, the names of which every 'boomer' will at least recognise.

Japan was enjoying its postwar economic 'miracle', and we were beginning to be flooded with everything Japanese: from watches and transistor radios (trannies) to TV sets and Nissan Bluebirds, Glorias and Cedrics.

Australia's own car industry was going through an interesting evolution, too. For a time we couldn't work out whether we were Arthur or Martha — the Australian car, the Holden in its various guises of the fifties, started out looking like a Pommy family saloon and even gave a nod, albeit a very timid one, in the direction of Detroit with the Yankee excesses of chrome flashings and fins — although in the Holden's case, the fins were more 'finettes'. The sixties would introduce the 'Coke bottle' look, and that's what we went for, with the odd aberration of some funky metal like the R and S series Valiants, and the 'land crab' Austin 1800.

The miniskirt arrived with a gasp of horror when Jean Shrimpton traumatised the Toorak Road set by wearing what was later to prove to have been a very modest mini to Flemington during the lead-up to the Melbourne Cup. J F K was killed in Dallas, and we all knew precisely what we were doing when we got the news. Marilyn was found dead 'in the nude', and Neil Armstrong made 'one giant leap for mankind'. The so-called free love and peace movements arrived on a cloud of strange-smelling smoke, and many opted out under an avalanche of mind-altering hallucinogens. Perhaps the entire sixties *was* an hallucination.

THE SOUNDTRACK
TO THE SIXTIES

BIRTH OF THE BACKBEAT

From the early sixties, the popular music scene began to take on its own identity, rather than being the amorphous mess of the fifties popular music charts. The kids started to take certain styles, in particular rhythm and blues and its progeny, rock-and-roll, and make them something of their own.

The legendary American muso Muddy Waters is reputed to have said, 'The Blues had a baby and they called it Rock and Roll.'

The baby boomers who began proliferating at the end of the Second World War were starting to gain some independence as they entered their teenage years, and they grasped it with a vengeance. They had music which was (almost) their own, clothes which set them apart, and attitude with a capital 'A'. It was either thrilling or terrifying, depending upon which age group you slotted into.

Bill Haley and the Comets first brought their sanitised version of rock-and-roll music to the white masses with the smash hit 'Rock around the Clock', which featured in the fifties flick, *The Blackboard Jungle*. Black Americans had been rocking and rolling for years, they just didn't know it was called that.

The Blackboard Jungle also spawned a certain 'look' for young people: tight jeans, T-shirts and hair slicked back at the sides for boys, or 'bodgies' for the more radical looking, and tight sweater tops, wide glossy belts and 'sway' dresses for the girls or 'widgies', as the hard core were called. Any self-respecting town had their bodgies and widgies, although the bigger the town the greater the prevalence of the species.

The Brits had their version of the bodgie, called teddy boys, pretty similar to the Aussie version but generally spivvier.

Cliff Richard in his early career looked like a mild teddy boy, as did other Brit stars like Adam Faith and Billy J Kramer. Cliff was one artist who managed to carry his career into the sixties and continue to thrive by adapting to the changing musical styles, but never venturing too far from accessible pop. Cliff even managed to sport a sedate Beatle haircut when the Beatles were popular.

Other performers, solo artists and groups were far edgier, and these were the people who would wield most influence and change popular music forever.

In the US looks mattered far more than musical ability, so a gaggle of almost interchangeable pop stars sprang up who were drop-dead gorgeous to look at, but who couldn't sing or act, as we found out when they appeared in 'teen' movies. Fabian, Frankie Avalon, Paul Anka and Ricky Nelson were among the main offenders, although to be fair to Ricky Nelson he could sing a bit *and* act a bit.

As far as pop music went, the Yanks had it all over the Poms in the fifties, mainly because of the thriving (if still not mainstream) black rhythm and blues scene. However it wasn't too far into the new decade when the tables were turned. The so-called 'British Invasion' left the Americans shell shocked, and it took them some years to recover and attempt a catch up.

In Australia we sort of limped along with local acts copying overseas artists as best they could. Some of them made a fair fist of it, but frankly most of them were pretty bloody awful.

Australian radio stations had dipped their toes tentatively into the tepid waters of popular music, although it wasn't until the sixties were underway that programmers and advertisers alike recognised the enormousness of the burgeoning youth market, or the baby boomers, before they were called that.

Top 40 radio stations sprang up in all Australia's major centres, although in the country the stations would often dedicate an hour or so at night for a countdown of the popular songs of the time. If you tuned in to a countdown of the Top 10 songs in 1960 you'd hear, not necessarily in the following order:

'Are You Lonesome Tonight?' — Elvis Presley
'It's Now or Never' — Elvis Presley
'Little Boy Lost' — Johnny Ashcroft
'My Old Man's a Dustman' — Lonnie Donegan
'Tie Me Kangaroo Down Sport' — Rolf Harris
'Save the Last Dance for Me' — The Drifters
'Walk Don't Run' — The Ventures
'Boom Boom Baby' — Crash Craddock
'She's My Baby' — Johnny O'Keefe
'Running Bear' — Johnny Preston

The evolution of popular music in the sixties is probably best illustrated by looking at a Top 10 countdown for the rest of the decade, the most radical shift occurring around the middle sixties, with a dramatic downturn in the number of novelty or ballad-type songs which had dominated through the fifties and very early sixties.

1961
'Runaway' — Del Shannon
'Wooden Heart' — Elvis Presley
'I'm Counting on You' — Johnny O'Keefe
'I'm Gonna Knock on Your Door' — Eddie Hodges
'My Boomerang Won't Come Back' — Charlie Drake
'Crying'/'Candy Man' — Roy Orbison
'Milord' — Edith Piaf
'Rubber Ball' — Bobby Vee
'Surrender' — Elvis Presley
'Travellin' Man' — Ricky Nelson

1962
'The Lonely Bull' — The Tijuana Brass
'Can't Help Falling in Love' — Elvis Presley
'I've Been Everywhere' — Lucky Starr
'Silver Threads and Golden Needles' — The Springfields
'Working for The Man' — Roy Orbison
'Si Senor (I Theenk)' — Rob E G
'The Wanderer' — Dion
'Multiplication' — Bobby Darin
'Good Luck Charm' — Elvis Presley
'Sheila' — Tommy Roe

1963
'Pipeline' — The Chantays
'Tamoure' — Bill Justis Orchestra
'The Boys' — The Shadows
'Bombora' — The Atlantics

'From a Jack to a King' — Ned Miller
'Move Baby Move' — Johnny O'Keefe
'Do You Love Me?' — Brian Poole and the Tremeloes
'Not Responsible' — Helen Shapiro
'Blue Bayou' — Roy Orbison
'Then He Kissed Me' — The Crystals

1964

'I Saw Her Standing There'/'Love Me Do' — The Beatles
'I Feel Fine'/'She's a Woman' –The Beatles
'I Want to Hold Your Hand' — The Beatles
'All My Loving' — The Beatles
'A Hard Day's Night' — The Beatles
'I Should Have Known Better'/'If I Fell' — The Beatles
'You're My World' — Cilla Black
'She's a Mod' — Ray Columbus and the Invaders
'Leader of the Pack' — The Shangri-Las
'Poison Ivy' — Bill Thorpe and the Aztecs

1965

'Que Sera Sera'/'Shakin' All Over' — Normie Rowe and
the Playboys
'Rock and Roll Music'/'Honey Don't' — The Beatles
'Mrs Brown, You've Got a Lovely Daughter' — Herman's
Hermits
'I'll Never Find Another You' — The Seekers
'Help' — The Beatles
'A Walk in the Black Forest' — Horst Jankowski
'Ticket to Ride' — The Beatles
'Il Silenzio' — Nini Rosso
'Under the Boardwalk'/'Walking the Dog' — The Rolling
Stones

'The Carnival is Over' — The Seekers

1966
'We Can Work It Out'/'Daytripper' — The Beatles
'These Boots Are Made for Walkin'' — Nancy Sinatra
'Yellow Submarine'/'Eleanor Rigby' — The Beatles
'Friday on My Mind' — The Easybeats
'Strangers in the Night' — Frank Sinatra
'Step Back'/'Cara Lyn' — Johnny Young
'Born Free' — Matt Monro
'Too Much'/'I'll Make You Happy' — The Easybeats
'Nowhere Man'/'Norwegian Wood' — The Beatles
'Hitch Hiker' — Bobby and Laurie

1967
'The Last Waltz' — Engelbert Humperdinck
'Snoopy versus the Red Baron' — The Royal Guardsmen
'This is My Song' — Harry Secombe/Petula Clark
'All You Need is Love'/'Baby You're a Rich Man' — The Beatles
'Itchycoo Park' — The Small Faces
'Up Up and Away' — The 5th Dimension
'A Whiter Shade of Pale' — Procol Harum
'Penny Lane'/'Strawberry Fields Forever' — The Beatles
'Snoopy's Xmas' — The Royal Guardsmen
'The Green Green Grass of Home' — Tom Jones

1968
'Hey Jude'/'Revolution' — The Beatles
'MacArthur Park' — Richard Harris
'Sadie (the Cleaning Lady)' — Johnny Farnham
'Love is Blue' — Paul Mauriat

'You Keep Me Hanging On' — Vanilla Fudge
'This Guy's in Love with You' — Herb Alpert and the
    Tijuana Brass
'Honey' — Bobby Goldsboro
'Lady Madonna' — The Beatles
'The Unicorn' — The Irish Rovers
'Hello Goodbye'/'I am the Walrus' — The Beatles

1969
'Star Crossed Lovers' — Neil Sedaka
'Where Do You Go to (My Lovely)?' — Peter Sarstedt
'Ob-La-Di, Ob-La-Da'/'While My Guitar Gently Weeps'
    — The Beatles
'Get Back'/'Don't Let Me Down' — The Beatles
'Honky Tonk Women'/'You Can't Always Get What You
    Want' — The Rolling Stones
'Something'/'Come Together' — The Beatles
'The Ballad of John and Yoko' — The Beatles
'Penny Arcade' — Roy Orbison
'Part Three into Paper Walls'/'The Girl That I Love' —
    Russell Morris
'The Real Thing Parts 1 and 2' — Russell Morris

HEARD IT ON THE RADIOGRAM

There was always music in our house. No one played a musical instrument but my mum and dad were big radio listeners, and because the fifties saw them in their twenties and early thirties, they were pretty much into popular music stations, or what were to evolve into the Top 40 stations, as the popular broadcasters became known.

I'm not all that convinced about their musical tastes, though. An enduring memory is of my dad wandering around the place, or driving along in the car whistling such memorable numbers as 'When the Red Red Robin Comes Bob Bob Bobbing Along' or 'The Yellow Rose of Texas', which had been a huge hit in the mid-fifties for Mitch Miller and the Singalong Gang, the latter translated much better to Dad's whistling because a couple of times during the song there are some piccolo breaks, and a piccolo is probably the instrument which most closely approximates a human whistle. In Dad's case, 'approximate' was the operative word.

Things took a turn for the better in the late fifties when we got a brand new Philips radiogram. It had a massive speaker behind some pretty elaborate stained timber and cloth grille work on the front, with doors on either side to store records. To begin with, these were mostly 78s, but as the years crept by microgroove became the go and the old

78s disappeared, seemingly overnight, to be replaced by single 45s and long-playing 33⅓ discs.

Our 78 collection consisted of about two dozen discs given to us by an aunt, mainly what we considered olden-days stuff by people like Hank Snow, Slim Dusty and that 'other' Slim, Whitman. I'd never seen Slim Whitman so I couldn't comment on him, but I had seen pictures of Slim Dusty, and even back then he didn't seem all that slim to me.

The 78s I liked best were by a woman who actually toured Australia and eventually settled here. She was a black pianist called Winifred Atwell, and she could really tickle the ivories. My favourite record of hers was something called 'Black and White Rag'.

The working bits of the radiogram were really something, because you pushed the top of the cabinet towards the rear, and as you did so the front came down on chrome hinges to form a shelf where you could stack records before and after you played them.

The outside of the cabinet was a rich mahogany colour, and the inside was lined with mega-trendy blondwood. To the left-hand side was the felt-covered turntable. It had a small centre spindle for single plays, and a taller spindle you placed over that for stacking records.

The ability to stack records indicated your player was state-of-the-art, and was a feature to be shown off with more than a little pride. The fact the stacker often malfunctioned and dropped two or three records onto the turntable at a time was a minor inconvenience, given the brag value.

A lever to one side of the turntable was the ejector which was also something of a feature; if you'd heard a bit too much of Slim Whitman in his too-tight underpants wailing

away in the 'Indian Love Call' — 'When I'm calling you ...
ooo ... ooo ... ooo ... ooo' — one flick of the ejector lever
and Slim left the stage.

Other knobs covered the operation of the turntable's
speed.

The right-hand side of the radiogram was taken up with
the radio itself, with bands descending down the glass screen
to indicate the radio stations in each of the states of Australia
— for example all the stations in Victoria had 3 in front of
their call letters, ie. 3DB, 3AK etc. South Australia was 5,
Western Australia 6, and so on. All the stations were on the
AM band, because in the sixties FM, or frequency
modulation, hadn't been heard of.

In very tiny red print, alongside the stations in larger
centres, were the names of the towns. The screen was pretty
busy, and your eyesight needed to be spot on to tune in to
the station you were looking for.

If you lived in the country, as we did, you also needed a
very large aerial, usually a long piece of wire strung out the
nearest window and up onto the roof.

Because our Philips was the bells and whistles version it
also had a short-wave tuner, which didn't get used very much
unless we played with it to hear the BBC with their posh
Pommy voices, or the *Voice of America*. During the Vietnam
War you could tune in to hear a Vietnamese woman with
rather poor English describing us Australians as 'America's
running dogs'.

Before everyone had a TV set, radio serials were extremely
popular, from the kids' serials played after school, like
Biggles, *Hop Harrigan* and *Ginger Meggs*, to the various clubs
the different radio stations had for their young listeners.

The most famous kids' club was the ABC's Argonauts,

and those who joined got ridiculous names and took the pledge:

> *Before the sun and the night and the blue sea, I vow to*
> *stand faithfully by all that is brave and beautiful, to seek*
> *adventure, and having discovered aught of wonder, or*
> *delight, of merriment or loveliness, to share it freely with*
> *my comrades, the Band of Happy Rowers.*

The ABC also led the charge with kids' educational programs, and there were few Australian primary school students of the fifties and sixties who didn't gather around the classroom radio to listen to *Let's Join In*.

In the early evening, about the time many people sat down to dinner, there were popular Australian serials like *Dad and Dave* and *Life with Dexter*, which starred Willie Fennell and followed the day-to-day misadventures of Australia's own Dagwood Bumstead, the character Dexter Dutton.

More serious radio plays and serials were on later in the evening, and daytime was the domain of the soaps, among the most popular *Portia Faces Life*, *When a Girl Marries* — 'To all those who are in love, and to all those who can remember' — and, of course, the biggest one of all, the ABC's long-running serial, *Blue Hills*, which began on radio as *The Lawsons* in 1944 and ran an amazing thirty-two years.

Because technology was beginning to change rapidly, radiograms were soon replaced by the latest big thing, stereograms. And it was all pretty galling to think our pride and joy was suddenly out of date. We soon overcame that, though, with the addition of a 'stereophonic head', which contained a different type of needle and supposedly changed your radiogram into a stereogram. This, of course, was complete bullshit, but a scathingly brilliant marketing ploy by the companies involved.

The arrival of microgroove 45 and 33⅓ records coincided almost precisely with the groundswell in popular music. By the end of the fifties, the 78 was gone, and rock-and-roll was king.

Certain artists never changed or even modified the style that had made them famous; like the Platters, who remained true to their lush arrangements and beautiful melodies, and endured. We had two of their most popular singles — 'Twilight Time' and 'Smoke Gets in Your Eyes'.

I'm not sure what other black artists thought of them, but it seemed they'd been very carefully packaged so as not to scare the horses, and to appeal to as large an audience as possible. My parents thought the Platters were 'lovely'. Mind you, in the same instance, they also had records by Bill Haley and the Comets, 'Rock around the Clock' and 'See You Later Alligator'; Chuck Berry's 'You Never Can Tell'; and 'But I Do' by Clarence 'Frogman' Henry.

As the sixties dawned, they were clearly not as far over the hill, musically speaking, as I might have thought, even though I always referred to any time more than five years previous as 'the olden days'. The real test of any parent's coolness was just around the corner, and manifested itself as those four 'long-haired gits' from Liverpool.

Because adults were in charge of most radios, something had to give to get the music to the kids. So-called crystal sets were a feature of just about every boy's bedroom in the fifties, but even with the more elaborate sets, the sound was weak and barely adequate for appreciating music at any level.

The Japanese came to the rescue. In the economic miracle which took place in the decade following the war, the Japanese flooded the world with stuff they were able to mass-produce. Most people thought of it as cheap junk, but they were at the forefront of the development of transistors.

Transistors meant that suddenly radios, which were cumbersome and heavy in the most part because they were weighed down with outmoded valve technology, could be made much more compact, and would weigh only a fraction of their bakelite and timber ancestors.

Kids all over the world were suddenly getting to control the radio, their *own* radio. In our house it was in the form of my older brother's red plastic HMV transistor radio. It was powered by a battery half the size of a house brick, which lasted no time at all and was bloody expensive, but who cares, we could listen to pop music all day (or until the battery went flat) if we wanted to.

AND THE HITS JUST KEEP ON COMING

In 1960, at the turn of the decade, the big hits were hardly subversive and shouldn't have panicked too many parents. The biggest songs that year were 'Running Bear' by Johnny Preston, 'What Do You Want to Make Those Eyes at Me For?' by Emil Ford and the Checkmates, 'Handy Man' by Jimmy Jones, 'What in the World's Come Over You?' by Jack Scott, 'Little Boy Lost' by Johnny Ashcroft, 'My Old Man's a Dustman' by Lonnie Donegan, 'Tie Me Kangaroo Down Sport' by Rolf Harris, 'What a Mouth' (What a North and South) by Tommy Steele (in one country town I heard about, there was a big scandal when some high school kids sent this song as a cheerio over the radio to the town gossip), 'Just a Closer Walk with Thee' by Jimmie Rodgers, 'Everybody's Somebody's Fool' by Connie Francis, 'Itsy Bitsy Teeny Weeny Yellow Polka Dot Bikini' by Brian Hyland, 'Walk, Don't Run' by the Ventures, 'It's Now or Never' and 'Are You Lonesome Tonight?' both from Elvis Presley, and 'Save the Last Dance for Me' from the Drifters.

All these songs made it to number one on the Australian charts, and there was nothing scary among them, unless you listen too closely to the lyrics of 'Tie Me Kangaroo Down Sport'. There was, however, one other song which made it to the coveted number one position, and that was by an Australian bloke who would give parents a lot to worry about in the next few years. He became known as 'the Wild One'. Johnny O'Keefe hit the top with the rockingest number one of the year, 'She's My Baby'.

If Johnny O'Keefe was the scariest teen act of 1960, he must have given parents some breathing space in 1961, when his love song, 'I'm Counting on You', went to number one. In fact in popular music terms the Wild One could easily have been the Mild One. In retrospect he wasn't at all outlandish, but in his day, J O'K represented every parent's nightmare as the type of boy their daughters might bring home.

Mild might also describe those early popular music charts. Among the really big hit songs that year were 'Milord' by Edith Piaf, 'When the Girl in Your Arms Is the Girl in Your Heart' by Cliff Richard, 'Crying' by Roy Orbison, 'Travellin' Man' by Ricky Nelson, 'A Scottish Soldier' by Andy Stewart, 'Runaway' by Del Shannon, 'Rubber Ball' by Bobby Vee, and 'One Last Kiss' by Crash Craddock. And, of course, the ubiquitous Elvis, who topped the charts twice in twelve months with 'Surrender' and 'Wooden Heart'.

The only chart topper of 1961 that might even loosely fit the category of rock-and-roll came just before Christmas when the Sandy Nelson instrumental, 'Let There be Drums', hit number one.

At last 1962 saw a genuine shift in the style of music which had dominated the Top 40 charts for so long. The gimmick songs were still there, the ballads were still there, but even some mainstream artists started to deliver a little more grit and freneticism in their style. Among the vanguard were Dion with 'The Wanderer', Elvis's 'Good Luck Charm', 'Do You Wanna Dance?' and 'The Young Ones' from Cliff and the Shadows, 'Working for the Man' by Roy Orbison,

'Sheila' by Tommy Roe and 'Big Girls Don't Cry' from the Four Seasons.

There was still plenty to make the olds wrestle back control of the radio, though, with big hits like the piano tune, 'Alley Cat' by Bent Fabric, and the hit which began a phenomenal run for Herb Alpert and the Tijuana Brass, 'The Lonely Bull'.

In the novelty category, Aussie Lucky Starr hit the jackpot with 'I've Been Everywhere', and Mike Sarne, with an uncredited Wendy Richards, had 'Come Outside'; Wendy went on to play Miss Brahms in the British comedy, *Are You Being Served?*

Songs from '62 to be avoided at all costs were James Darren singing 'Gidget Goes Hawaiian' and Richard Chamberlain proving he couldn't sing when he recorded the theme from the hit TV series in which he starred, *Dr Kildare*. The resulting atrocity was called 'Three Stars Will Shine Tonight' — a pretty theme slaughtered.

The highlight of the year for me was when I first heard the voice of a girl called Dusty. Dusty, with her brother Tom Springfield and friend Tim Field, topped the Australian charts as the Springfields with 'Silver Threads and Golden Needles'.

The era of protest songs certainly hadn't started in '62, yet an overtly political song stopped the charts when Toni Fisher hit number one with a song called 'West of the Wall'. As the title suggests, the song was about the erection of the Berlin Wall.

The Wall had been erected virtually overnight in August 1961. While citizens of Berlin were mostly asleep, the East German government closed its borders and began to lay out fences and entanglements of barbed wire. Within months a massive concrete and stone wall had sprung up.

People began escaping over the wall from East Berlin in search of a better life in the West, so in early 1962 another wall was built to make the barrier more secure. The tension between East and West at the time was incredible, and the Berlin Wall dominated news bulletins and newsreels for months on end.

In 1963, when US President John F Kennedy visited Berlin, he made his famous Wall speech which ended with the words:

Freedom is indivisible, and when one man is enslaved, all are not free. When all are free, then we can look forward to that day when this city will be joined as one and this country and this great Continent of Europe in a peaceful and hopeful globe. When that day finally comes, as it will, the people of West Berlin can take sober satisfaction in the fact that they were in the front lines for almost two decades. All free men, wherever they may live, are citizens of Berlin, and therefore, as a free man, I take pride in the words Ich bin ein Berliner *(I am a Berliner).*

Before the year was out, JFK was shot dead in Dallas, and it would be another twenty-six years before the Berlin Wall was finally torn down.

JUST WAVING

1963 was the year the big waves washed over Australia. For the first time it was kids' music which dominated the charts, and it didn't come from the expected direction of rock-and-roll, it came from the beach or, more precisely the surf.

Number one hits included 'Surfside' by Digger Revell's Denvermen, 'Pipeline' by the Chantays, 'Surf City' by Jan and Dean, 'Wipeout' by the Surfaris, and 'Bombora' by the Atlantics. Little Pattie almost made it to the top but stalled at number two with her double-sided hit 'Stompin' at the Maroubra'/'He's My Blond Headed, Stompie Wompie, Real Gone Surfer Boy'.

Perhaps the most remarkable hit of '63 was Kyu Sakamoto's 'Sukiyaki', sung in Japanese. The song's real title, 'Ueo Muite Arukou', would have ensured it never got airplay, but some smart cookie decided 'Sukiyaki' was one of the very few Japanese words that western DJs could handle.

The inexorable rock-and-roll march continued with big hits like 'Tell Him' by the Exciters, 'Ruby Baby' by Dion, 'How Do You Do It?' by Gerry and the Pacemakers and 'And Then He Kissed Me' by the Crystals.

None of this meant we'd lost our taste for novelty songs, because '63 saw the release of Sheb Wooley's 'Hootenanny

Hoot', 'Hello Mudduh, Hello Fadduh' from Allan Sherman and 'On Top of Spaghetti' by Tom Glazer.

The real excitement on the music scene in 1963 was caused by the Fab Four, though at this stage they were not quite fab. In September they reached number three on the national charts with 'She Loves You', then just before Christmas the surf wave which had started the year turned into the Merseybeat tidal wave when 'I Wanna Hold Your Hand' swept all before it to top the charts.

Every Top 40 radio station in Australia jumped aboard the Beatle wave and rode it for all it was worth. In fact, because of the enormous excitement and publicity they'd created in Britain and Europe, the Beatles were famous in Australia before their music had even been heard here, thanks to the popularity of fan magazines or 'fanzines'.

Any serious observer would no doubt agree that in Australia the music world changed over the summer of 1963–64. During the Christmas holidays, the Beatles were horrifying parents all over the country with their number one hit 'I Want to Hold Your Hand'. The release of 'I Want to Hold Your Hand' was an event of national significance, at least for the younger portion of the population, and every self-respecting teenager in the country had a spotty ear glued to the tranny.

Parents pretty much wrote the Fab Four off as 'those long-haired gits', or with 'they can't sing, otherwise why would they go on with all that yeah, yeah, yeah nonsense?'

But we could hear what the Beatles were singing about, and we loved what we heard. And, at least in those early days, there was nothing remotely subversive or sinister about their songs, they were basically fairly straightforward and simple little love songs, delivered in a way that no one had before.

The pop ship entered somewhat murkier waters in the first week of 1964 when Roy Orbison's Christmas hit 'Pretty Paper' displaced the Beatles, but the tide had at last turned, and what the Americans described as the British Invasion was about to sweep over Australia as well.

THE BEATLES TAKE NO PRISONERS

The Beatles directed the British Invasion and led by example. Their hits just kept on coming: 'I Saw Her Standing There', 'Twist and Shout', 'Roll over Beethoven', 'All My Loving', 'Can't Buy Me Love', 'Please Please Me', 'Boys', 'A Hard Day's Night', 'I Should Have Known Better', 'I Feel Fine', 'She's a Woman'.

The Beatles made their only tour of Australia in 1964, immediately after they'd finished filming *A Hard Day's Night*. If you thought the movie was frenetic, with the Fab Four being chased all over the place by screaming fans, the tour was even more so.

The only cloud over the visit as far as the Beatlemaniacs were concerned was that for the early part of the tour Ringo had to stay at home in London to recover from a bronchial infection he'd contracted during the filming of *A Hard Day's Night*.

Coming in from Hong Kong, their BOAC 707 touched down at Darwin at about a quarter to three on the morning of 11 June and hundreds of screaming fans were waiting at the airport to catch a glimpse of them.

After refuelling, their flight continued onto Sydney, arriving at around a quarter to eight in the morning. Sydney was experiencing one of its torrential downpours, as only Sydney knows how. It was bucketing down, and the Beatles got soaked to the skin, despite the fact they were clutching TAA umbrellas as they paraded before thousands of fans.

In the days before heavily focused targeted marketing, the umbrellas with the Australian airline logo was suddenly became familiar all around the world because of the enormous print media, TV and newsreel coverage the Beatles' tour was receiving.

Ringo's replacement was a drummer called Jimmy Nicol. He wasn't paid much attention because he wasn't a 'real' Beatle, and he didn't look like a Beatle. Despite the fact he dressed the same as John, Paul and George, his hair was way too short, even if he did attempt to brush it forward like the mop tops.

Jimmy quietly flew out of Australia with the Beatles manager, Brian Epstein, when Ringo had recovered sufficiently to join the tour in Melbourne. At last the Ringo fans got to see their man.

The Beatles had already developed a reputation around the world for their cheeky sense of humour, and press conferences were often hilarious comedy shows with one-liners flying thick and fast. John Lennon proved to be particularly quick witted. At their first press conference in Sydney, a journalist asked them, 'What do you expect to find in Australia' to which Lennon replied, 'Australians.'

Their offbeat humour set the tone for what was to be a memorable, if brief, tour.

Everyone had their favourite Beatle: John was the funny one, Paul the pretty one, George the serious one, and Ringo was considered cute, although in reality he was as ugly as buggery.

The first of their four performances in Australia was to be in Adelaide. On 12 June they landed at Adelaide airport, and the largest crowd ever gathered in South Australia before or since, an estimated 350,000 people, turned out to line the route from the airport to the city.

They did two shows at Centennial Hall, one at 6 pm followed by another at 8 pm, each show virtually identical to the ones they'd been performing during the rest of their international tour. In a tight set they belted out 'I Want to Hold Your Hand', 'All My Lovin'', 'She Loves You', 'Long Tall Sally', 'Til There was You', 'Can't Buy Me Love', 'I Saw Her Standing There', 'Roll over Beethoven', and to make sure that every single hysterical fan in the audience went completely over the top, 'Twist and Shout'.

From the TV news reports of the Beatles' concerts, it was pretty tricky working out whether they were singing or not. They *looked* like they were singing, but for all I knew their guitars might not have even been plugged in. You couldn't hear anything except girls screaming. It was one constant screech, punctuated every so often by an increase in intensity every time John or Paul wiggled his bum.

Parents were now seriously alarmed.

On Saturday 13 June, they did two further concerts, same time same venue. Living in the country, we didn't get a chance to see the Beatles live, and being only thirteen at the time, I wouldn't have been allowed to go anyway. There was a bonus in that we did get to hear a bit of the concert broadcast on the radio.

Actually for all you could hear it might have been a local rock-and-roll band playing, because nothing of a musical nature could be heard above the screaming.

In Melbourne, the Beatles did six shows over three nights at the Festival Hall. The media scrutiny was intense, though George did manage to slip away briefly to take a spin in an MG that someone had lent him.

On Thursday 18 June, the Beatles returned to Sydney to give a further six shows over three nights at the Sydney Stadium. The brevity of their performances was underlined by the fact that a local newspaper threw a birthday party for Paul at 9.30 that evening, after their 8 pm show.

Ten thousand girls had entered a competition run by the paper to win an invitation to the party, and a dozen or so were selected, but, apart from reports that Ringo got horribly pissed, according to the hangers-on and those in the know, there was no hard evidence of any hanky-panky.

After a week touring New Zealand, the Beatles flew back to Brisbane, again to the same hysterical welcome from thousands of fans. Two more shows over two nights at the Festival Hall and it was over.

When pressed by journalists about their Australian tour, an exhausted John Lennon said simply, 'It was good.' The Beatles' tour of Australia was the most successful of their brief career, not bad going for a country of only eleven million people.

AURAL SEX — ELVIS IN THE SIXTIES

It was the established American acts that suffered most as a result of the Beatles and the British wave, even 'the king', Elvis Presley, had his wings clipped slightly in 1964, scoring a hit with the double sider 'Ask Me'/'Ain't That Lovin' You Baby', and not quite making the top with: 'Viva Las Vegas' and 'Kissin' Cousins', the title tracks from a couple of Elvis' movies, and a song called 'Such a Night'.

A look at the enormous catalogue of songs which Elvis put out through the sixties is quite astounding. No fewer than thirty-six Elvis singles made the Australian charts, and twenty-six of them made the Top 10, nine to number one. They were: 'It's Now or Never', 'Are You Lonesome Tonight?', 'Wooden Heart', 'Surrender', 'Can't Help Falling in Love', 'Good Luck Charm', 'Ain't That Loving You Baby', 'Crying in the Chapel' and 'In the Ghetto'.

It was really a cause of wonder that Elvis ever managed to get near a recording studio given the number of movies he churned out, some of them not half bad and some fairly excruciating — still, they were popular with the kids, and the Elvis filmography clearly indicates the popular attractions on the silver screen during the late fifties and sixties.

Elvis was an instant big screen star when, in 1956, he headlined in 'Love Me Tender'; then the Hollywood juggernaut began to roll. And, to be fair, although not Marlon Brando, he was a reasonable actor. Certainly there were and still are worse actors among the pop stars who have tried the switch to the silver screen.

1957
Loving You
Jailhouse Rock

1958
King Creole

1960
GI Blues
Flaming Star

1961
Wild in the Country
Blue Hawaii

1962
Follow that Dream
Kid Galahad
Girls Girls Girls

1963
It Happened at the World's Fair
Fun in Acapulco

1964
Kissin' Cousins
Viva Las Vegas

Roustabout

1965
Girl Happy
Harum Scarum
Tickle Me

1966
Frankie and Johnny
Paradise Hawaiian Style
Spinout

1967
Double Trouble
Easy Come Easy Go
Clambake

1968
Stay Away Joe
Speedway
Live a Little Love a Little

1969
Charro
The Trouble with Girls
Change of Habit

When you look at the workload that Elvis (or his manager) took on, it's no wonder the poor bugger slipped off the perch too young.

There were some compensations, though. Throughout his film career, Elvis starred with hundreds of the loveliest starlets and actresses of the time, among them Carolyn Jones, Juliet Prowse (whose legs went on forever), Barbara Eden, Tuesday Weld, Hope Lange, Stella Stevens, Ursula Andress, Teri Garr, Ann-Margret, Barbara Stanwyck, Raquel Welch, Shelley Fabares, Mary Ann Mobley, Donna Douglas, Nancy Sinatra (who later stated that Elvis was among the most polite and naturally funny people she'd ever met), Sheree North, Barbara McNair and Mary Tyler Moore.

By comparison, the Beatles, movies, *Help!*, *A Hard Day's Night* and *Yellow Submarine*, seem almost sparse, yet each was a huge success in its own right.

THE BRITS BLITZ THE KNOWN WORLD

Having decided to go solo, after a couple of folkie hits and enormous success with the Springfields, Dusty Springfield cemented her position as Britain's pre-eminent female artist by charting in quick succession with 'I Only Want to be with You', 'Stay Awhile', 'Wishin' and Hopin'', 'I Just Don't Know What to Do with Myself' and 'All Cried Out'.

Another British female star, Cilla Black, under the mentorship of John Lennon, hit the charts in '64 with 'You're My World' and 'It's for You'. Small wonder the Americans were feeling the squeeze.

Making their mark for the first time in this extraordinary sea change in popular music were Brian Poole and the Tremeloes, the Dave Clark Five, Gerry and the Pacemakers, the Bachelors, Peter and Gordon, Billy J Kramer and the Dakotas, the Hollies, the Swinging Blue Jeans, Chad Stuart and Jeremy Clyde, Sounds Incorporated, the Searchers, the Zombies and the Kinks. And Cliff and the Shadows also kept churning them out.

Then, in one fell swoop, a scruffy-looking mob of louts called the Rolling Stones suddenly made the Beatles look respectable, at least in the eyes of a lot of increasingly panicky parents.

Because Mick Jagger wore a T-shirt with a boat neck, three-quarter sleeves and horizontal stripes, we all had to have one too. Mine turned up under the Christmas tree that year, and it might have been okay on ol' snake hips, but it was not a good look on me I now realise when I see old photos.

Despite the avalanche of new artists and new sounds coming out of the UK, Australians quickly detected the changing times and, given the competition from overseas, there were some remarkable feats in terms of record sales. Digger Revell and the Denvermen hit the Top 10 with a shocking thing called 'My Little Rocker's Turned Surfie', while Judy Stone scored with '4,003,221 Tears from Now'. Johnny O'Keefe continued down the 'mild' path with 'She Wears My Ring', and Rob E G, with a couple of successful releases to his name, veered away from his previously highly successful instrumental format to release 'When You're Not Near'.

The closest Australian acts came to emulating the excitement of the new sounds out of Britain was Billy Thorpe and the Aztecs. With their electrifying on-stage presence and string of hits, Aussies proved we could mix it with the best with hits like 'Poison Ivy', 'Mashed Potato', 'Sick and Tired' and, from *waaayy* out of left field, 'Over the Rainbow' from *The Wizard of Oz*. At least my folks now had one Billy Thorpe song they liked.

A couple of inoffensive New Zealanders called Bill and Boyd had a hit called 'Chulu Chululu' and, because they were popular, we instantly adopted them as Australians, while a group of (slightly) offensive Kiwis' Ray Columbus and the Invaders, hit number one with 'She's a Mod'. Because of their undeniable success, they too had to be adopted as honorary Australians.

If 1964 had seen the British Invasion of popular music engulf the world, 1965 saw the completion of the extraordinary triumph. Added to the list of artists who not only appeared on but dominated the Australian charts was former child star Petula Clark, who under the guiding hand of composer and band leader Tony Hatch, had a string of hits beginning with 'Downtown', 'I Know a Place' and 'You're the One'.

Crooner Matt Monro created a diversion from the mainstream with his ballad 'Walk Away'. There were some other quirky diversions in '65 with two number one instrumental hits 'A Walk in the Black Forest' by Horst Jankowski and his Orchestra, and the haunting 'Il Silenzio', a pop reworking of the 'Last Post', by Italian Nini Rosso.

Other artists to make their mark in the big time were Herman's Hermits, Georgie Fame and the Blue Flames, the Moody Blues, Marianne Faithfull, Tom Jones, Donovan, the Yardbirds, Wayne Fontana and the Mindbenders, Manfred Mann and Freddie and the Dreamers.

The first of the so-called 'protest' songs appeared in quantity in 1965, among them 'What Have They Done to the Rain?' by the Searchers, Dylan's 'Blowin' in the Wind' sung by Peter, Paul and Mary, 'Wake up My Mind' by the Uglys, 'Eve of Destruction' by Barry McGuire, 'Universal Soldier' by Donovan, and Hedgehoppers Anonymous's 'It's Good News Week'.

Suddenly the optimism of the popular music revolution had taken a darker and unnerving turn, when issues of the day were being reflected through popular culture.

And in 1965, desert boots got rhythm when folk-rock was invented with Bob Dylan releasing the LP, *Bringing It All Back Home*. Although it took a little time to catch on in more Top 40-oriented music, it did lead to a wave of ever so 'seriously meaningful' songs from the likes of the Byrds, Simon and

Garfunkel, Donovan, Thunderclap Newman, Buffalo Springfield, the Mamas and the Papas and Crosby, Stills, Nash and Young.

There was still room for frivolity and escapism though, as a glance at the chart toppers for the year suggests. 'Ferry Cross the Mersey' from Gerry and the Pacemakers, '20 Miles'/'Devoted to You', 'Pride' and 'Fool, Fool, Fool' by Ray Brown and the Whispers, 'Under the Boardwalk'/'Walking the Dog' from the Rolling Stones, 'Rock and Roll Music'/'Honey Don't', 'Ticket to Ride', 'Help' and 'We Can Work It Out'/'Daytripper' from the Beatles, 'Mrs Brown, You've Got a Lovely Daughter' from Herman's Hermits, 'Crying in the Chapel' by Elvis, 'I Told the Brook' from Billy Thorpe and the Aztecs, 'Que Sera Sera'/'Shakin' All Over' from Normie Rowe and 'She's So Fine' by the Easybeats.

The year 1965 saw the rise of Australia's first truly international 'supergroup' when the Seekers burst onto the charts with music which could hardly be pigeon-holed, it was 'folksy' but it wasn't folk, there were some rock elements, yet it wasn't rock.

The demise of the Springfields in the UK was quite fortuitous for the quartet from Australia who decided to try their hand at the big time, and in the mid-sixties the place to be was London. The Seekers hit number one immediately with the Tom Springfield-penned 'I'll Never Find Another You', then in quick succession 'A World of Our Own', 'Morningtown Ride', 'Georgy Girl' and 'The Carnival is Over'.

With Judith Durham's pretty face, feminine dress sense and bell-like voice, and the clean-cut wholesome appearance of the boys, what was there to dislike about the Seekers? Mums and dads loved them and kids loved them. With some well-chosen TV specials, the Seekers received massive coverage and widespread approval — perhaps there was redemption from the increasingly dishevelled and ragtag bunch that was more the norm on the pop charts.

Following their phenomenal overseas success, Judith Durham, Keith Potger, Bruce Woodley and Athol Guy made a triumphant homecoming when they performed in front of a rapturous crowd estimated at over 200,000 at the Myer Music Bowl in Melbourne.

It seemed that the Americans were getting over their initial shellshock of the British Invasion, and even if they weren't topping the charts, enduring names like P J Proby, the Righteous Brothers, Roy Orbison, Bobby Goldsboro, Wayne Newton, Roger Miller, Gene Pitney, Bob Dylan, Dean Martin and Sonny and Cher joined the perennial Elvis in the Top 40.

Any ardent chart watcher with a teenager's viewpoint must have almost caved in to despair in the first three months of 1966. Prominent in the higher echelons of the charts were 'Spanish Eyes' by Al Martino, 'Maria' (from *West Side Story*) by P J Proby, 'Where Does Love Go?' by Charles Boyer and 'Some Sunday Morning' by Wayne Newton. However, redemption for the rock-and-roll heart wasn't far away.

With one or two notable exceptions, number one hits for most of 1966 reflected pretty much the prevailing trends. They included 'Women' (make you feel alright), 'Too Much'/'I'll Make You Happy (Just Like Your Mama Wants)', 'Come and See Her' and 'Friday on My Mind' all by the great Aussie group the Easybeats, 'These Boots Are Made for Walkin'' by Nancy Sinatra, 'Nowhere Man'/'Norwegian Wood' and 'Yellow Submarine'/'Eleanor Rigby' from the Beatles, 'Elusive Butterfly' by Bob Lynd, 'Hitch Hiker' by Bobby and Laurie, 'Tar and Cement' by Verdelle Smith, 'Strangers in the Night' from Frank Sinatra, the theme from the incredibly popular movie about Elsa the lioness, 'Born Free' by Matt Monro, and 'The Green Green Grass of Home' by Tom Jones.

Western Australia provided a new 'sensation' in 1966 when a kid called Johnny Young burst onto the national scene after enjoying somewhat more limited success in the West. Johnny Young hit number one with 'Step Back'/'Cara Lyn' and the EP *Let It be Me*.

With the Vietnam War dominating the news, Sgt Barry Sadler hit the jackpot on the pop charts with his jingoistic 'Ballad of the Green Berets'. Among the more interesting and eclectic mix which didn't fit into the pop mainstream, but nevertheless made it to the charts in 1966, were the instrumental 'No Matter What Shape (Your Stomach's In)' by the T Bones, 'Jake the Peg' by Rolf Harris, 'Somewhere My Love', the theme from the film *Dr Zhivago* by the Ray Conniff Singers, 'Guantanamera' by the Sandpipers and 'Winchester Cathedral' by the New Vaudeville Band.

Amazingly, 'The Loved One' by Australia's blues-influenced the Loved Ones, the Beach Boys' 'Good Vibrations', 'Ooh La La' by Normie Rowe and 'You Don't Have to Say You Love Me' by Dusty Springfield failed to top the charts, all having stalled at number two.

And the big news for 1966 was the (brief) appearance of an American group called the Knickerbockers. They dressed in suits à la the Beatles, they sounded just like the Beatles, they were packaged just like the Beatles. They got to number six on the charts with a Beatle clone song called 'Lies' and got a lot of press, especially in the United States where they were busting to have their own Beatles. Their own publicity got to them, however: they made the public statement 'We're going to be bigger than the Beatles!' They weren't.

LOVE AND UNDERSTANDING, AND OTHER WEIRD VIBES

In 1967 the Beatles started going strange on us.

Here in Australia we'd just caught up on the dark suits with the stovepipe pants, collarless jackets and thin black ties with pointy-toed boots, not to mention the mop-top hair, then suddenly it's all lank (much longer) hair, beads, sandals and paisley patterns. And I don't think it was Peter Stuyvesants the Fab Four were smoking.

Speaking of Peter Stuyvesants, we were bombarded at the pictures and on TV with cool-looking guys with beautiful birds hanging off them, jetsetting all over the world to places like New York, Rome, Amsterdam, London and Rio, presumably just because they smoked Peter Stuyvesant cigarettes.

One of my cousins smoked Peter Stuyvesants, and her life didn't appear to be any more or less glamorous than anyone else's. Maybe Marlboro was a better bet, at least perhaps you could live out your cowboy fantasies — mind you, little did he know it, but the Marlboro Man was to come to a sticky end, precisely because of the product he was flogging.

I digress ... the Beatles were going strange, and rapidly. Their last big hit of 1966 was the double-sider, 'Yellow Submarine' and 'Eleanor Rigby', which were quite quirky, and a bit of a departure for the group. But nothing quite prepared us for their first chart outing in 1967, another double-sider, 'Penny Lane' and 'Strawberry Fields Forever'. The first time I heard the latter, I thought, 'What are the boys doing?' It took at least three days to grow on me, which was a worrying sign, because the Beatles were usually instantly accessible.

But, either I'd got used to the evolving Beatles, or the charts generally had taken a psychedelic lurch, because by the time 'All You Need is Love' was launched with much fanfare — including a live worldwide satellite telecast, with some blurry black and white pictures, beamed into the lounge rooms of Australia — they seemed perfectly normal, even if my dad clicked his tongue repeatedly and remarked, 'Just take a look at them, would you ... what's the world coming to?'

The Beatles rounded out the year with yet another double-sided number one, 'Hello Goodbye'/'I Am the Walrus' — yep, the Beatles had changed, and so had we all.

In their own way the Beatles truly called the shots as far as music trends went. In '67, among the big hits were Procol Harum's 'A Whiter Shade of Pale', 'Itchycoo Park' by the Small Faces, and 'Living in a Child's Dream' by the Master's Apprentices.

Some other notable chart appearances were from a cleverly packaged group from the US called the Monkees. With their eponymous TV show acting as a vehicle for their light pop music (the term 'bubblegum music' had not yet been invented), the Monkees were an immediate success, and in '67 alone charted with 'I'm a Believer', 'I'm Not Your Stepping Stone', 'A Little Bit Me, a Little Bit You', (theme from) 'The Monkees', 'I Wanna be Free', 'Pleasant Valley Sunday', 'Daydream Believer' and 'She'.

Davy Jones, the cute Pommy member of the Monkees, also had a solo spoken hit with an incredibly schmaltzy thing that had all the girls wetting their pants called, 'Theme for a New Love'.

Snoopy, the dog from the popular Peanuts comic strip, had a big year in 1967. First there was 'Snoopy versus the Red Baron' a catchy novelty song which hit number one for the Royal Guardsmen, and featured the word 'bloody', which had to be 'beeped' when played on radio (oh, such innocent times). And just to prove it wasn't a fluke, the Guardsmen were back with 'Return of the Red Baron', which almost made the Top 10, and then in November they appeared with the cleverly marketed 'Snoopy's Xmas', which hit number one.

Among the more memorable hits of '67 which didn't make it all the way to the top were Sandy Posey's 'Single Girl' (a feminist's nightmare), 'Ruby Tuesday' by the Rolling Stones, 'Gimme Some Lovin'' and 'I'm a Man' from the Spencer Davis Group, 'Matthew and Son' by Cat Stevens, 'Happy Together' by the Turtles, 'Groovin'' by the Young Rascals and 'New York Mining Disaster 1941' from the Bee Gees.

Incredibly, the Bee Gees only got to number twenty-two with that song, however the Gibb brothers did somewhat better over the next few months with 'To Love Somebody', number six, and 'Massachusetts', number three, before slipping back to fourteen with their next release, 'World', in December.

At this stage it started to look like the Bee Gees might be heading down the Beatles' path; they had become remarkably hairier, paisley shirts became the go and some of their lyrics became confusing to say the least, 'Jumbo' a good example:

Jumbo says to say goodnight, see you in the morning
Please don't lose your appetite, he knows who is yawning
Tomorrow you can climb a mountain
Sail a sailboat through a fountain
Jumbo said to say goodnight, he's a friend of yours

Although, for some people, the Bee Gees' hit song from later in the sixties, 'I Started a Joke', was perhaps their most self-revelatory.

Other (slightly) less odd hits of the year were 'Silence is Golden' by the Tremeloes, 'Waterloo Sunset' by the Kinks, 'Don't Sleep in the Subway' by Petula Clark, 'It Must be Him' by Vicki Carr, and 'Respect' from Aretha Franklin.

Number twenty-five was all the legendary Doors could manage with 'Light My Fire'. Another carefully marketed band from America, a family called the Cowsills, was immediately popular with a jaunty little song with a slightly psychedelic edge called 'The Rain, the Park and Other Things'.

Around 1966, mainstream rock and pop had started to develop a somewhat harder edge, influenced no doubt by Bob Dylan's revolutionary 1965 LP, *Highway 61 Revisited*, and its single, 'Like a Rolling Stone', the likes of which had never been heard in popular music before.

And rather than pure entertainment, some of the songs edging onto the charts had serious social comment. San Francisco became the focal point for the hippie movement, especially the Haight-Ashbury area of town near the university. Thousands of hippies flocked to festivals like the 'First Human Be In' and the 'Trips Festival' — many of them fuelled on LSD taken via a spiked punch.

The hippies referred to the punch as the Kool-Aid acid test. The vast majority of America's hippies were white and, as one commentator put it, 'voluntarily poor'. The bands at the centre of the scene included The Grateful Dead, Big Brother and the Holding Company, The Doors, and Jefferson Airplane.

The hippies scared the living daylights out of the grown-ups, but soon fizzled out on their own excesses. That is apart from the few who whacked their brains so hard they've remained in a 1966 state of mind and can still be found tootling around in Volkswagen kombis, gazing at their navels on Indian mountains, or staring blankly into the distance in places like Nimbin and Byron Bay.

As for the people who started it all, in 1967 Abbie Hoffman, Jerry Rubin, Allen Ginsberg and about 150,000 other hippies attempted to levitate the Pentagon in Washington DC. It didn't work.

The closest I managed to get to psychedelia was when I dried out some banana skins and smoked them. This was supposed to be the 'mellow yellow' that Donovan sang about. Smoking the dried skins was supposed to give you a high. It doesn't!

Herb Alpert's phenomenally successful run continued through 1967 when he had four tracks which made a modest impact on the charts, 'Mame', 'Casino Royale', 'A Banda' and 'Carmen'.

Although the single releases didn't set the charts on fire, they did propel the sales of Alpert's albums, and there were few homes in the country that didn't have at least one Herb Alpert collection in the record bin.

Surprisingly, although he had a few chart successes, Elvis didn't manage a number one in 1967, others who did included the Mamas and the Papas with 'Dedicated to the One I Love', featuring the wonderful voice of 'big fat Mama Cass' (as the DJs used to call her, political correctness hadn't been heard of in 1967, and besides 'avoirdupoisally challenged' doesn't have quite the same ring to it).

Frank and Nancy Sinatra also had a hit with 'Something Stupid', and the Charlie Chaplin-penned theme from his film *A Countess From Hong Kong*, 'Love This is My Song', a lushly orchestrated sentimental love song which was a number one hit for *both* Petula Clark and ex-Goon, steam-driven singing Welshman, Harry Secombe. Other hits were 'Up Up and Away' from the 5th Dimension, and 'The Last Waltz' by Engelbert Humperdinck, while an apprentice plumber from Melbourne had a very merry Christmas when his song 'Sadie (the Cleaning Lady)' topped the charts. 'Johnny' Farnham had arrived and was here to stay.

Procol Harum were not to repeat the dizzying success of 'A Whiter Shade of Pale' when their follow-up, 'Conquistador', struggled to make it to number twenty-eight at the beginning of 1968. The Beatles continued their strange journey, producing brilliant music along the way, the *Magical Mystery Tour* EP reaching number two, and the two further releases that year number one: 'Lady Madonna' and the double-sided 'Hey Jude'/'Revolution'.

Bubblegum music officially arrived when an American record label called Buddha Records had an incredible string of excess with a series of formulaic 'studio' bands. The Ohio Express had hits in '68 with 'Yummy Yummy Yummy (I've Got Love in My Tummy)', 'Down at Lulu's' and 'Chewy

Chewy' — the latter no doubt giving rise to the bubblegum label. At the same time The 1910 Fruitgum Company were churning out 'Simon Says', '1, 2, 3, Red Light' and 'Goody Goody Gumdrops', hardly pop's finest hour.

One of the first really big pop music festivals was held at the fairground in Monterey, California, in 1967. The Monterey festival was the largest ever attempted and must have been a logistical nightmare. Around 200,000 mostly young people turned up for a weekend of 'music, peace, flower power and love', and you can bet your sweet bippy there was more than love wafting through the air.

Many of the acts at Monterey weren't paid, the proceeds of the festival went to charity. But for some of the artists it was an opportunity to strut their stuff before record companies and producers, and acts that pre-Monterey might have been totally unheard of, or at least obscure, were thrust into the spotlight, with a number of them going on to enjoy breathtaking success.

Monterey was the model for the Woodstock festival a couple of years later.

What a long weekend it must have been. On the Friday the bill was filled by Simon and Garfunkel, The Animals, Johnny Rivers, Lou Rawls, the Paupers and the Association; on Saturday it was Country Joe and the Fish, Big Brother and the Holding Company (with Janice Joplin up front, loud and dangerous), Al Kooper, The Butterfield Blues Band, Quicksilver Messenger Service, The Steve Miller Band, Canned Heat, The Electric Flag, Moby Grape, Hugh Masekela, The Byrds, Laura Nyro, Jefferson Airplane, Booker T and the MGs and Otis Redding; and to top off the weekend, on Sunday there were Ravi Shankar, The Blues

Project, Big Brother and the Holding Company, The Group With No Name, Buffalo Springfield, The Who, Grateful Dead, The Jimi Hendrix Experience, Scott McKenzie and The Mamas and the Papas. Monterey was the first appearance before a US audience for The Who and Jimi Hendrix, and the first major gig for Janis Joplin and Big Brother and the Holding Company.

1968 — THE SUMMER OF LURV

The number one hits of '68 were as eclectic as ever, and probably accurately reflected the tastes of the Australian record-buying public.

Leading the fresh number ones for the year was a French orchestra led by Paul Mauriat with 'Love is Blue' (L'Amour Est Bleu). An excruciating tear-jerker called 'Honey' by Bobby Goldsboro had everyone running to the record stores then to the tissue boxes — and some went running to the toilet. The Irish Rovers hit the top with 'The Unicorn', and at last the ubiquitous Herb Alpert had a number one, and to everyone's amazement, it wasn't with his trademark brass instrumentals but with a vocal by Herb himself. What made the success of 'This Guy's in Love with You' even more remarkable was the reason Herb had no doubt avoided vocalising on his earlier records, he proved once and for all he *couldn't* sing! But, his lack of vocal prowess didn't impede 'This Guy ...' soaring to the top.

Another amazing performance came from Richard Harris when he delivered the chart topper 'MacArthur Park'. Penned by prolific songwriter Jimmy Webb, 'MacArthur Park' was everything a pop song shouldn't have been ... overly long, overly produced, over the top and completely nonsensical — psychedelia gone mad! But perhaps that's why it was a success, it was in fact everything a pop song *should* be. Whatever, there were many discussions late into the evenings of 1968 about what was the true *meaning* of the song. As far as I could work out it was about a nutter who took a hell of a long time to bake a cake, had subsequently iced it with green icing, lost the recipe to boot, then foolishly left the end product out in the rain!

The raucous Vanilla Fudge swung the charts back on a more normal course with 'You Keep Me Hangin' On', only to be upstaged later in the year by veteran performer Neil Sedaka's opus to love lost, the saccharine-soaked 'Star Crossed Lovers'.

Among the more enduring songs of 1968 were 'Tin Soldier' by the Small Faces, 'Judy in Disguise' (With Glasses) by John Fred and his Playboy Band, 'Monterey' and 'Sky Pilot' both from Eric Burdon and the Animals, and the quirky, laid-back, ultra-cool Hombres' song which pretty much summed up the sixties, 'Let it All Hang Out'. Then there were 'Green Tambourine' by the Lemon Pipers, 'Words' from the Bee Gees, which only reached number fifteen, 'Mighty Quinn' by Manfred Mann, 'To Sir with Love' (from the smash hit film of the same name) by Lulu, 'Jennifer Juniper' by Donovan, 'Valleri' by the Monkees, 'Pictures of Matchstick Men' by Status Quo, 'The Dock of the Bay' by Otis Redding, and 'If I Were a Carpenter' by the Four Tops, and returning, this time with 'Jumpin' Jack Flash' were the Rolling Stones. Spawning a film of the same name was 'The Harper Valley PTA' by Jeannie C Riley, which was quickly joined on the charts by 'Little Arrows' by Leapy Lee, 'Jesamine' from the Casuals, 'Elenore' from the Turtles, 'White Room' by Cream, 'With a Little Help From My Friends' by Joe Cocker, 'Magic Carpet Ride' by Steppenwolf, 'All Along the Watchtower' by the Jimi Hendrix Experience,

'Wichita Lineman' by Glen Campbell, 'Eloise' by Paul Ryan, 'Going Up the Country' by Canned Heat and, by no means least, 'Son of a Preacher Man' by the great Dusty Springfield.

All in all, 1968 was a vintage year for popular music, and probably marked the end of yet another era as the last year of the decade dawned.

And 1968 can't be left without at least a passing nod to some of the 'extraordinary items' which shared the charts with so many sixties classics. These included 'Lapland' by the Baltimore and Ohio Marching Band, 'Cinderella Rockefella' ('You're the fella, you're the fella who rocks me ...'), with versions from Esther and Abi Ofarim and Anne and Johnny Hawker, 'Underneath the Arches' with Johnny Farnham really getting down and dirty, the theme from the children's TV series *Skippy* by Eric Jupp and 'Lily the Pink' by Scaffold.

WHERE DID YOU GO TO, MY LOVELY?
THE END OF THE ERA

If a script had been written for the perfect collection of popular music charts to wrap up the decade, no one could have come up with what actually transpired. The 1969 charts managed to encapsulate everything that had happened in the previous nine years, and to also provide a clear pointer into the direction of the seventies.

Fleetwood Mac appeared in the charts for the first time in 1969 with the instrumental 'Albatross', which gave no hint whatsoever as to the direction the music that the various incarnations of Fleetwood Mac would take in future.

The Beatles were imploding to a messy end, but still managed to consistently top the charts with what could only be described as an eclectic mix, even for them: 'Ob-La-Di, Ob-La-Da', 'While My Guitar Gently Weeps', 'Get Back', 'Don't Let Me Down', 'Something', 'Come Together' and 'The Ballad of John and Yoko'.

The other number one hits of 1969 included Peter Sarstedt's 'Where Do You Go to, My Lovely?', while cute little Johnny Young had people agog when he wrote the psychedelic epic 'The Real Thing Parts 1 and 2' for Russell Morris. Herman's Hermits had 'My Sentimental Friend', and Elvis got right back up there after what had been a bit of a drought with 'In the Ghetto'. One-hit wonders Zager and Evans had the eerie 'In the Year 2525', while the Rolling Stones managed to get a song straight to the top when they released the double-sided hit single, 'Honky Tonk Women'/'You Can't Always Get What You Want'. Russell Morris repeated the success of 'The Real Thing' with another epic which might as well have been called 'The Real Thing Part 3'. Instead it was called 'Part Three into Paper Walls', featuring the overblown production of the previous hit, but this time the flipside of the single showcased Russell Morris's sweet voice on the hit 'The Girl that I Love'. Rounding out the 1969 number ones were 'One' by Johnny Farnham, 'Penny Arcade' by Roy Orbison, 'I'll Never Fall in Love Again' by Bobby Gentry, 'Raindrops Keep Falling on My Head' from both Johnny Farnham and B J Thomas, and the Hollies with 'He Ain't Heavy, He's My Brother'.

Nothing underlined the demise of the Beatles more definitely than the formation of the Plastic Ono Band, an experimental outfit formed by John Lennon and Yoko Ono with various odd hangers-on. Fans desperate to perpetuate the Beatle magic bought sufficient quantities of 'Give Peace a Chance' to get it into the Top 10, but the release just before Christmas 1969 of a visceral rant appropriately called 'Cold Turkey' tested the patience of even the most loyal fan, and accordingly they failed to gobble it up and 'Cold Turkey' struggled to reach as high as number twenty-two.

Serious Beatle fans laid the blame squarely at the feet of a small, plain Japanese woman who, to their minds, was clearly as mad as a barking coot.

The Bee Gees featured constantly in pop music mags, and there was always plenty to gossip about, love affairs, break ups, reconciliations and phenomenal success — especially internationally.

Despite the fact the Bee Gees hadn't appeared on the charts until late '65 with the little known 'Wine and Women', before the end of the decade they charted with 'Spicks and Specks', 'New York Mining Disaster 1941', 'To Love Somebody', 'Massachusetts', 'World', 'Words', 'Jumbo', 'I've Just Gotta Get a Message to You', 'I Started a Joke', 'The First of May'/'Lamplight', 'Tomorrow Tomorrow' and 'Don't Forget to Remember'. But not one of them managed to crack the elusive number one on the Australian charts.

Songs which stood the test of time from '69, but, like all the Bee Gees releases, failed to hit the top were 'For Once in My Life' by Stevie Wonder which only reached number nineteen, 'Hooked on a Feeling' by B J Thomas, 'Galveston' by Glen Campbell, and Creedence Clearwater Revival's string of great songs 'Proud Mary', 'Bad Moon Rising', 'Lodi', 'Green River', 'Fortunate Son' and 'Down on the Corner'. There were also 'Time of the Season' by the Zombies, 'The Boxer' by Simon and Garfunkel — no doubt inhibited by the fact it was banned by some stations for the inclusion of the lyric 'whores on Seventh Avenue' — 'Pinball Wizard' from the Who's overblown rock opera *Tommy*, 'Israelites' by Desmond Dekker and the Aces, who first brought reggae music into the mainstream, 'Dear Prudence' by Doug Parkinson In Focus, 'Spinning Wheel' from Blood Sweat and Tears, 'Ruby, Don't Take Your Love to Town' by Kenny Rogers and the First Edition, and 'Polk Salad Annie' by Tony Joe White. Having written hits for others, Neil

Diamond continued to struggle to hit the top himself with 'Sweet Caroline'. Also failing to reach the top were 'Everybody's Talkin'' by Nilsson, 'Crimson and Clover' by Tommy James and the Shondells, and 'Time is Tight' by Booker T and the MGs. And Tammy Wynette gave the feminists something to get their knickers in a twist about when music fans in their droves snapped up the country crossover 'Stand by Your Man'.

In terms of numbers of releases and the variety of musical styles which made the charts, the closing year of the sixties was no doubt the most prolific and diverse.

But despite the plethora of pure pop, driving rock, some ballads, some instrumentals, some nostalgia and a lashing or two of psychedelia, it was hard to shake the novelty hit, as evidenced by the chart success of 'Feelin' So Good S.K.O.O.B.Y.-D.O.O' and 'Sugar Sugar' by the Archies, 'Boom Bang a Bang' by Lulu, 'Gitarzan' by Ray Stevens, 'La La' from the Flying Circus and 'Jam up Jelly Tight' by Tommy Roe. Frankly, if it weren't for the fact it was the Beatles, 'Ob-La-Di, Ob-La-Da' would have fitted very neatly into this category.

The last number one hit of the 1960s was the Hollies' 'He Ain't, Heavy He's My Brother'. Given what had gone down in the last ten years when we let it all hang out, somehow that seems quite appropriate!

WOODSTOCK — THREE DAYS OF MUSIC, MARIJUANA AND MUSH

What started out as a reasonably low-key event on Max Yasgur's farm in New York State in August 1969, developed into the biggest festival yet staged. Fittingly, the sixties ended with a bang *and* a whimper of great music, of mud and slush, and of good and bad trips, man, at a music festival that has become one of the iconic moments in the history of rock music and in the story of the sixties.

The festival was called Woodstock because that's the name under which it was originally promoted. It was to be held at a town called Woodstock, but the locals didn't fancy the idea of all those dope smokers and long-haired gits descending on their sleepy little town. So Max Yasgur's son, Sam, persuaded his dad to allow the festival to be held on their dairy farm, not too far from Woodstock.

Max might have thought twice if he'd known what he was in for. Sam told his dad that maybe ten or twenty thousand people might attend what was officially called 'The Woodstock Music and Art Festival', though no one remembers too much about the 'art' bit. As the weekend drew near, people began turning up at Yasgur's farm, causing traffic jams across New York State. More than 400,000 young people turned up, despite the rain and the quagmire that the farm had turned into. Cars had to be parked miles away, and the final part of the journey made on foot.

The weekend was marked by flower power, peace and love. Drugs were taken openly, peace signs were everywhere and it was indeed remarkably peaceful. Thousands took their clothes off, and in the pictures we saw afterwards, the question 'why?' has to be asked. It looked freezing.

The mood of Woodstock was reported to be fantastic, with people sharing what little food or shelter they had, at an event which had been seriously under catered for.

The music kicked off on Friday 15 August and didn't wind up until the following Monday morning. The performers were the cream of the popular music world, Joan Baez, The Band, Jeff Beck Group, Blood, Sweat and Tears, Paul Butterfield Blues Band, Canned Heat, Joe Cocker, Country Joe and the Fish, Creedence Clearwater Revival, Crosby, Stills, Nash and Young, Grateful Dead, Arlo Guthrie, Tim Hardin, Keef Hartley, Richie Havens, Jimi Hendrix, The Incredible String Band, Janis Joplin, Jefferson Airplane, Mountain, Quill, Melanie, Santana, John Sebastian, Sha-Na-Na, Ravi Shankar, Sly and the Family Stone, Bert Sommer, Sweetwater, Ten Years After, The Who and Johnny Winter.

Two people died at Woodstock and two babies were born, and despite the fact the crowd was praised for how well it behaved, terrified local authorities across America rushed through laws to make sure nothing like Woodstock could happen again.

Spoilsports!

OUT OF THE GARAGE AND INTO BATTLE

In the latter half of the sixties, the confectionery giant Hoadleys — of Violet Crumble and Pollywaffle fame — sponsored a national 'Battle of the Sounds'. Another big sponsor was the Sitmar cruise line, which provided the main prize, a cruise to the UK so that the winning band might try their luck in the big smoke. The Battle of the Sounds caught the imagination of kids across the country, and was immediately popular at its inception in 1966.

The format was simple (if flawed), and literally hundreds of would-be rock stars gave it a go. Radio stations around the country were the linchpin and helped promote the various heats. Youth-oriented magazines like *Everybodys* and *Go Set* also gave the contest a push along.

The Beatles' brief visit to Australia in 1964 in some way seemed to galvanise young musos or would-be musos all over the country. Because the Beatles' early music was so simplistic, lots of aspiring rockers could pick up an electric guitar and amplifier reasonably cheaply, find another kid who fancied himself as a drummer, and within a short time, could be sending the neighbourhood mad each day after school and every weekend as they practised at full volume in the garage.

In 1966, as well as the return trip to the UK, the winning band would receive $1000 spending money, and a contract with GO records.

Over eighty radio stations nationwide became involved and organised heats in church halls, sheds, community centres and footy clubs, and more than five hundred bands entered the first competition with one hundred and twenty from Melbourne alone.

Most bands were mediocre, many bloody dreadful, and some not half bad! At each of the heats, a compere (most often a DJ from a participating radio station) would introduce the bands to the adoring fans. Even being the DJ at one of the heats of Hoadley's carried a certain cachet, so local announcers would compete pretty vigorously to get the gig.

The bands were then given three minutes each to do their thing. They were judged on sound, originality, audience reaction and presentation — extra bonus points could be accumulated for something extra like an unusual instrument.

Some of the rules for the Battle of the Sounds were a bit suss, to say the least. For instance, a band could have a maximum of five members. Why this was so was never clear. Some used to say it was because Sitmar didn't want to fork out extra fares for the winners, another school of thought was because the popular Merseybeat of the time featured drums, three guitars and a singer. Bands could enter only one heat on a given day, however they could enter another heat on another day, provided that heat was held within a designated geographical zone corresponding to the band's place of residence. Many groups entered several times, although there's no hard evidence of any of them ever enjoying great success.

After the eliminations the finals would feature a judging panel of four or five people, usually drawn from the music industry, for example a record producer, a popular singer, someone from the sponsors and perhaps someone from the press.

The rules were tested first up in 1966 because the band which eventually won, the Twilights from Adelaide (and as a fifteen-year-old South Australian kid, wasn't that a buzz), had six members, including two vocalists. They had to drop one of the vocalists. The remaining vocalist, Glen Shorrock, went on to stardom with Axiom and the Little River Band and, of course, as a solo artist.

Another member of the Twilights, Terry Britten, gained fame as a songwriter and producer, delivering hits to Tina Turner and Cliff Richard among others.

The winners of Hoadley's National Battle of the Sounds for the seven years it ran were: the Twilights, Adelaide, 1966; the Groop, featuring a young Brian Cadd, Melbourne, 1967; the Groove, Melbourne, 1968; Doug Parkinson In Focus, Sydney, 1969; the Flying Circus, Sydney, 1970; Fraternity, Adelaide, 1971; and Sherbet, Sydney, 1972.

Among the bands who got so near yet so far, but still managed to make a mark, to a greater or lesser extent, were the Masters Apprentices, Perth's Beat'N Tracks (Phil Manning on lead guitar who was later to go on to great success with Chain), the Affair (lead singer Kerrie Biddell), the Valentines (with Bon Scott, later to lead AC/DC), Autumn, La De Das, Piranha, Zoot, Freshwater, Elm Tree (vocalist John Paul Young) and Jeff St John and Copperwine.

As a result of the proliferation of bands which had aspirations to make the big time, the country was flooded with so-called 'pub' bands, and a lot of them were really quite good, belting out cover versions of the popular hits at the time to packed-out Sunday sessions at thousands of pubs all over Australia. The bands that comprised kids who were too young to be on licensed premises would often get a gig playing at the Y dances, organised by the local YMCA.

There was no doubt that the huge numbers of kids who wanted to make it as pop musicians fuelled the popularity of the burgeoning pub band scene that flourished in the sixties. Popular local bands, sometimes two different bands on one night, would perform at the huge suburban beer halls Australian pubs had become. Hundreds of young people (many of them under age) would have a favourite band they'd follow around, and the pubs themselves competed fiercely for the patronage of the kids at the Sunday sessions.

LURID-VISION SONG CONTEST

Whenever conversation should turn to the question of popular music's finest hours, the Eurovision Song Contest deserves a mention. This peculiar song contest has always been hugely successful in Europe, but it wasn't until the late sixties when some British artists recorded some wins that Australians began to take notice, although given the quality of some of the offerings, probably not too many people would volunteer the information that they have a contest winner or two in their vinyl collection. The winners from the beginning of the decade were:

1960 France — Jaqueline Boyer, 'Tom Billibi'.
1961 Luxembourg — Jean Claude Pascal, 'Nous Les Amoureux'.
1962 France — Isabelle Aubret, 'Un Premier Amour'.
1963 Denmark — Grethe and Jorgen Ingmann, 'Dansevise'.
1964 Italy — Gigliola Cinquetti, 'Non Ho L'Eta'.
        (For the first time, that year a 'known' British artist appeared at Eurovision when Matt Monro sang 'I Love the Little Things'.)
1965 Luxembourg — France Gall, 'Poupee de Cire, Poupee de Son Lux'
        (Kathy Kirby represented the UK with 'I Belong'.)

1966 Austria — Udo Jurgens, 'Merci Cherie'.
(The UK veteran performer Kenneth McKellar
sang 'A Man Without Love' that year.)

1967 UK — Sandie Shaw, 'Puppet on a String'.
(At last the Poms began to take Eurovision slightly
more seriously. The competition was fierce to
represent the UK, with Sandie Shaw winning a
nationally televised sing-off. The song was a piece
of pure pop fairy floss and, of course, went on to
win in Austria.)

1968 Spain — Massiel, '(He Gives Me Love) La La La'.
(The Brits couldn't quite take out the quinella,
when Cliff Richard's 'Congratulations' was beaten
into second place by a single point by the Spanish
entry which went on to become a minor hit
internationally)

The Eurovision decade closed in spectacular fashion, when
four separate countries managed to come up with enough
collective dross to tie on points, with eighteen votes each:

Spain — Salome, 'Vivo Cantado'.
UK — Lulu, 'Boom Bang a Bang'.
Netherlands — Lenny Kuhn, 'De Troubadour'.
France — Frida Boccara, 'Un Jour, Un Enfant'.

The Eurovision song contest began as a showcase of kitsch
and, in some cases, dire mainstream pop music, and has
continued to cultivate that very fertile ground, with some
breathtakingly appalling performances over the years.

THE CREAM OF BRILL

Before the British pop invasion began, the Americans had established what our DJs used to call 'The Hit Factory'. Teams of young songwriters worked out of the Brill Building on Broadway in New York.

The Brill Building was the idea of a young songwriter, Don Kirschner, who'd had some modest success in the late fifties. His great genius was in getting together teams of songwriters to literally churn out songs.

Many of the biggest international hits came out of the Brill Building, penned by teams like Gerry Goffin and Carole King, Howard Greenfield and Neil Sedaka, 'Doc' Pomus and Mort Shuman, Barry Mann and Cynthia Weil, and Jeff Barry and Ellie Greenwich.

Sometimes the more successful teams would collaborate with lesser-known songwriters, and the creative output from the Brill Building was quite staggering, even though the Hit Factory years of chart domination were relatively short. Among the hundreds of songs Gerry Goffin and Carole King churned out at Brill were the hits 'Can't Stop Talkin' about You', 'Don't Forget about Me', 'Goin' Back', 'Go Away Little Girl', 'Her Royal Majesty', 'Hey Girl', 'Hi De Ho (That Old Sweet Roll)', 'I Want to Stay Here', 'I Wasn't Born to Follow', 'I'm into Something Good', 'It Might as Well Rain (Until September)', 'Locomotion', 'Natural

Woman', 'Oh No Not My Baby', 'One Fine Day', 'Pleasant Valley Sunday', 'Some Kind of Wonderful', 'Some of Your Lovin'', 'Take Good Care of My Baby', 'Up on the Roof', 'When My Little Girl is Smiling', 'Will You Still Love Me Tomorrow?' and 'World I Used to Know'.

No wonder the Brill Building boomed, Don Kirschner was a shrewd businessman with an eye for a hit, and they just kept on coming. Howard Greenfield and Neil Sedaka wrote 'Breaking Up is Hard to Do', 'Calendar Girl', 'Happy Birthday, Sweet Sixteen', 'Little Devil', 'Oh Carol', 'Stairway to Heaven' and 'Where the Boys Are'.

Jeff Barry and Ellie Greenwich, often collaborating with producer Phil Spector, provided '(And) Then He Kissed Me', 'Baby I Love You', 'Be My Baby', 'Chapel of Love', 'Da Doo Ron Ron', 'Do Wah Diddy Diddy', 'I Can Hear Music', 'Hanky Panky', 'Friday Kind of Monday', 'Leader of the Pack', 'Spring Fever', 'River Deep Mountain High' and 'Right Back Where I Started From'.

Yet another Brill team, Barry Mann and Cynthia Weil, produced 'Blame it on the Bossa Nova', 'On Broadway', 'I Just Can't Help Believing', 'I Want You to Meet My Baby', 'I'm Gonna be Strong', 'Just a Little Lovin' (Early in the Morning)', 'It's Getting Better', 'Looking Through the Eyes of Love', 'Make Your Own Kind of Music', 'Saturday Night at the Movies', 'The Shape of Things to Come', 'We Gotta Get out of This Place', 'Who Needs It', 'You're My Soul and Inspiration' and 'You've Lost That Lovin' Feeling'.

As if the Hit Factory were not productive enough, apart from individual efforts 'Doc' Pomus and Mort Shuman contributed 'Can't Get Used to Losing You', 'His Latest Flame', 'Little Sister', 'Save the Last Dance for Me', 'Surrender', 'Suspicion', 'A Teenager in Love' and 'This Magic Moment'.

Consider that these were part of the outfit of one hit factory alone, and you can see why the output of popular music was so incredibly prolific and diverse.

But during the sixties, one songwriting team eclipsed all others. Often their songs were oddly arranged, the rhythms quirky, and the lyrics quite 'out there'.

Many performers found their music difficult and challenging to perform, yet Hal David and Burt Bacharach provided a good part of the soundtrack of the decade with 'Tower of Strength', 'The Man Who Shot Liberty Valance', 'Any Day Now', 'Make It Easy on Yourself', 'I Just Don't Know What to Do with Myself', 'Only Love Can Break a Heart', 'Don't Make Me Over', 'Blue on Blue', 'True Love Never Runs Smooth', '24 Hours from Tulsa', 'Wives and Lovers', 'Anyone Who Had a Heart', 'Walk on By', 'Wishin' and Hopin'', 'A House is Not a Home', 'You'll Never Get to Heaven (If You Break My Heart)', '(There's) Always Something There to Remind Me', 'What the World Needs Now is Love', 'What's New, Pussycat?', 'Trains and Boats and Planes', 'My Little Red Book', 'Message to Michael', 'Alfie', 'I Just Don't Know What to Do with Myself', 'Casino Royale', 'The Look of Love', 'I Say a Little Prayer', 'Do You Know the Way to San Jose?', 'This Guy's in Love with You', 'Promises Promises', 'I'll Never Fall in Love Again' and 'Raindrops Keep Falling on My Head'.

In the latter part of the decade, a songwriter called Jimmy Webb had a burst of creative genius to give us 'Didn't We', 'Up Up and Away', 'By the Time I Get to Phoenix', 'MacArthur Park', 'Wichita Lineman' and 'Galveston'.

DIAMOND IN THE SMOOTH

Although Neil Diamond had been prolifically writing songs since 1960, he had no real success until 1966, when he became a virtual one-man hit factory. In that one year, delivered, among heaps of others, 'Solitary Man', 'Cherry Cherry', 'I'm a Believer', a hit for the Monkees, 'The Boat That I Row', a hit for Lulu, and 'Red Red Wine'. It was a vintage year.

The following year he was on a roll with 'A Little Bit Me, a Little Bit You', which was a hit for the Monkees, 'Girl You'll be a Woman Soon', 'Thank the Lord for the Night Time', 'Shilo', 'Back from Baltimore' and 'Kentucky Woman'.

In 1968 his hits were 'Two Bit Manchild', 'Brooklyn Roads', 'And the Grass Won't Pay No Mind', 'Sunday Sun', and 'Honey Drippin' Times'.

Just to round out the sixties nicely, in 1969 Neil wrote 'Brother Love's Travelling Salvation Show', whose opening line gave him the title for a forthcoming and mega best-selling live album: 'Hot August night, and the leaves hangin' down, and the grass on the ground smellin' sweet …'. He also wrote 'If I Never Knew Your Name', 'Sweet Caroline' and 'Holly Holy'.

In five short years, Neil had pretty much set up his retirement nest egg.

THE MEANINGFUL MOANER

Bob Dylan's influence on the music and thinking of the sixties was quite profound. Sometimes it was a bit of a stretch to quite 'get' whatever it was he was on about in his lyrics, other times it was pretty clear. Dylan was one of those artists you loved or hated. I did both — loving his early material and going off him a bit later. He was also a songwriter whose songs seemed to be accessible to other artists. Some groups and performers took Dylan's songs and arranged them in such a way they were barely recognisable.

Among those who could thank Bob Dylan for giving their careers a kick along in the sixties with songs he'd penned were Peter Paul and Mary, ('Blowin' in the Wind' and 'Don't Think Twice, It's All Right'), The Byrds ('Hey Mr Tambourine Man' and 'All I Really Want to Do'), The Turtles ('It Ain't Me Babe'), Manfred Mann ('Just Like a Woman' and 'The Mighty Quinn'), Jimi Hendrix ('All Along the Watchtower'), Burl Ives ('I'll be Your Baby Tonight').

Dylan was one of the major reasons folk music received some serious mainstream attention and Top 40 success in the early sixties. He certainly spawned the whole protest music thing in the early to mid-sixties which resulted in hits like 'Wake Up My Mind', 'Eve of Destruction', 'Universal Soldier' and 'It's Good News Week' from a range of performers. He was also said to be a major influence on the development of the lyric style of The Beatles and to have introduced them to the psychedelic possibilities of mind-altering substances. They, in turn, would have been one of the influences on his 'going electric'.

Bob Dylan is also said to have invented folk-rock in 1965 with songs like 'It's All Over Now Baby Blue' and 'Maggie's Farm', acid-rock in 1966 with the swilling, amphetamine-fuelled double LP, *Blonde on Blonde*, and then country-rock when he recorded his LP *Nashville Skyline* in the country music capital in 1969. It included a duet with country music star Johnny Cash on the opening track, 'Girl from the North Country'.

Remarkably, for an artist with limited musicianship and a more than limited voice, Dylan re-invented himself and popular music more often than anyone else in the sixties.

Through the decade he produced the memorable albums, *Bob Dylan, The Freewheelin' Bob Dylan, The Times They are A-Changin', Another Side of Bob Dylan, Bring It All Back Home, Highway 61 Revisited, Blonde on Blonde, Bob Dylan's Greatest Hits, John Wesley Harding* and *Nashville Skyline*.

Despite this staggering output, Dylan's success on Australian singles charts was limited. In 1965 he reached number five with 'Like a Rolling Stone' and number twenty-six with 'Positively 4th Street', and in 1966 with 'Rainy Day Women Nos. 12 & 35' he reached number ten, while 'Just Like a Woman' got to number six. Incredibly, Bob Dylan didn't chart again until the seventies.

GLUED TO THE BOX

WHEN THE WORLD WAS BLACK AND WHITE

In the sixties, Australia really started to warm to television. We might not have had TV introduced to the country as early as we did had it not been for the fact that Melbourne was to host the Olympic Games in 1956. With the eyes of the world focused down-under, it would have looked rather backwards had we not had TV, especially as Britain and the US had been watching it for years. The necessary legislation was passed through the federal parliament, and we were on our way to becoming a nation of square eyes.

For a start, TV sets were really rather scarce. In 1956 there were about five thousand TV licences; like most things in those days, everything seemed to require a licence, no one was quite sure why it was deemed necessary to licence a TV set, but it basically boiled down to a revenue-raising exercise.

By 1960, the number of sets in Australia had grown to around a million. For a start they were prohibitively expensive. In 1956 the average family man earned around £850 a year, and with TV sets costing between £200 and £400, you were looking at between a third and a half of average yearly earnings.

Another inhibiting factor was the availability of a TV signal. Outside the large metropolitan areas, you needed an antenna which was high enough to endanger low-flying aircraft, and a so-called 'booster' which was supposed to improve the picture but which, in reality, only sharpened up the 'snow'. Despite teething problems, by 1960 one in three Australian homes had TV — we had taken to the newish technology like ducks to water.

Electrical stores were crammed with TV sets, some even specialised in just TVs, radios and record players, and would have their floor displays set up so that each appliance could be seen (or heard) in its optimum environment.

Many stores would display a dozen or so sets stacked in their front windows, providing a mesmerising array of test patterns. Very often transmission didn't begin until later in the day, so the test pattern and some pretty dubious music were all you got.

TV sets ranged from pretty basic-looking seventeen-inch models on spindly legs, to the big 'solid state' numbers. The bulky twenty-one-inch models, with highly polished timber cabinets and cloth-covered speakers, were the ultimate, but only for the seriously well-off.

The salespeople were pretty good with TV jargon, and could easily blind you with science; of course they'd always recommend a 'console' over a 'lowboy', basically because they were more expensive, but they did look and sound better than the cheaper models, and many families who really couldn't afford to found themselves on the hire-purchase slippery slope.

TV spread quickly. From its introduction in Melbourne and Sydney, services began in Queensland, South Australia and Western Australia in 1959, with Tasmania in 1960 and the ACT in 1962. The Northern Territory had to get through the sixties without TV.

There was much debate about what was a safe amount of

viewing per day, but no real consensus was reached on this so it varied from household to household. For a start we were restricted to a couple of hours a day, but restrictions gradually loosened as the passing of time proved none of us were going blind or suffering from radiation sickness.

ALL SET

Whatever television set your family had was clearly the best, and people would swear that the sharpness of picture or quality of tone on their brand was light-years ahead of all the others. And there was an array of 'others' to choose from: Philips, Astor, Kirby-Crosley, HMV, Thorn-Atlas, Admiral, AWA and Healing.

We had a Healing twenty-one-inch console, and in truth it did look pretty swish for its time, even though the plastic channel changer broke off rather quickly. From then on, the channel had to be changed with a pair of pliers, which rested on top of the console alongside the TV lamp.

There was also a problem with damp. In the depths of winter if things got a bit damp in the corner of the sunroom where our TV eventually sat, the valves would fizz and crack alarmingly, sending bursts of white lightning across the twenty-one-inch screen.

In 1965 you could trade in your old TV on a brand new Astor Devon twenty-three-inch console. After getting £95 for the trade-in, you paid a further £114. Alternatively you could rent a TV from eighteen shillings and sixpence weekly. Considering that a top-grade fireman was paid £10/9/6 a week, it was pretty steep either to buy or rent a TV.

For a brief time there were some metal cabinet, vinyl-covered TV sets on the market. These looked particularly space age, because the cabinet followed the curve of the picture tube, and you could order different vinyl finishes to match your décor. The popularity of the metal-cased sets waned rather rapidly when authorities warned that you could be electrocuted by the metal cabinet if something came adrift inside. I knew some people who fitted rubber suction caps to the feet of their metal set to act as insulators 'just in case'.

Enterprising retailers of TV sets soon sussed out that there was a whole world full of accessories which any self-respecting TV-watching home just had to have. Suddenly an ordinary lounge chair became a 'TV chair', a footstool became a 'TV stool', a side table a 'TV table', and so on. Some genius even came up with the idea that you must watch TV with a TV lamp, otherwise you might damage your eyes. Accordingly virtually every home had a TV lamp sitting on top of their set.

The lamp was a spindly thing, often on three metal legs, with the anodised aluminium shade shaped a bit like a large dinner plate clipping directly onto the globe. The shade, of course, came in a range of colours to suit your décor, but given the décor, which was all the go at the time, it didn't matter particularly what colour it was.

To go with the rest of your TV paraphernalia, you could purchase a TV tray. This was simply a tray with fold-out legs which you could place across your lap to eat from while you watched TV. Some families actively resisted eating in the lounge room, but it wasn't too long before dining rooms became virtually redundant.

TUNE IN, VEG OUT, TUCK IN

With the coming of television, the food industry soon realised the potential of lounge-room dining, and it wasn't too long before we were slavishly following the Americans with the introduction of TV meals.

TV meals might have been a greater success had microwave ovens been around at the time, but because you had to thaw the frozen meals, then heat them slowly in the oven, it all became too much of a bother.

A typical TV dinner would have three or four separate compartments on the one tray, each compartment containing a food which was sometimes easily identifiable, and at other times a complete mystery. TV dinners tasted about as good as they looked, in other words bloody awful, and apart from in exceptionally indolent households, they were not a roaring success.

They must have been somewhat more popular in the US because in his 1964 hit 'You Never Can Tell', Chuck Berry sang, 'The coolerator was crammed with TV dinners and ginger ale.'

More successful were TV snacks. These could be anything from nuts, chips and fruit, to biscuits and chocolate, just packaged up with 'TV' on the wrapping, and they were instantly welcomed into the lounge.

THE BIG PULL (AS SEEN ON ABC TV)

Once you had your television, you were set. We couldn't have been too choosy about what we watched. Most viewers in the major cities had at least three channels to select from, in the country it was a bit more potluck.

A typical Monday's viewing in any Australian capital city in 1965 looked something like this:

ABC Channel 2

10.30	*For Schools*
1.00	*Weekend Magazine*
1.25	*Women in the Army*
1.30	*For Schools*
4.45	*Kindergarten Playtime*
5.00	*The Magic Roundabout*
5.30	*The Magic Boomerang*
5.55	*Cartoons*
6.00	*King's Outlaw*
6.30	*Mr Justice Duncannon*
6.55	*Sports Report*
7.00	*News Newsreel Weather*
7.30	*Doctor Who*
7.55	*Export Action*
8.00	*Doctor Kildare*
8.50	*William Clauson in Concert*

9.00	*Impact*
10.00	*The Big Pull*
10.30	*Weather*
10.40	Close

Channel 7

12.25	*Mahalia Jackson Sings*
12.30	*Fractured Flickers*
1.00	*Take the Hint*
1.30	*Concentration*
2.00	*It Could be You*
2.30	*Monday Matinee*
4.00	*Beauty and the Beast*
4.30	*Children's Channel Seven*
6.00	*Superman*
7.00	*Quiz Show*
7.30	*Mr Novak*
8.30	*Eastside Westside*
9.30	*The Jack Benny Show*
10.00	*Project 65*
11.00	*Late News*
11.10	*Reflection*
11.15	Close

Channel Nine

5.00	*Magic Circle Club*
5.30	*Bomba the Jungle Boy*
6.30	*News Weather Probe*
7.00	*Tycoon*
7.30	*The Virginian*
9.00	*The Ed Sullivan Show*
10.00	*Victorian Football League Playback*

| 11.00 | *Late News* |
| 12.00 | Close |

The cheapest programming for the flourishing new stations came from America, where TV production had been up and running for years. Whatever the genre, Americans could provide the programming, from the spooky *Alfred Hitchcock Presents* — opening to quirky music and the profile of the portly director — to the long-lived *Star Trek*, *The Time Tunnel* and *The Outer Limits*, which my parents banned us from watching because we'd have nightmares. Ditto *The Twilight Zone* and *Land of the Giants*. *Lost in Space* was more our speed.

If the folks were out and we were being babysat, we could sneak out of bed and watch some of the banned shows, and the parents were right, they did give you nightmares, but it was worth it. I thought *The Twilight Zone* was best of the lot, because it combined science fiction with the supernatural, and you had a sort of ancestor of *The X Files*.

Every kid in the country must have wondered why their mum wasn't like Donna Reed in *The Donna Reed Show*. In the show she played Donna Stone, wife of Dr Alex Stone, played by Carl Betz, and mother of Mary, played by the gorgeous (if sometimes whiney) Shelley Fabares, and Jeff, played by Paul Peterson, who later in the sixties had a hit record with 'A Little Bit for Sandy'.

Donna Stone kept her house beautifully, was always happy, doted on her husband and kids, was always working out treats for them, and always had milk and cookies on the table the moment the kids stepped in the door from school. I was convinced that was the way all of America lived, and what a dud stroke of luck I had had to be born in Australia.

Usually, if there was a hit show of a particular type, the clones would pop up all over the place, like *Bewitched* and *I Dream of Jeannie*, *The Addams Family* and *The Munsters*.

When it came to westerns the list was lengthy, including *Wagon Train* with Ward Bond, *Rawhide* with a very young Clint Eastwood as Rowdy Yates, *Gunsmoke*, *Maverick*, *Have Gun Will Travel*, *Bonanza*, and even *The Lone Ranger*, with Clinton Moore as the Ranger and Jay Silverheels as his faithful sidekick Tonto. Kids all over Australia would belt home from school in time to catch the sound of the 'Wilhelm Tell Overture' on the opening credits of the Lone Ranger, with the Ranger calling out 'Hi-ho Silver awaaaaaaaayy!'

Situation comedies flourished in the sixties with Lucy in her many guises, *Gilligan's Island*, *The Beverly Hillbillies*, *F Troop*, *The Ghost and Mrs Muir*, *My Favourite Martian*, *Gomer Pyle*, *The Dick Van Dyke Show*, *Greenacres*, *Petticoat Junction*, *Bewitched* and *Mr Ed*, just to scratch the surface.

Of course we watched all of these in black and white because, despite the fact the Americans had been making a lot of them in colour for years, colour TV in Australia was still a long way off.

In 1969, when Neil Armstrong stepped onto the moon, every electrical shop in Australia had its front window full of the blurry images coming back from space. Anyone who didn't have a TV at that stage could watch history being made in the main street of their town. It was probably just as well there was a continuous commentary during the moon landing and subsequent walk because the pictures themselves weren't all that clear.

By the time all the TV channels had replayed the vision a

thousand times over, and the still pictures with explanatory graphics appeared in all the newspapers, it was certainly driven home that we had witnessed one of the most significant scientific feats in history.

About that time there were millions of kids around the world, including me, who thought that being an astronaut might be a fairly good gig. The one minor stumbling block of course was that you had to do well at school and go on to university. Having been invited to leave school at fourteen, I could rule out a career as an astronaut.

WE WISH TO INTERRUPT THIS PROGRAM
TO BRING YOU AN AD

The first 'ad' on Australian television was for Rothman's cigarettes, which seems somehow appropriate given the swamping of TV with cigarette commercials which were to endure through the sixties. We were exhorted to 'get with it' and enjoy Alpine, Ardath, Benson & Hedges, Cambridge, Camel, Capstan, Craven A, Dunhill, Escort, John Player, Kent, Kool, Lucky Strike, Marlboro, Peter Stuyvesant, Rothmans, Turf, Winfield, or any one of a zillion other brands.

I could never quite work out what the difference was between the brands, but then I could never quite get what the big deal was about cigarettes. I gave them a try from time to time, and you could tell the difference with the mentholated ones like Kool, but the rest seemed much of a muchness to me.

As my teen years rolled on, cigarettes became even less attractive when I was told that if you weren't a smoker yourself and you kissed a girl who was, it was like 'licking out an ashtray'.

The power of TV advertising wasn't highlighted by just the cigarette ads; many products became household names on the strength of the images they presented on the box.

We were exhorted daily to 'Join the Escort club — just 42 cents to become a member.' Trouble was the price kept going up, so they had to keep changing the ads. Stuart Wagstaff used to tout for Benson & Hedges, 'When only the best will do,' and we learned 'Wherever you go in this happening world — you'll find Peter Stuyvesant' while, based on its advertising image, the House of Dunhill was presumably a more upmarket means of getting lung cancer.

Ardath had a trite little jingle to the tune of 'Twinkle Twinkle Little Star': 'Ardath Ardath you're a star, beats the other smokes by far.' Australians, being what they are, reworked that jingle in school playgrounds to 'Stuart Wagstaff you're a star, beats the other fags by far.'

And at former Governor-General Viscount Slim's memorial service in 1970, a bloke was arrested for singing, 'Light up a Viscount, a Viscount, a Viscount, light up a Viscount, the best of them all.'

Louie the fly first appeared to flog Mortein flyspray in 1957, but really took off and became something of a cult figure in the sixties. 'Louie the fly, I'm Louie the fly, straight from rubbish tip to you.' Who can't remember Louie? *And,* more importantly, who doesn't associate him with the product Mortein? The 'bad and mean and mighty unclean' Louie had a roguish charm about him, and though he got his comeuppance in every commercial, when a new ad came along there he was, ready to fight another day, filling our houses with every germ imaginable.

Louie was so popular that he even had his own cartoon series in the Sydney *Sunday Telegraph.*

Flytox was a poor second in the advertising race, and the only reason it remains embedded in my grey matter is because my dad reckoned that sarsaparilla (root beer in some places) tasted like Flytox. I'm not sure how he knew what Flytox tasted like.

Through the sixties lots of people, especially in the country, bought their favourite insecticide in liquid form, then dispensed it with a pump-action atomiser — that way you could kill every creeping crawling thing in your home and, no doubt, make the whole joint completely toxic at the same time.

The soap battles for the hearts and minds was raging, with some of the leading brands like Lux, Palmolive, Lifebuoy and Solyptol. You could often detect what soap a particular household used by the perfume left lingering around the place.

That's if you could get past the heavier fog of Dettol or Pine O Cleen hanging in the air. We must have been a scrupulously clean lot in the sixties to have locked away in the brain things like the White King song: 'White King is wonderful, oh by gosh, it kills all the germs as it whitens your wash.'

Come to think of it, we must have been pretty fixated with germs because we were bombarded with every germ killer and cleaner imaginable, there were Ajax, Bon Ami, Surf, Rinso, Fab, Phenyl and Airwick — to keep the toilet 'nice to be near'. And there were Mum, Odorono and any number of deodorant sticks to keep ourselves nice to be near, 'to take the worry out of being close.'

Because hairstyles reached their peak of absurdity in the sixties, especially for women, hair spray manufacturers had to come up with a product that could hold a pile of hair a foot high and a foot wide in position, no matter what the climatic conditions. Alberto VO5 to the rescue. After a good fogging with VO5, a bird could fall head first off her Vespa at thirty miles an hour and walk away with a mild headache. Ditto with Gossamer Invisible Net.

Depending upon your age, guys dressed their hair with Brylcreem ('a little dab'll do ya'), Old Spice hair cream ('masculine freshness, makes it great to be a man'), California Poppy or Texan. Old blokes greased their hair down with Brylcreem and California Poppy, while younger blokes did it with Texan. (Actually, for young men interested in some serious self-abuse, Brylcreem — as its name suggests — was in fact very handy, but a nightmare to get off. Well, that's what I've heard.)

Texan looked greasy when you first slathered it all over your head, however it dried to more of a matt finish, and hardened to form a carapace a crayfish would be quite proud of.

It was essential to hold your hair in place with some kind of product, otherwise you couldn't get the desired swept-forward-and-across look that The Beatles had made so popular. And any self-respecting kid who wasn't a bodgie or a rocker had a Beatle haircut.

IS IT AUSSIE, IS IT, LIZZIE?

In between the ads and all the American shows, we did have some Australian stuff, a lot of it pretty turgid. *Homicide* was one of the more popular local programs, and another cops and robbers show, *Division Four*, began late in the sixties.

Apart from the shows that had a bit of money spent on them, a lot of Australian shows looked and were pretty wooden. There was a particularly hideous thing on the ABC called *Stormy Petrel*, and it was followed by another show which sort of carried on the early Australia theme called *The Outcasts*, and that title pretty much summed up the quality of what was being churned out.

Once again the difference between how lucky the Americans were was highlighted when you compared our early television productions with the stuff they were producing. With the possible exception of Jackie Gleason's *The Honeymooners*, the American sets looked real. The houses they lived in looked solid and comfortable, the furniture was beautiful, they had fabulous cars, beautiful gardens, wide streets and perfect weather.

The sets on shows like *Stormy Petrel* looked as though they were rejects from a local amateur dramatic society production. Even in black and white, nothing looked too convincing, and the sets weren't helped any by shocking acting and dreadful costumes.

Action scenes were virtually impossible to stage in any convincing fashion, so most of the action happened offstage and all you heard was the sound effects, or some breathless thespian lurching in front of the camera to explain what had gone on. For a good part of the early sixties when we suspected a show might be an Australian production, it was the cue for a beeline to the channel changer.

Little kids were surprisingly well catered for on sixties TV. Some of the material offered to them was dire enough, but other stuff went on to become smash hits, some even selling overseas.

The ABC was pretty reliable in showing stuff with fairly broad appeal for kids, even if *Torchy the Battery Boy*, *Captain Pugwash* (with sidekicks, Master Bates and Seaman Stains) and *Clutch Cargo* and his pals Spinner and Paddlefoot wouldn't get a look in with today's more sophisticated anklebiters.

There was a very campy show called *The Magic Circle Club* on the commercials, it sort of 'evolved' into *Adventure Island* with characters like Fester Fumble, Lisa and Clown camping it up outrageously in the Kingdom of Diddle Dum Diddle. The people who put the show together were John Michael Howson and Godfrey Phillipp. Howson camped it up outrageously as one of the show's characters, and Jason Donovan's mum, Sue, was the presenter.

Here's Humphrey saw the debut of the mute bear, there was high drama on the South Seas with *The Adventures of the Seaspray* — this was actually filmed at sea, at least it looked like it was, and it was a refreshing change from the programs which looked like they'd been made for two bob in a shed somewhere.

The ABC produced a science fiction show called *The*

Stranger, which made the *Doctor Who* sets look positively lavish, and there was more out-of-this-world action from *The Magic Boomerang* and *Phoenix Five*. There was something called *Smugglers Beware*, which was supposed to be a comedy for kids — it wasn't!

The star of the decade was definitely *Skippy* the bush kangaroo. Skip had kids doing kangaroo vocal impressions in schoolyards all over the country. The story-lines for *Skippy* were pretty much interchangeable, but at least it too was shot on location, and there was always plenty of action with the added bonus of a helicopter. For its day it must have cost a fortune to make.

There were even a number of quiz shows directed at kids, the most popular being *The Quiz Kids*, hosted by John Dease, in which smarmy little smart-arses made the majority of kids watching feel like out-and-out thickheads.

For adults there were plenty of quiz and game shows to choose from. On Bob Dyer's long-running *BP Pick-a-Box*, Barry Jones reigned as undefeated champion for years. Other popular shows were *I've Got a Secret*, *It Could be You*, *Concentration* and *Coles $6000 Question*.

We even had our own home-grown western in *Whiplash*, a big-budget series about the early days of the Cobb and Co coaches. It had an American star, Peter Graves, in the lead role.

Easily the most controversial Australian program of the sixties was *The Mavis Bramston Show*, starring Gordon Chater, Carol Raye and Barry Creyton. I never really knew what it was all about — it was banned in our house for being too rude — but lots of kids would whisper about the more salacious bits.

The ABC had a long-running serial each week night just before the seven o'clock news. It started out at only fifteen minutes long, but with its enormous popularity it was later expanded. *Bellbird* was based on the lives of the people in a small country town.

The main characters were Joe and Olive Turner, played by Terry Norris and Moira Charleton, John Quinney played by Maurie Fields, Charlie Cousens (Robin Ramsay), Fiona Davies (Gerda Nicholson), Constable Des Davies (Dennis Miller) and Laura Chandler (Meg Morris). Others in the show were Lynette Curran, Penne Hackforth-Jones, Elspeth Ballantyne, Terry McDermott, Gary Gray, John Stanton, Anne Lucas, and Carmel Millhouse and Peter Aanensen as Marge and Jim Bacon, proprietors of the local pub.

Probably because of the subject matter, *Bellbird* was more popular in the country than in the bigger cities, although everyone knew about it when Charlie Cousens, one of the most popular central characters, came to a sticky end when he fell to his death from the top of the town's grain silo.

It was also the first Aussie TV show that, reportedly, some viewers actually believed was about a real town and that the characters were real people (who said TV doesn't adversely affect the brain).

LIP SYNC

For some reason, despite the fact that Australian drama and comedy was pretty flaccid in the early days of TV, we did seem to be able to produce reasonable music shows. Well, the sets at least looked like a bit of money may have been spent on them.

Here kids' pop shows led the way, among them *The Johnny O'Keefe Show* and various permutations of it like *Six o'Clock Rock*, *Teen Scene*, where Olivia Newton-John made her TV debut, and *Sing Sing Sing*, which came to a very sticky end with presenter Johnny O'Keefe's highly publicised nervous breakdown.

Other shows were *Where the Action Is* and *Bandstand*, which ran for years with the totally square-looking Brian Henderson enjoying tremendous popularity. Each week you'd anxiously wait to hear who the special guest stars would be, and each week you'd be mildly disappointed to discover they were going to be pretty much the same ones who had appeared last week or the week before that.

There was also *Kommotion*, with Ken Sparkes presenting and a whole load of people miming atrociously; *Juke Box Jury*, where a group of guest panelists would listen to the latest 45s and declare each one a 'hit' or a 'miss'; *It's All Happening*; *Go*; *Dig We Must*, with Laurie Allen and Bobbie Bright; *Turning On*, hosted by 'Baby' John Burgess; *Ten on the Town*, with Mike Walsh and a little later Ricky May; *Club 7 Teen*, *Surf Sound*, with compere Rob E G; and, marking the return of Johnny O'Keefe, *Where the Action Is*.

Probably the biggest drawback to Australian music shows was the outrageous miming that went on. Some super-cheap Saturday afternoon 'fillers' actually featured actors lip-syncing to songs which were hits for overseas artists, the worst part being the fact we all knew who the artists were that we were listening to, and it certainly wasn't the poor hapless wretch trying to look cool on the TV.

FOR OLDER GROOVERS

Shows which catered more for grown-ups were *The Lorrae Desmond Show*, *In Melbourne Tonight*, with Graham Kennedy, *Here's Dawn*, featuring Dawn Lake, *Sunnyside Up*, with the Happy Gang, *Thank Your Lucky Stars*, *Top of the Town*, and the ill-fated *Tony Hancock Show*. Tony Hancock was incredibly popular and had enjoyed great success with a long-running British radio show called *Hancock's Half Hour*, and he'd come to Australia to make a series of thirteen television shows, but only three got to air. Tony had been working on the series when he committed suicide in Sydney.

Although Australian variety shows weren't particularly awful, they looked pretty much the ugly duckling in comparison to some of the overseas variety shows.

Top of the heap for variety in the sixties was probably *The Dean Martin Show*, which first aired in 1965. Small wonder it was an instant hit when the premier episode featured guest stars Frank Sinatra, Bob Newhart, Diahann Carroll, Joey Heatherton, Danny Thomas, Steve Allen, and Les Brown and his 'band of renown'.

People who regularly appeared on the Dean Martin show were Buddy Hackett, Dom Deluise, Rodney Dangerfield, Caterina Valente, Don Rickles, Florence Henderson, Gene Kelly, George Burns, Jack Klugman, Jonathon Winters, Kate Smith, Lainie Kazan, Liberace, Mahalia Jackson, Peggy Lee,

Petula Clark, Phyllis Diller and Rich Little. As well as the regulars, Deano's show featured more than three hundred guest stars who read like a who's who of the world's entertainment industry.

On the strength of his ability to promote his new releases through his show, Dean Martin regularly featured on the pop music charts in the sixties with songs like 'Everybody Loves Somebody' (the theme from the show), 'Chapel in the Moonlight', 'Little Ole Wine Drinker Me', and 'In the Misty Moonlight'.

The Ed Sullivan Show was also a must-watch on a Saturday night, especially if he had on one of the more popular bands or performers

Without doubt one of the most popular shows on sixties TV was the ABC's *The Avengers*. Hard to categorise, *The Avengers* was a heady mix of action, espionage, science fiction, fantasy and sex, the latter mainly from the delightful leading women and the cutting-edge clothes they wore.

John Steed, played by Patrick McNee, was the debonair bowler-hatted lead man, and in early episodes his partner, Cathy Gale, was played by Honor Blackman. Later episodes featured Diana Rigg as Mrs Emma Peel, arguably the most memorable of Steed's partners. When Emma Peel appeared in a tight black leather catsuit, the drool factor for the male audience went off the scale.

The series ran for almost the entire sixties and, towards the end, after Diana Rigg left the show, Linda Thorson came in as Tara King, but unfortunately she couldn't fill Emma Peel's fashionable boots.

Many people thought the John Steed character was based on James Bond, but in fact *The Avengers* began on TV the year before the first Bond movie was released.

In a similar vein of espionage with a slight comic twist was a groundbreaking American show called *I Spy* — groundbreaking in that it was the first TV series to feature a black actor (Bill Cosby) in a lead role. Robert Culp played Kelly Robinson, a top tennis player who was really a spy, and Bill Cosby played Alexander Scott, who was a language expert posing as Kelly Robinson's trainer.

The show was filmed in exotic locations all over the world as they went about the spying business.

Up until *I Spy*, Bill Cosby had been known only as a stand-up comedian, and the popularity of the show really gave his career a kick along.

Another big-budget spy show, at least by British standards, was *Danger Man* starring Patrick McGoohan. *Danger Man* was shown on the ABC and was hugely popular. Described as Bond without the girls, there were still plenty of spy gadgets to fool around with. 'My name is Drake, John Drake' set the scene for each episode and Drake's cover was as an employee in the travel industry, when in reality he was a top British agent.

Other shows aimed squarely at adults were *The Fugitive*, where Richard Kimble, played by David Janssen, went on the run week after week after being wrongfully accused of killing his wife. *Z Cars,* from the UK, was a great police drama, though the Zephyrs they drove looked a bit dinky, and *Combat*, a Second World War drama, which had a different story each week.

Somewhat frothier were a couple of private investigator shows out of America: *Hawaiian Eye*, starring Robert Conrad as Thomas Jefferson Lupaka and, to keep a younger audience interested, Troy Donahue as Phil Barton, Connie Stevens as 'Cricket' and Kazuo Kim as 'Poncie Ponce'; and, also achieving the crossover, *77 Sunset Strip,* which had a teen cult following because of the character 'Kookie', Gerald Lloyd Kookson III, played by Ed Byrnes.

Kookie was always running his comb through his hair to attract the chicks. There was even a popular song, 'Kookie, Kookie Lend Me Your Comb', sung by Ed Byrnes and Connie Stevens.

Comb sales skyrocketed, and for a few seasons comb and brush sets in small zippered vinyl cases were very popular as gifts for teenage boys. I had about fifty of the bloody things.

KARTOON KAPERS

Cartoon shows were incredibly popular, some of them as popular with grown-ups as they were with kids. The moment the lyrics 'Meet George Jetson, his boy Elroy, daughter Judy, Jane his wife' were heard we'd be agog. Same goes for *The Flintstones*:

> *Flintstones, meet the Flintstones, they're the modern Stone*
> *   Age family.*
> *From the town of Bedrock, they're a page right out of*
> *   history.*
> *Let's ride, with the family down the street,*
> *through the courtesy of Fred's two feet.*
> *When you're with the Flintstones, have a yabba dabba doo*
> *   time,*
> *a dabba doo time, we'll have a gay old time.*

Head and shoulders above the rest was *Thunderbirds,* a glorified puppet show put together by a British couple, Gerry and Sylvia Anderson and incredibly popular with kids and teenagers. The puppets were completely unconvincing, but they sucked you in anyway with marvellous stories each week about the trials and tribulations of 'International Rescue'.

Set many years into the future, *Thunderbirds* featured

fabulous characters like International Rescue's London agent Lady Penelope, who got chauffeured around in a spage-age hot pink Rolls-Royce with the numberplate 'FAB 1'. Everything about Thunderbirds was fab!

Although not animated, another sixties television show which crossed generational lines was *Batman*. It was so ridiculously over the top it was screechingly funny, especially with 'WOP!', 'KAPOW!' and 'SHAZAM!' flashing onto the screen in the action sequences — and the shows were *all* action.

Starring Adam West as Batman and Burt Ward as Robin, the 'Caped Crusader' attracted guest stars, some of whom became regular characters, like bees to a honey pot. Among the Hollywood legends who queued up to get on the show were Anne Baxter, Burgess Meredith, Carolyn Jones (Morticia from *The Addams Family*), Cesar Romero, Cliff Robertson, Julie Newmar, Milton Berle, Vincent Price, Eartha Kitt, Edward G Robinson, Hermione Baddeley, Ida Lupino, Glynis Johns, Eli Wallach, Joan Collins, Tallulah Bankhead, John Astin, Liberace, Lesley Gore, Jill St John, James Brolin, Steve Allen, Teri Garr, Allan Hale (the skipper from *Gilligan's Island*), Gypsy Rose Lee, who thankfully kept her clothes on — at this stage of her career she was well into her fifties, Gerry Mathers (the Beaver from *Leave It to Beaver*), Art Carney, Robert Montgomery, Rudy Vallee, Sammy Davis Jnr and Zsa Zsa Gabor. Clearly there was a certain cachet attached to appearing on *Batman*.

Another great attraction of the show was all the fabulous gear that Batman and Robin had, including the Batmobile, the Batplane and the Batboat. Not to mention the Batcave — oh to have *that* in your backyard.

AT THE FLICKS

THE LOOK

What set the bulk of the movies made in the sixties apart was the fact they *looked* like movies made in the sixties. Whether the movie was a western, a historical drama, a Shakespearean classic or a 'sword and sandals' extravaganza, the male actors all had sixties haircuts, including a good many Beatle cuts, and the female actors invariably had the big hair which was so fashionable for much of the decade, not to mention the distinctive make-up — mascara trowelled on, blue eyeshadow, and various shades of fluorescent and frosted lipsticks.

A perfect case in point was the hugely popular and award-winning movie *Dr Zhivago* starring Julie Christie and Omar Sharif. Despite the fact Boris Pasternak's novel was set during the First World War and the Russian Revolution, you'd swear from the make-up and hairstyles in the movie that it was set in the year the movie was made — 1965. Still who cared, as long as the blokes could drool over Julie Christie, and the ladies over Omar.

Success at the American Academy Awards pretty much meant box office success too, with a few exceptions. The movies to pick up the big gong through the sixties were *The Apartment*, *West Side Story*, *Lawrence of Arabia*, *Tom Jones*, *My Fair Lady*, *The Sound of Music*, *A Man for All Seasons*, *In the Heat of the Night, Oliver!* and *Midnight Cowboy.*

Midnight Cowboy is the only movie in my life that I saw again immediately. Having sat through a screening, I then went out to the box office to buy another ticket. Something about the bleakness of the film appealed to me. I was eighteen at the time, so perhaps it was just a growing-up thing. The performances of Dustin Hoffman and Jon Voigt no doubt helped the success of the film in no small way.

Music from movies also had an enhanced chance of making it across to the popular music charts. Some of the Academy Award-winning songs from movies in the sixties which did just that were 'Never on Sunday', 'Moon River', 'Days of Wine and Roses', 'Call Me Irresponsible', 'Chim Chim Cheree', 'Born Free', 'Talk to the Animals', 'The Windmills of Your Mind' and 'Raindrops Keep Falling on My Head'.

THE HORROR OF HAMMER

Some of the most popular movies of the sixties were churned out by Britain's Hammer studio. They were mostly horror movies and mostly dreadful, but we lapped them up. Every once in a while the studio would produce something of merit, but given their prolific output, the law of averages would suggest that was bound to happen.

Hammer relied heavily on a pool of actors who appeared time and time again in their features, the most prominent among them Peter Cushing and Christopher Lee.

Often the drive-in theatres would run a 'Hammer Horror' as the first feature of a double bill, with a more serious film shown second and, on very special occasions, at least as far as I was concerned, they'd promote a 'fright night', with two Hammer movies on the same bill.

Because I had quite prominent canine teeth, I could do a passable vampire impression. One night at the drive-in we were watching a particularly scary movie where a young couple were stranded in Transylvania in a broken-down Kombi van. Just at that heart-stopping moment, you-know who returned to the car. I put my face to the window and, baring my fangs, scared my girlfriend shitless. She refused to go to any more horror flicks after that.

Among the more memorable (in the broadest sense of the word) Hammer movies of the sixties were:

The Curse of the Werewolf (Oliver Reed)
The Brides of Dracula (Peter Cushing)
The Two Faces of Dr Jekyll (Christopher Lee)
The Phantom of the Opera (Herbert Lom)
The Damned (McDonald Carey)
Kiss of the Vampire (No one I'd ever heard of)
The Evil of Frankenstein (Peter Cushing)
The Devil Ship Pirates (Christopher Lee)
The Curse of the Mummy's Tomb (No one I'd ever heard of)
She (Ursula Andress)
The Nanny (Bette Davis)
Dracula, Prince of Darkness (Christopher Lee)
The Plague of the Zombies (A heap of zombies)
Rasputin, the Mad Monk (Christopher Lee)
The Old Dark House (Robert Morley)
The Witches (Joan Fontaine)
One Million Years BC (Raquel Welch)
Frankenstein Created Woman (Peter Cushing)
The Mummy's Shroud (Mummies)
The Anniversary (Bette Davis)
The Devil Rides Out (Christopher Lee)
Dracula Has Risen from the Grave (Christopher Lee)
Frankenstein Must be Destroyed (Peter Cushing)

A few of these movies fall into the category of 'odd man out', for instance *The Nanny* and *The Anniversary*, both starring Bette Davis, were a cut above the rest, if only for Bette's amazing acting skills. Through the sixties Bette was going through a slow patch in her career, so directors exploited her fairly shamelessly in a series of low-budget horror flicks. The two she did for Hammer were among the better ones before her career again took an upturn.

The other two to stand out from the normal Hammer genre are *She*, starring Ursula Andress, and *One Million Years BC,* with Raquel Welch. Both movies would have been entirely forgettable had it not been for the fact they both featured two of the most beautiful (and large-breasted) women in the world cavorting around in scanty bits of strategically draped animal hide. I can't for the life of me remember anything about the plot of either movie, but I remember vividly Ursula and Raquel's attributes, but then I was sixteen or seventeen, so I would, wouldn't I?

NO. 007, WITH A BULLET

'Bond, James Bond' arrived with a martini in hand and girl on arm when Sean Connery first appeared in *Dr No* in 1962. The movie was a worldwide hit, and set a solid foundation for the Bond franchise. The suave character of Bond, the beautiful women, the exotic locations, the quirky support characters, the gadgetry and the unlikely plots ensured a wide audience for years to come.

Sean Connery was a busy boy through the entire decade. As well as his other projects he managed to churn out *From Russia with Love* in '63, *Goldfinger* in '64, *Thunderball* in '65 and *You Only Live Twice* in '67, before taking a spell.

The Bond movies had a bit of an identity crisis in 1967 when *Casino Royale* was released. I never really thought of it as a 'real' Bond movie, and it wasn't that the spoof, starring Peter Sellers wasn't enjoyed by some people, but I didn't get it.

Australian actor George Lazenby became the new official James Bond in 1969 when he starred in *On Her Majesty's Secret Service*. But it was a disaster and he didn't have his licence to thrill extended.

The Bond movies were also remarkable for producing theme songs which became popular music hits. Starting with the original 007 theme by the John Barry Seven in 1962 'Dr No', the movies spawned hits for Matt Monro with 'From Russia with Love'; Shirley Bassey, 'Goldfinger'; Tom Jones,

'Thunderball'; Nancy Sinatra, 'You Only Live Twice'; and Herb Alpert and the Tijuana Brass, 'Casino Royale'.

Despite the array of voluptuous beauties who have fallen for the charms of James Bond over the years, no one has come even remotely close to the vision of Ursula Andress as Honey Ryder emerging from the sea in *Dr No*.

When *Playboy* magazine published a list of 'The 100 Sexiest Stars of the Century' in 1999, the sixties were well represented by Ursula Andress, Kim Novak, Gina Lollobrigida, Brigitte Bardot, Jane Fonda and Jacqueline Bisset.

Every other spy movie (and there were a rash of them in the sixties) attempted to mimic the Bond formula in style and music, with varying degrees of success.

Among the more popular spy movies and TV shows following the Bond genre was *The Man from UNCLE* (United Network Command for Law and Enforcement) starring, as the TV show's top secret agents, Robert Vaughn as Napoleon Solo, David McCallum as Illya Kuryakin, and Leo G Carroll as their boss, Alexander Waverley.

The men from UNCLE fought a constant battle against arch enemy THRUSH. (No one ever quite spelt out what THRUSH stood for, but among us fans it was generally thought to be Technical Hierachy for the Removal of Undesirables and the Subjugation of Humanity.

The TV series was made between 1964 and 1968, and with its one-hour episodes it was hugely popular in Australia. The worldwide popularity of the series was evidenced by the fact that the producers were able to cobble together bits and pieces of the TV series, usually episodes which had run as two parters, and repackage them as movies which went into general release.

The UNCLE movies were not high art but found a keen

audience, especially among teenagers and young adults. The cinema screens were literally bombarded with UNCLE movies over a four-year period beginning with:

The Spy with My Face, 1965
One of Our Spies Is Missing, 1966
One Spy Too Many, 1966
The Spy in the Green Hat, 1966
The Karate Killers, 1967
The Helicopter Spies, 1967
How to Steal the World, 1968

Like so many popular TV series of the sixties which managed to develop a cult following, *The Man from UNCLE* had no difficulty attracting a galaxy of special guest stars, among them Telly Savalas, Barry Sullivan, Herbert Lom, Joan Crawford, Eleanor Parker, Leslie Nielsen, John Carradine, Julie London, Carol Lynley, Bradford Dillman, Lola Allbright, Senta Berger, Fritz Weaver, Curt Jurgens, Terry Thomas, Kim Darby, Janet Leigh, Jack Palance, Joan Blondell, Dorothy Provine and Rip Torn.

Columbia pictures, which had originally been offered the Bond movie idea and declined (much to its chagrin later), eventually climbed upon the spy bandwagon, even if it was a little late. In 1966 they brought to the screen a movie called *The Silencers*, which was very loosely based on a secret agent, Matt Helm, created by author Donald Hamilton in a swag of books.

Although the original stories were really about a bloke who was little more than a hired assassin who went around bumping off anyone deemed to be a threat to the United States by the 'US Intelligence and Counter Espionage'

(ICE), in the series of movies Dean Martin played Matt Helm as a sort of comedic James Bond. At the time it was thought that Dean Martin was a rather strange choice to play Matt Helm, however his career was at its peak at the time — he was hugely popular as a recording artist and actor, and he had a top-rating TV show.

The first Matt Helm film co-starred the luscious Stella Stevens and was a massive hit. In the same year the studio rushed out another Helm film, *Murderer's Row*, with Karl Malden and Ann-Margret. Though not as popular as the first, and with a sillier story line, *Murderer's Row* did well enough to encourage the producers to press on.

The Ambushers, with Senta Berger, was churned out in 1967 and, to completely flog the dead horse, it was followed by *The Wrecking Crew*, featuring Sharon Tate in her last movie, and Chuck Norris in his first.

Just think, if the powers that be had decided not to make *The Wrecking Crew*, we might have been spared the acting ability of Chuck Norris, and the world would have been a better place.

In November 1969, a mob of maniacs who dubbed themselves the Manson family, followers of a psychopath called Charles Manson, broke into Sharon Tate's home in Beverley Hills. At the time Sharon was married to director Roman Polanski and was eight months pregnant with their child. Sharon and the guests at her house were all butchered in a senseless and indescribably vicious crime which shocked the world.

GETTING DOWN AND GETTING DIRTY

As if the music scene weren't enough to give any parent of the sixties a serious case of palpitations, the movies suddenly got sexy, and a new classification scheme was introduced by the federal government. If a movie got an 'adults only' classification, AO, we were banned from going.

Not that the classification stopped us, especially when you sneaked into the drive-in in the boot of a car.

More and more movies were getting an AO classification, and the studios seemed to be trying to outdo each other when it came to presenting erotica on the screen. The Brits produced a highly popular movie in *Tom Jones*, starring Albert Finney and Susannah York, in which a young bloke gallivanted around the countryside, bonking as many fair maidens as possible.

The slippery slide to debauchery was rather steep when you consider the changing standards. By 1968, when Roger Vadim released his movie, *Barbarella*, starring Jane Fonda, *Tom Jones* would have looked like an Enid Blyton tale. Jane Fonda's Barbarella, some time far in the future, is set the task of saving the Earth from the evil Durand Durand. Just why she had to bonk her way across the universe in order to do so is never quite explained, but then no one went to see *Barbarella* for the story anyway.

Andy Warhol's dirty, trashy and completely unwatchable films started turning up in Australia in the late sixties — *Flesh*, *The Chelsea Girls*, *Eat*, *Kiss* and *Blow Job*. And the most controversial was the late sixties release of the Swedish film, *I Am Curious — Yellow*, which was the first to show pubic hair and a flaccid penis. This film was perhaps the beginning of a fine tradition, a movie which would have quickly sunk without a trace if not for the controversy.

SMUTTY CARRY ON

The producers of the *Carry On* films were highly prolific throughout the sixties. They turned out a swag of low-budget 'tits and bums' flicks, with a core cast of British character actors, including Sid James, Kenneth Connor, Charles Hawtrey, Joan Sims, Kenneth Williams, Hattie Jacques, Lis Fraser and Bill Owen.

The movies were low on class or any kind of sensitivity whatsoever, but high on entertainment value, at least to a certain audience, and that was an audience they targeted particularly well.

Cobbling together a collection of corny and very often smutty jokes and one-liners, the movies would often parody news of the era, and even in some cases other movies, as was the case of *Carry On Cleo* in 1964, after the big-budget *Cleopatra* starring Liz Taylor, which had bombed out in a tidal wave of publicity the year before.

Other *Carry Ons* from the sixties were:

Carry On Regardless, 1960
Carry On Cruising, 1962
Carry On Cabby, 1963
Carry On Jack, 1964
Carry On Spying, 1964
Carry On Cowboy, 1965

Carry On Screaming, 1966
Carry On Don't Lose Your Head, 1966
Carry On Follow That Camel, 1966
Carry On Doctor, 1968
Carry On up the Khyber, 1968
Carry On Camping, 1969
Carry On Again Doctor, 1969

THE BIG AND MOST GROSS

In 1968, one of the decade's most important films was released, Stanley Kubrick's *2001: A Space Odyssey*. Up until then science fiction movies had been pretty low-rent. They had been made on a shoestring, and looked like it. But they were not quite as dire as the crap dished out the decade before — which included stuff like *The Thing (From Another World)*, *Earth versus the Flying Saucer* and *I Married a Monster from Outer Space*.

2001 was different, it was a big-budget movie with a highly regarded director. Most of the money which went into the movie went on the special effects and, for their time, they were awesome — no one had ever seen anything quite like it. And the director's use of classical music with the stunning scenes in space left an indelible impression on the moviegoer.

The critics panned it but the audiences, especially young people, loved it. I couldn't wait to see it, but when I did, eventually, at our local drive-in, I was bitterly disappointed. I loved the special effects, I loved the music, but I didn't get it! It seemed to me to be overblown arty-farty crap!

Despite the fact the movie industry was in a serious downturn in the sixties, in part due to the popularity of television, the decade still managed to produce some blockbusters. The highest grossing films at the box office were:

One Hundred an One Dalmatians (1961)
Jungle Book (1967)
The Sound of Music (1965)
Thunderball (1965)
Goldfinger (1964)
Doctor Zhivago (1965)
You Only Live Twice (1967)
The Graduate (1967)
Butch Cassidy and the Sundance Kid (1969)
Mary Poppins (1964)

Given the amount of money spent on it, *Cleopatra*, starring Elizabeth Taylor and Richard Burton, should have been a huge hit. Especially as every single gossip column in the world was chronicling the steamy romance between the two stars.

Cleopatra was the most expensive film ever made up to 1963, and turned out to be a disaster for the Fox studio. The studio narrowly escaped going under, thanks largely to the success of two smash hits, *The Longest Day* (1962) and *The Sound of Music* (1965).

Because of the enormous cost of making films in Hollywood, many of the sixties' biggest movies were made in Britain, notably among them *Lawrence of Arabia* (1962) and *Doctor Zhivago* (1965).

Australian cinema had still not come of age, but occasionally we did manage to churn out something with reasonable audience appeal, like *They're a Weird Mob* (1966).

THE DRIVES

Despite the advent of television, drive-in picture shows thrived throughout the sixties. Any town of reasonable size had at least one drive-in and in the cities there were heaps of them. The walk-in picture theatres had slowly been declining in popularity at the same time as the drive-ins boomed.

For kids the drives weren't so much about what was on the feature bill but more to do with hanging out with your mates, and when you got a bit older and started developing an interest in sex, your car (or your dad's car if you could wheedle it out of him) was your own private parlour for a 'bit of the other'. And because there were always two movies on with a break at half-time, you had plenty of time for whatever took your fancy.

Australian cities had numerous drive-ins dotted around the suburbs, and in the country towns which were large enough to support a theatre, they were usually located on the outskirts where there was ample space for the rather extensive area required for all the cars.

For some reason drive-in names often ended in '—line': across Australia there was at least one Moonline, Skyline, Mainline, Pineline, Borderline, Starline or Beachline drive-in theatre in every state.

Some places were clearly not meant to have drive-ins, but that didn't deter the developers because they sprung up all over the place. In regions of the country prone to heavy and prolonged fog, it was common for screenings to be cancelled. In areas where rainfall was particularly heavy, long-suffering patrons could spend the evening trying to make out what was happening on the big screen through a screen of water, which picked up any tiny amount of glare from any source, or condensation, which made the windscreen almost completely opaque.

The location of the drive-in could cause additional hassles, especially if the area was low-lying. This invariably meant fog in winter and mozzies in summer. If you didn't want to be eaten alive, you'd sit in the car with all the windows wound up tightly, slowly suffocating to death.

Certain towns really took the drive-in theatre to heart. Albany, on the south coast of Western Australia, were I spent my late teen years, was a relatively small town in the sixties, yet it had no fewer than three drive-in theatres: the Orana, the Central 70 (so named for the big screen) and the Boronia.

The drive-in kiosk was always located at the back of the parking area underneath the projection room. Wherever you went in Australia, kiosk fare was pretty much the same; you'd swear that someone had the franchise for the lot of them.

Just before half-time, you'd get the waft of hot fat drifting along on the night air as the chips and Chiko Rolls were prepared for the rush. As well as all the stuff dripping in fat, you could get steak sandwiches with fried onion and tomato sauce. These were prepared well ahead, so that by half-time they'd be lukewarm at best, and the contents of the greaseproof wrapping would be starting to congeal rather nicely.

Coca-Cola, Fanta and Passiona were probably the most popular fizzy drinks, although this could vary depending upon the geographical location of the drive-in, when a localised brand might be popular.

The one *constant*, wherever the drive-in was located was the choc bomb . This was basically two scoops of vanilla ice-cream in a wafer bucket, with the ice-cream top dipped in melted chocolate then shoved in the freezer to set. Some drive-ins had a bit of a reputation for making the bombs too far ahead, and that, too, could lend a rather unappealing sogginess to the wafer bucket.

Though the movies being screened were often secondary to the social experience of the drive-in, they tended to be features which had appeared in the walk-in theatres some months before, and in some cases that could be up to a year before.

Like the standard theatre, the usual fare was advertisement slides, followed by a cartoon, followed by more advertisement slides, then the first feature, usually a B-grade western or something similar. After half-time, more advertisement slides, then the main feature.

The choice of car to take to the drive-in was of critical importance, especially if some smuggling was going to be attempted. A Holden or Falcon sedan was pretty good: you could fit two large or three small kids in the boot.

My dad's Chev Belair was grouse, because you could fit four kids in the boot. Even a mate's Renault Ten, with its boot in the front, was able to accommodate my girlfriend and me (very cosy, indeed). Trouble is, the bastard wouldn't let us out when we got inside, instead diving around, and around going over the speed humps until we were sick as dogs.

There was a certain art to getting out of the boot once you were in the drive-in. Parked as far away from the ticket box as possible, the driver then made great play of getting a blanket out of the boot, and holding it up as if straightening it, screening the smuggled kids and the slide around the dark side of the car and into the back seat.

Then the fights started over which window the speaker went in, how loud the volume should be and then, of course, who put the speaker back on the stand after the show when it was freezing.

One cunning stunt that parents would pull, when you were younger, was to stick you into your pyjamas and dressing-gowns so that you'd be ready for bed the moment you got home. This, of course, was a double-edged sword because you couldn't nag to go to the canteen at half-time, just in case some of your schoolmates should spot you.

Once a bit older, it was great fun wandering around while the feature was under way. Up the back in the darkest part of the drive-in was where all the serious pashing went on. On any given night you could get enough perving in to last you a week. And, with a couple of mates, you could suddenly start rocking up and down on the bumper at a strategic moment. Sticking a matchstickin a tyre valve would also provide some fine entertainment when the flicks had finished.

At the end of the night the projectionist would quickly throw up a slide reminding people to replace the speakers on their stands before driving off. Many a car ended up with speakers dangling inside as they drove off, or worse still with their windows dangling off speaker stands.

JAFFAS IN THE STALLS

With the popularity of the drive-ins, the traditional movie houses found the going tough. In the larger cities these were mainly grand old theatres, taking up enormous amounts of valuable real estate in prime locations. As a result, sadly, many of them met their demise, or were later converted into multi-screened 'plexes' to increase the economy of scale.

The old theatres all seemed to have certain elements in common. Horsehair padded seats which flipped up when you stood up. Rich-toned, though often threadbare, carpets, and literally kilometres of lavish velvet curtains hung in great swags across and around the screen, and often around the walls as well. The smell of old leather, mingled with dust and often a little damp, was all pervading.

Typically, the cheap seats were in the downstairs stalls, the better seats upstairs and the premium seats, the two-seater lounges in the boxes, along the side balconies. Some of the very old and large theatres also had cheap seats way up the back, in the 'gods'. Invariably these seats would have splits in the leather with horsehair and springs sticking out, ready to snag, pinch or prick the gear of the unwary.

Some really grand old theatres had extra features like a Wurlitzer organ, which would come up through the stage floor to entertain patrons before the movies began and again at half-time.

The fare at the kiosks of the walk-in theatres varied somewhat from the drive-ins, probably because they didn't want the smell of hot fat permeating the carpets and drapes. Despite the lack of the deep-fried stuff, the rest of the consumables were pretty much the same. The ice-cream choc bombs, and over-priced packets of Jaffas, Fantales, Maltesers, Columbine caramels, Milkshakes (the lolly, not the liquid variety) Violet Crumbles, Pollywaffles, Jersey toffees and white chocolate.

If it happened to be a Saturday matinee, the biggest sellers were likely to be Choo Choo bars, White Knights, Chicos, Smarties, Milk Bottles, the little packets of sugar cigarettes, called Fags, complete with bright 'burning' red tips, and Nigger Boy licorice. If you were particularly flush, you could buy the long red and yellow box of assorted licorice straps — the box featured the faces of two black boys, Rastus and Sambo. Political correctness did not rule in the sixties.

During one Saturday matinee I recall in the early sixties, a kid fell from the balcony onto some kids below. He wasn't seriously hurt, but it sure disrupted the show for a while. We couldn't tell Mum and Dad that we were downstairs when the kid fell, because we were supposed to be upstairs, as all the rough kids we were meant to avoid were downstairs. But we went downstairs because the seats were cheaper and therefore there'd be more to spend on lollies.

ON THE HOME FRONT

DÉCOR IS NOT A DIRTY WORD

With the arrival of television, households all over the country were suddenly exposed to styles and fashion fads from overseas. This, of course, had a subtle, and in some cases not so subtle, effect on how we saw ourselves and our homes.

Up until the sixties, most lounge rooms might have been furnished with a three-piece suite, usually a three-seater overstuffed lounge and two bulky overstuffed chairs, with possibly a china cabinet, a standard lamp and a couple of occasional tables to complete the picture.

Now, with TV we could check out how the other half lived, and it looked pretty darned good. Out went the overstuffed suite and in came the new vinyl modular lounge suite. At best it might be plain green, yellow or red, but at its most atrocious it could be a ghastly travesty of taste.

At the time we thought it was gorgeous, but in 1960 my family bought a new suite to replace the old brown patterned overstuffed one. The new suite comprised of five pieces, three of which could be placed together to make a lounge, thus two had one arm each and the middle bit, of course, was armless. The other two pieces had the standard two arms. The arms were a pale timber, which had been bent in a trendy curve.

So far so good, but the rock upon which our décor

consultant (Mum) perished was the fact the suite was five different colours. Each piece a different pastel shade. One was yellow, one was pink, one grey, one lime and the other blue.

The carpet in our lounge room was pale blue, while the curtains were every colour available in 1960 — featuring a Dali-esque print of huge multicoloured autumn leaves on a creamish background.

We thought the whole room looked fabulous, especially as it was topped off with nests of tables and an ashtray on a chrome stand with a plastic spinner on the top. Even though no one in our house smoked, it was proper etiquette to provide the facility for visitors. There was also a magazine rack, made out of black wrought iron, to hold the latest copies of *Women's Weekly*, *Woman's Day*, the daily paper and the *TV Times*, and against a wall was a lowboy china cabinet featuring sliding glass doors. But sitting in pride of place in one corner of the room, like a shrine, was the Healing twenty-one-inch solid-state console TV with the anodised aluminium TV lamp on top, and the gently buzzing antenna booster box alongside on the floor.

We really did think that the whole look was fab.

But my Aunty Iris had a lava lamp, with coloured globs moving about in an oily morass. If only we'd had one of those our lives would have been complete.

WE HAVE CONTACT ... AND VINYL

No one could have made it through the sixties without vinyl, it was an extremely popular product. Kitchen suites, lounge suites, bar stools, car seats all came in new vinyl colours. Anyone who at sometime in the sixties didn't have a mustard-coloured lounge suite had truly missed out.

Even the floors were covered in vinyl, at least in work areas. It seemed the floor pattern for vinyl coverings was as limitless as the designers' imagination, fake tile patterns were popular as were mosaic patterns, fake wood grain and even fake pebbles.

The pebble look was not terribly practical because although the pebbles were relatively flat, they had behind them small pockets of air which raised them slightly. Unfortunately the early sixties also saw stiletto heels enjoying incredible popularity among some women. A couple of weeks walking around in stilettos on a pebble-look vinyl floor would pretty much take care of the pebbles, covering the floor with hundreds of tiny punctures.

The fifties craze of painting every cupboard door a different colour and, in some cases, every wall, had started to die out, but the 'feature' wall was very much in vogue. If you had your lounge room painted, say, a soft grey, it would not be uncommon to have the feature wall a pale lemon colour. This, of course, sometimes got a bit out of hand and you could wind up with some hideous combinations.

With the gradual arrival of easy-to-hang wallpaper, there was no end to the decorating permutations budding amateur interior designers could inflict on their houses. The first really popular wall covering was Contact.

In our kitchen, at one time, we had a wall covered in Contact featuring fake white bricks with ivy creeping all over them. Because it had been applied as a homemade job, the bricks, unfortunately, had a few creases in them and the whole thing looked a bit wonky.

Still, Contact was coated in tough vinyl, which meant you could scrub it pretty vigorously without the pattern disappearing before your eyes. And, of course, any leftover bits could be used to line the insides of the kitchen cupboards. For years newspaper had been used for this purpose, but it got yucky fairly quickly, and besides, mice used to love eating it. They (the rodents) got their comeuppance with the arrival of Contact. Many people used Contact only for lining cupboards and cutlery drawers, and there must have been thousands of homes across the country with the contents of their cupboards resting on the red basket-weave-pattern Contact, which was among the most popular.

The generally conservative styling favoured by most Australians for their homes took a rapid turn in the sixties with a new 'space-age' look becoming suddenly popular as the space race began.

Flat or near flat low-pitched roofs replaced the traditional gables. Large sliding windows and doors replaced the conventional timber doors and lap and sash windows, carports replaced the detached garage and, inside, open-plan living became all the go.

Very often the lounge and dining room became one room, and a peculiar idea called a 'conversation pit' emerged. This was simply a lowering of the floor, usually around a central feature, typically a fireplace. The idea was to confine people to a more intimate space where they could lounge around on cushions or lounge chairs placed facing each other in the pit, and make conversation. Why people couldn't make conversation in a conventional lounge room escaped me. It must have escaped nearly everyone else too, because conversation pits were a passing fad.

The sixties kitchen grew larger to include family space, thus we saw the beginnings of what was to be ubiquitously known as the family room.

By no means was the influence of TV restricted to the inside of the house. Because of shows like *The Donna Reed Show*, *Bewitched*, and *I Dream of Jeannie*, outdoor living areas, which before might have been called gazebos, or even just semi-enclosed verandahs, suddenly became patios, because that's what they called them in America.

And as our houses changed, so too did the gardens. Traditional English-style gardens with flowerbeds, lawns, hedges and fences, gave way to a more open look with wide expanses of lawn sweeping to the footpath, and palms and spiky-leafed plants giving a more exotic and uncluttered look.

The huge back yards remained pretty much unchanged, with Hills hoist clothes lines dominating the scene, and a galvanised metal shed now having to house the Victa lawnmower and all the half-empty paint tins, bikes, car parts, tools and boxes of bric-a-brac which had once resided in the back of the garage.

Only seriously well-off families could afford swimming pools, but everyone could afford a canvas or vinyl wading pool. These invariably only lasted one summer, if that, with the fabric giving out through having been left in the sun for months on end. The result was a pool of stagnant green water in the bottom, which provided a breeding ground for millions of mozzies.

IN THE ENGINE ROOM

Despite the coming of television, as with previous decades, the kitchen, specifically the kitchen table, was still at the heart of family life in the sixties. Although usually at the back of the house, the kitchen door was in effect for family and most visitors, the front door. In fact, particularly in the country, the actual front door was often stuck fast from disuse.

As well as the actual eating of meals, most things were done at the kitchen table, from entertaining to dealing with family crises and from homework to the annual tax return.

The kitchen was overwhelmingly the domain of the ladies. Most Aussie males didn't know a pot from a pan, a soufflé from a salad — and were bloody proud of it.

Wall ovens, which were pretty much unheard of until the sixties, started to gain in popularity, although they took a somewhat circuitous route. As people changed over from the old slow combustion, or even the old Metters stove to new gas or electric upright models, choices became more varied. The smartest kitchens gradually started having side-by-side and split-level stoves installed, before eventually the fully blown wall oven, with separate hob top, took over.

Suddenly the island bench became popular, and the really 'out there' designs included the stove top or sink.

Single sinks would no longer do, not that anyone was

washing any more dishes, but double sinks were the go.

Dishwashers, although increasingly available, were hideously expensive and relatively unreliable, so their surge in popularity came after the sixties had ended.

Laminex and Formica were no longer the only toppings for benches and facings for kitchen and laundry cupboards, as designers moved away from the green or red marble-look tops for tables and benches. Patterns were still popular but tended to be a little more subtle than previously, basket-weave patterns, leaves and even plain colours featured more and more.

During the sixties the kitchen gradually featured more and more mod cons, and if you had some luxury appliances, like a Mixmaster, you'd display them on a benchtop. This practice was most successful when the colour of the appliance, in the case of the Mixmaster white or pale green, blended with the rest of the décor. In those kitchens where every cupboard door was a different colour, it didn't matter particularly much.

Toasters were still mainly the type with drop-down sides, the pop-ups the preserve of the very well-to-do or kitchen fanatic, while the electric kettle was the bulbous chrome variety with a bakelite handle or the ceramic Hecla with the disposable element.

Electric frypans were becoming commonplace, and when one of these arrived in a kitchen for the first time, the lady of the house experimented for weeks, determined to prove that this marvelously modern appliance was so versatile you could cook virtually anything in it. You could poach or fry eggs (although why you'd want to poach eggs in an electric frypan when you had a purpose-built poacher with individual egg holders sitting in the cupboard, I still haven't worked out), you could make curries and roast vegetables and meats, and there were even cookbooks devoted to the frypan.

One of the least successful recipes for the pan was the 'bake in the frypan cake'. I'm not sure if it was something my mum did wrong, but I don't recall the frypan cake being made more than the once.

Thanks to White Wings and Betty Sydney, cake making enjoyed quite a renaissance in the sixties. No more the drudgery of a million ingredients tediously combined in the big old mixing bowl, now it was a case of rip open the packet, chuck the contents of the big sachet into the Mixmaster, add the milk or water or whatever was called for on the instructions on the back of the pack, and Bob's your uncle. Then it was into the oven (once you'd given up on the frypan), wait for the cake to cook and then after it had cooled down, the icing or topping would be the contents of the smaller sachet in the cake mix box.

The variations were endless, from plain vanilla and butter cakes right up to the wonderful rainbow cake, which was a favourite in our house.

The rainbow cake was simply a cake of three different coloured cake mixes (chocolate, strawberry and vanilla) prepared separately then very gently swirled together so that when the cake was baked you ended up with an impressive marbled effect. I'm not sure if there was any difference in the taste of each different colour, but it looked good.

The sixties saw the beginning of the end of Irish stew, rissoles with mashed spuds, peas and gravy, Sunday roast lamb, tuna casserole, bright orange smoked fish in white sauce with big lumps of carrot, boiled spuds and cabbage (which spent so long on the slow combustion stove, any hint of green disappeared), boiled custard with jam roly-poly and wine trifle dominating the tables across the nation.

Margaret Fulton and the *Australian Women's Weekly* were leading the charge to more exotic fare, such as fried ham steaks garnished with fried pineapple rings and, if you wanted to really impress, a glacé cherry stuck in the hole in the pineapple. Come to think of it, the sixties must have been boom years for Golden Circle because pineapple rings also featured on that pinnacle of haute cuisine Chicken Maryland, made even more special with a lump of boiled corn and a fried banana.

On special occasions, if you were really going all out to impress, the Marie Antoinette champagne glasses came out, each one of them a different pastel shade, and each one filled with Sparkling Starwine, Porphyry Pearl or Cold Duck, depending upon how determined one was to impress.

MOUNTING AND STUFFING
WITH SOPHISTICATION

With improvements in kitchen appliances and the increasing range of produce and other foodstuffs came an increased sophistication in Australian cuisine, with old stalwarts like meat and three veg complemented by more exotic fare.

When a particular dish became popular it would sweep the country and turn up regularly on the dinner party menu, at least until the next fad came along.

Starting with the soup, favourites like tinned tomato might now be jazzed up a little with a swirl of cream, croutons and chopped parsley sprinkled on top. The lamb shank and vegetable, and pea and ham soup now had competition from pumpkin, French onion and, for the downright avant garde, gazpacho.

When the chilled soup craze first hit, there were many embarrassed moments as guests sat down at the table only to find that the hostess seemed to have forgotten to heat the soup. For the untrained palate, the first spoonful of chilled gazpacho was positively gag territory.

Weird combinations began finding their way into our salad bowls — celery, apple and walnut for instance — we didn't know then it was called Waldorf salad. Grated carrot and sultanas started to appear, and one that came as a shock to the sensibilities of kids, watermelon and onion, which to my mind was not a marriage made in heaven.

As hostesses endeavoured to outdo one another, increasingly bizarre concoctions graced the table. Grated carrot set in a bowl of orange jelly, and — when you're on a good thing, why not stick to it? — minted peas set in a bowl of lime jelly.

I'm not sure who Stroganoff was, but he sure was popular with Australian cooks in the sixties. Stewed beef pieces with sour cream stirred through was a regular feature on the dinner party menu. Because sour cream was not common in supermarkets, you very often had to buy fresh cream then sour it with lemon juice or vinegar. This was not a particularly good look if the cream curdled.

A sure-fire way to ensure your beef stroganoff didn't embarrass you come serving time was to replace the cream with Carnation or Bear brand milk, and sour the taste of that with lemon juice or vinegar.

Kitchen 'managers' were always coming up with new and innovative ideas. Dips were very fertile ground for bursts of creative genius. Mayonnaise and celery dips were decidedly plain alongside the new arrivals. You could do anything with a packet of Philadelphia cream cheese.

Although 'Philly' first became really popular with the advent of cheesecakes, it didn't take some bright spark long to wake up to the fact it made a great base for dips. You could bung in chopped gherkins or pickled onions, even a packet of dried French onion soup or (the height of innovation) a small jar of sweet corn relish. With the omnipresent packet of Jatz crackers in the cupboard, dips were the hostess's best friend.

Chicken divan was an instant hit, although where it got its name from is another mystery. If guests should drop in unexpectedly you could invite them to stay for a meal, and while the man of the house poured them a beer or a Starwine in the lounge room, the lady of the house could quickly rip the flesh off the carcass of a cooked chook and fling it into a large flattish casserole dish. Then she'd quickly blanch a heap of broccoli flowerets and throw them over the chicken, then tip two tins of cream of chicken soup over the lot.

If you were extremely sophisticated you'd splash a bit of sherry over that, then, with a handful of grated cheese over the top, it was into the oven. Half an hour later your guests would be swooning in admiration as they sat down to your haute cuisine.

The level of admiration could be doubled or even trebled, if you'd bothered to quickly mix up a packet of vanilla-flavoured Instant Pudding, to which you'd added a little nutmeg. As soon as it was set you could place a few pieces of candied ginger in syrup on the top, with chocolate grated over. That way, upon presentation to the astonished (and by now thoroughly intimidated) guest, you could lie shamelessly about it being one of your own 'little numbers'.

And what would any sixties housewife have done without Rice-a-Riso, marketed as 'a meal in a box'? Whoever dreamed up the idea of flavouring rice, packaging it up and flogging it off at a premium, must have made a squillion.

Towards the end of the sixties another cuisine 'essential' arrived in Australia — the fondue set. If you were particularly unlucky, you could be given anything up to a half-dozen of these as wedding presents — enough fondue sets to last you the rest of your life.

Legend has it that the fondue originated in Switzerland as

a cheap and easy way for peasants to eke out their meagre food supply during the long freezing winter. But it wasn't simply the peasants who took to the fondue in a big way in Australia, it was everyone. Fondue cookbooks abounded, even though quite frankly the limitations of the set were rather obvious.

The set consisted of a metal saucepan or bowl into which you'd put a couple of different types of cheese and some white wine. This was then placed over a small spirit burner, and when the mixture was all nice and melty, you'd dip in chunks of bread and vegetables.

Then for dessert you could clean out the pan and start all over again, this time with chocolate, cream and perhaps a liqueur from your Vok range, into which you could dip fruit such as strawberries, chunks of banana, some marshmallows or plain biscuits. The chocolate fondue was, frankly, more successful than the cheese.

On American TV shows we saw in the sixties, individuals helped themselves from serving plates and bowls in the centre of the table; the idea soon caught on in Australia.

In a family the size of ours this was a godsend as it had been quite a feat to serve up separate plates then deliver them to the table without everything going stone cold.

There was another up side to the American way of serving meals — you could avoid that steaming bowl of brussels sprouts like the plague, that is until the heads of the table sussed out what was going on, and you'd be watched like a hawk to make sure you'd taken your proper share of both the disgusting stuff and the less disgusting stuff.

When it came dessert time, and time to divvy up the ice-cream brick, you could depend upon fairness in portion size by appointing an ice-cream slicer. The appointee would slice the ice-cream brick into the required number of portions, then each person at the table would choose their slice before the slicer. This ensured that the ice-cream was divided up so accurately it could have been done with a laser measuring tool. Only lasers weren't around then.

AUSSIE BARBIE (AND KEN) — IN APRON AND THONGS

Most households had a barbecue of some description in the backyard, and these ranged from a simple metal plate over a couple of bricks stacked on top of each other to the more elaborate monumental-type constructions for those who fancied themselves as something of a 'tong master'.

Eating outside wasn't a good idea unless you had a patio enclosed with flywire, because the flies were so bad you gladly stood in the smoke from the barbie with your eyes watering just to stop the little buggers eating you alive.

In our house, the barbie was invariably chops and sausages. Dad would cook the shitters out of the meat, and at the risk of getting a clip under the ear, we'd refer to barbecue meals as 'charred chops and limp lettuce.'

Certain apparel was essential for the proper use of the barbie.

1. Barbecue apron. The louder the better. In the sixties really vulgar aprons hadn't appeared, but you could get aprons with slogans like 'Chief cook and bottle washer' or 'Champion of the chops', or something equally inane. Many aprons featured prints of tomato sauce bottles or snaggers, or something pertaining to the barbecue.

2. Barbecue implements. These would usually consist of long-handled tongs, a long-handled two-pronged fork and a knife. A very good set might include a bottle opener, often on one end of one of the implements. Barbecue sets could be given each year for Christmas or birthdays because they were so shoddily made they were guaranteed not to see out the season.

3. Sunglasses and hat for obvious reasons, and zinc cream to cover exposed bits of the arms.

4. Aerogard. In a vain attempt to deal with Louie and his thousands of mates.

5. Your metal esky with a couple of frozen lumps of ice and a few 'king browns'. Stubbies had not yet caught on. The metal esky most commonly featured a bright red tartan design on the outside. These, too, were ideal Christmas gifts because they rusted out each year after having been left in the yard for months on end half full of melted ice.

6. The tranny — in the time it took to char the chops and griddle the snags into anonymity, you could get in a good quarter of your local footy game or several overs of the Sheffield Shield match.

7. Cricket set. This was actually for the after-barbecue game of cricket, but you'd be using a tennis ball after the cricket ball went through the kitchen window or sleep-out louvres on Boxing Day.

8. Aspros or Bex for how you're going to feel after a day of hot sun, king browns and greasy food.

Among the accompanying salads for the barbie were invariably lettuce, finely shredded with chopped hard-boiled eggs stirred through with homemade mayonnaise made from Grandma's recipe featuring tinned condensed milk, powdered mustard and white vinegar — delicious.

There'd also be a huge bowl of tinned beetroot, and a salad made by layering sliced tomatoes and white onions then drizzling over a little vinegar and adding a sprinkling of pepper and salt.

If the barbie was a special occasion, there might be the three-bean salad straight out of the tin.

Fortunately coleslaw didn't become essential fare at *every* barbecue until much later in the sixties.

ON TOP OF SPAGHETTI

One food fad of the sixties which didn't go away and therefore, I guess, couldn't have been a fad, was Italian food. With the enormous number of migrants from Italy came their food, and methods of preparing it.

Australians, of course, knew all about spaghetti, after all we'd been eating it out of tins for yonks and — how much more adventurous than the Italians were we? — we even had it for breakfast on toast sometimes. Thing was, apart from the name, there was no similarity whatsoever between what we and the Italians called spaghetti.

By the sixties, Italians were running cafes and restaurants all over the country. At the start menus were pretty basic, and a mainstay was spaghetti bolognaise, possibly because this was an easy introduction to the further delights of the Italian kitchen.

With our increasing awareness of the difference between what we'd been calling spaghetti and the real thing, more and more supermarkets and grocery stores began to stock packets of San Remo spaghetti (we still hadn't started calling it pasta, though the Italians did) and San Remo tomato paste in tiny tins.

Garlic was not nearly as taboo as it had once been, and herbs like rosemary, oregano and basil were no longer complete strangers, even if they were mostly the dried variety in a jar.

Many Australians may have had an idea of what lasagna, cacciatore, fettucine, carbonara, gelato, linguini, marinara, ravioli, veal scallopini and risotto were, but focaccia, pesto, gnocchi, aioli, antipasti, bruschetta, cannoli, carpaccio, osso buco, frittata, panettone, penne, prosciutto, tiramisu, tortellini and zabaglione were, at the start of the sixties, all just double Dutch — or, to be more precise, double Italian. But the change, when it did come, was remarkably rapid. It was to improve Australian cuisine in general — thankfully.

PLONK

The European immigrants who arrived in Australia in large numbers after the Second World War were wine drinkers, and the sea change in the drinking habits of the Australian population generally began in the sixties.

Many Italian families made their own wine, although I think you had to have been born in Italy to truly appreciate it. But in 1956, when the Orlando company released its Barossa Pearl wine and it was immediately successful, the love affair with wine took root.

By the sixties the variety of Australian wines on the market had increased exponentially, even if the favourites were the ones which now tend to be seen as having a bit of a cringe factor.

Jumping on the fizzy plonk bandwagon was a particularly virulent number out of Western Australia's Swan Valley called Skip and Go Naked. This was popular with the ladies, always got a smirk from the blokes and would often feature with Porphyry Pearl and Sparkling Starwine at cabarets and weddings.

Also popular with the ladies was Bacardi and Coke. Up until the sixties, a shandy or a port and lemonade or perhaps a small sweet sherry was about the extent of it for the ladies, but by the time the decade of liberation was over, wines and spirits were all acceptable and, shock horror, they even started coming out of the ladies' lounges.

Home bars started to become popular, some built-in, some timber or Formica portable items. Bar fridges were tucked away behind the best bars; these were just scaled-down versions of the standard kitchen fridge. At the back of a typical home bar would be mirror-backed glass shelves, so it looked as though you were twice as well stocked as you actually were. On the shelves, Vok liqueurs, in their distinctively shaped bottles, would be lined up; typically yellow advocaat, cherry advocaat, cherry brandy, crème de banana, crème de cacao, crème de menthe and blue curaçao.

The favourite was usually yellow advocaat because of the popularity of Fluffy Ducks, an incredibly sweet cocktail which was basically yellow advocaat and lemonade. Everyone had a variation on this — some people would variously add crème de cacao, a dash of gin, orange juice or cream.

A well-stocked bar would also have, alongside the liqueurs, bottles of scotch, brandy, gin, vodka, bourbon, sherry, port, muscat and marsala.

On another shelf was the glassware (if it was good enough to display): beer glasses, sherry glasses, spirit glasses and the multi-shaded Marie Antoinette-shaped champagne glasses.

On top of the bar itself, the bar set. Dangling from a little wooden and chrome 'tree' were a jigger measure, a small whisk, a knife and a mixing spoon. These made ideal Christmas or birthday gifts for the man of the house because, invariably, bits went missing, so you could give the same gift again and again.

GOIN' OUT FOR SOME FANCY GRUB

Although nowhere near the popularity they enjoy today, Chinese restaurants began to appear in the sixties, first in the capital cities then slowly throughout regional areas. The restaurants had exotic names like Imperial Court, The Great Wall, The Lotus, The Emperor's Garden, The Dragon Inn, The Jade Garden, The Golden Chopsticks — there was one in our town with the intriguing name The Double Happy.

The food in these pioneer restaurants wasn't particularly Chinese, it was more what the Chinese knew would appeal to the Western palate. Essential on the menu were chicken chow mein, sweet and sour pork, chop suey, spring rolls and fried rice. It was some time before we got into more exotic stuff like braised beef in black bean sauce or Peking duck.

Some people treated the early Chinese restaurants with great suspicion, and someone always knew someone who knew for sure what was happening to any cats which might have disappeared overnight.

The steakhouse made its debut in the sixties. Someone came up with the scathingly brilliant idea of opening a restaurant where the patrons cooked for themselves. On one side of the room would be a glass-fronted refrigerated cabinet displaying all the different steaks (a vegetarian's nightmare and a carnivore's heaven). You would make your selection of rump, sirloin, T-bone or fillet steak, take it to a massive barbecue at the back of the room, and there you would cook it. You therefore couldn't grizzle if your meat was underdone or overcooked.

Alongside the barbecue stood the bowl containing a pile of sliced onions for those who fancied them with their steak. Along another wall was a buffet, where there'd be a mountain of foil-wrapped hot jacket potatoes, various sauces, mustards and dressings, and a salad bar featuring the most popular salads of the day: potato, tossed tomato, sweet corn and rice, coleslaw and the ever-present beetroot. If the steakhouse had aspirations to 'haute cuisine', the beetroot would be the baby beet rather than the sliced variety.

Yet another refrigerated cabinet displayed desserts, like cheesecakes in several flavours, pavlova, fruit salad, chocolate mousse, Black Forest cake and apple pie, with a massive bowl of mock cream on the side.

Despite the fact staffing costs must have been minimal at the steakhouses, with just a few exceptions they soon disappeared as people grew tired of going out for the evening and cooking their own dinner, then returning home smelling of smoke and cooked onions.

WHAT'S UP, DOC?

Unless you were actually within a hair's breadth of death, most people in the sixties did not frequent the doctor's surgery. For kids, the most common ailments for which you simply *had* to see the doctor were things like tonsillitis, measles, mumps or chickenpox, but even then the doctor was a last resort. More often you were kept home and mollycoddled until you got over whatever ailment you had.

Most houses in the sixties had a mini-pharmacy in what we called the medicine cabinet. First aid kits were enormously popular, and ours was a white metal case with a red cross painted on the top of it. It was made by Sanax, and came with enough bandaging to wrap a mummy, a pair of scissors, which usually became pretty buggered because they'd be used for school projects, cutting up stuff to make kites etc., a pair of tweezers, Condy's crystals, Mercurochrome, petroleum jelly, a tourniquet, bandaids, safety pins, a thermometer and whatever other stuff the average family might require.

And the average family all seemed to need stuff like Vincent's Powders, Aspros or Bex, Kaomagma, to bind you up when you had the 'trots', and gunk called Antiflo, a poultice which came in a tin and was used for drawing boils, which nearly every kid in the sixties had, either on the back of their neck or on their bum.

The idea with the Antiflo was to put a blob of it on a couple of layers of gauze, cover it with some more gauze then stick it in the oven until it developed a lava-like quality. A parent (usually the dad) would then pick it up with a pair of tongs and, restraining the recipient of the treatment, slap the poultice on the affected area. This was quite memorable. Because the word was that you only got boils because you weren't cleaning yourself properly, after an Antiflo 'incident', necks and bums would be meticulously looked after for a least a few weeks.

There was another cure-all called Bates' Salve, which was supplied by the Rawleigh's man, a bloke who would drive around flogging potions out of the back of his Morris Minor van. He had all sorts of tonics, elixirs, pills and ointments, for humans and animals alike. Bates' Salve came in a caramel-coloured block, a bit like a large bar of soap, and when you heated it up it became soft, and could be used as a poultice for boils, or for drawing deeply embedded thorns or splinters. Some people also used it for school sores.

Most home medicine cabinets had Friar's Balsam, which was used to treat wounds and ulcers. Vicks Vaporub was in every home and was used for rubbing on the chest of anyone with a cold. You could also mix it into boiling water in a large bowl then, with a towel over your head to stop the fumes escaping, you would use it as an inhalant to help clear your airways. My dad always went for the big hit, and just stuffed the Vicks straight up his nose.

The Rawleigh's man also provided some stuff in a bottle which smelled like Vicks, only a billion times stronger. If you had a really bad cold or the flu, you'd use it in boiling water for the head-under-a-towel treatment. The vapour soon cleared out your nostrils and throat, and if you could have stayed under long enough it would probably have scoured you from top to tail. And it was not a good idea to open your eyes while in the steam tent.

If you lived in the country there was a fair chance you'd also have a snakebite kit in the house. This consisted of a one-sided razor blade, a roll of bandage with clips and a length of rubber.

The idea behind this kit was that should you be unfortunate enough to get bitten by a snake (as I did, but of course was away from home, and thus away from the snakebite kit), you made a tourniquet with the rubber strip above the wound, then you made a cut where you could see the puncture marks from the snake's fangs and — then comes the good bit — you then had someone suck the wound to remove the venom. After the suckee spat out the venom, they'd bind the wound tightly and get you to hospital pronto.

Many snake bite kits got discarded without ever being used because some medical authorities and snakebite 'experts' suggested it was not a real good idea to be slashing a snakebite wound and sucking out venom, especially if you had fillings. It made sense to me.

WETTING OURSELVES

LET'S BASTE AGAIN LIKE
WE DID LAST SUMMER

Given the enormous length of the Australian coastline and the fact that all our capital cities are on the coastal strip, it's small wonder Australians have a strong beach culture. This has pretty much been the situation throughout our history, but the strength and depth of that culture really only coalesced in the sixties.

On a hot summer weekend it wouldn't be atypical for a family to load up the car with an umbrella, windbreak, folding chairs, a small mountain of beach towels, an esky stocked with cool drinks and a couple of king brow's for dad, piles of sandwiches individually wrapped in greaseproof paper, sunglasses, hats and suncream.

The suncream of the time didn't have anything on the label about 'block-out factor' or protection ratings, I think it was more of an oil used to baste yourself, in much the same was as you'd baste a chook. We knew the perils of sunburn, but had yet to understand the full extent of the damage that the sun's rays would have on unprotected skin.

If you got to the beach early enough, especially in built-up areas, you could pick your prime piece of real estate, preferably with a bit of protection from the prevailing winds — and prevail the winds do in many parts of Australia, to such an extent you stand the real risk of having your skin sandblasted clean off your body if you're not careful.

If the beach had a groyne, that was always an ideal starting place for setting up camp for the day. With the umbrella strategically placed and the travelling rug spread on the sand, it was then standard procedure to have the riot act read before you could hit the water. 'Don't play too rough', 'No pushing others under', 'Don't walk on the reef or you'll cut your feet and the wounds will never heal', 'Don't muck around with any thing dead or alive that you find in the water', 'Don't go too deep', etc. etc.

By lunchtime most kids would have a good start on third-degree burns. And lunchtime was then interminable because, 'If you don't wait for an hour after you've eaten, you'll get cramp and sink to the bottom like a stone, never to be seen again.' Needless to say one was back in the water exactly one hour and one second after lunch.

If the day remained hot, it wasn't too hard to persuade your mum and dad to stay at the beach until dark. This meant that Dad would head off to get a pile of fish and chips, wrapped up in layers of newspaper to keep them hot, then spread them out on the travelling rug for everyone to 'bog in'.

Grown-ups would eat spooky stuff like gherkins and pickled onions with their fish and chips, but as far as I was concerned you could hold the lot, except for the chips, and the saltier the better.

By nightfall the mozzies would add their little contribution to the general discomfort of everyone. If you weren't quick on the draw with the Aerogard, itchy lumps were added to skin already burnt to a crisp, along with bathers which had dried on the body at least a dozen or fifteen times during the day and were now the texture of cardboard, with a nice little deposit of damp sand weighing down the crotch for good measure.

After the miserable trip home, the real fun began with the latest fad for taking the sting out of sunburn. In our house the remedy was usually something an aunt or other relative had heard of as 'absolutely marvellous and you'd never know you'd even been burnt in the first place.'

This, of course, proved on every occasion to be a vicious lie. The cold tea didn't work, the butter straight out of the fridge and smeared all over the body didn't work — that was just more basting of the chook as far as I could tell. The warm bath didn't work (continued the cooking process), the cold bath didn't work, the slices of lemon or orange didn't work — yet another marinade!

The only thing I recall that did work was sleep, and after the initial agony of having any part of your body too sore to even touch the sheets, twelve hours at the beach would take its toll and it was off to the land of nod.

The ensuing few days were a joy, as you slowly shed your skin like a moulting reptile, leaving bits of it in your bed, in the bathroom and over the car seat, grossing out anyone who wasn't in a similar predicament.

Why hadn't my ancestors come from Sicily or Croatia instead of the Highlands of Scotland? That way I might have stood a chance of retaining my skin each summer, and instead of spending December, January and February looking like the creature from the black lagoon, I could have gone nut brown, turning into deep copper by the end of the summer.

BEACH CLOBBER

Bikinis were still something you saw on newsreels in the early part of the sixties, there were also reports of girls getting arrested on Bondi Beach, in Sydney, for wearing what in reality were pretty modest bikinis, but they sure got the press going.

In rural Australia where the 'bold hussies' were not nearly so prevalent, unfortunately, beachwear was fairly conservative.

Beach bags enjoyed a few summers of popularity; these were cloth bags, often made out of a towelling material with a drawstring top. Only girls could be bothered with a beach bag, and in it they'd have any or all of the following: beach towel, bathing cap, bathers, suncream, brush, make-up, transistor radio (which were getting smaller each season, and often came in their own little leather carrying case with strap attached), thongs to get over the scorching hot sand without burning the soles off their feet, and a can of Fanta.

Boys drank Coke, girls drank Fanta, this anomaly has never been successfully explained.

Beach towels were something of a fashion accessory, and could vary from a modest striped number to something more the size of a single bed sheet, with garish images printed on it, like Spanish galleons under full sail on the high seas, or a Mexican enjoying a siesta under a palm tree on a beach being lapped by impossibly coloured water.

YO MAN, YO

Speaking of the Coke versus Fanta thing, one of the biggest crazes to sweep the world in the sixties was the yoyo.

These began as reasonably humble little toys made from wood or plastic on string, and took on a life of their own as they evolved.

Coca-Cola had cunningly jumped aboard the yoyo bandwagon very early on in the piece, and went as far as organising yoyo competitions right across the country. Like the dance crazes, yoyo competitions would often be held at half-time at the flicks, with prizes being vouchers for crates of Coke.

The Coke yoyos were particularly good because they were somewhat heavier than the ones you used to get out of show bags.

A really dedicated yoyo player could learn a stack of tricks to impress other players and the judges. There was 'The Eiffel Tower', 'Rock the Baby in the Eiffel Tower', 'The Trapeze', 'Rock the Baby in the Trapeze', 'Barrel Rolls', 'Bird's Nest', 'Flying Saucer', 'Three-Leaf Clover', and 'Walk the Dog'.

I couldn't do any of them, but I had a cousin who could do the lot.

OUT OF THE WAY, DICK DRAGGER, I'M HANGIN' TEN

Many older kids and teenagers discovered surfing in the sixties; my elder brother was one of these. He had a surfboard about the size of a small dinghy and, it seemed to me, slightly heavier than a small dinghy.

He carried his board around on a roof-rack fitted to the top of his Mini. This looked somewhat ludicrous and did nothing for the aerodynamics of the car.

Because it was what all the surfers did, the board had to be waxed, and over the summer with all the old wax discoloured and flaking, the texture of the surfboard looked a bit like my skin.

In the sixties, surfers would not be seen dead in the 'budgie smuggler'-type racing bathers, preferring the baggy Okanui board shorts.

The surfers developed a separate beach culture all of their own, with surf names for just about everyone and everything. Although I couldn't accuse my brother of falling exactly into the cool surfer category, he and his mates did use some surfing terms. I thought they sounded like wankers, even if I did have a couple of pairs of Okanuis.

Some of the more common surfing expressions were:

A three-sixty — spinning full circle on a wave.

Ace — to win or to beat someone.

Bag — to split the scene, to leave.

Barrel or barrelled — to ride through the tube of a wave and out the other end.

Bitchin' — cool, righteous, happening, or alternatively very bad.

Bump — a swell.

Choice — the best.

Crab — a bad surfer, poor style.

Dick Dragger — bodyboarder.

Full-on — really into something.

Grommet — young surfer.

Hang ten — pretty hard to do on a modern surfboard, but on my brother's log you could hang all ten toes over the nose of the board.

Kook — an unco surfer, highly derogatory.

Log — a very long surfboard, common in the fifties and sixties.

Sick — radical or dramatic.

WET CELLULOID

The sixties also spawned a swag of particularly dreadful beach movies. These were designed for a teenage audience and were mainly pretty sterile vehicles for minor pop stars to leap around in a beach setting, singing mostly forgettable songs.

Among the serial offenders were Frankie Avalon and Annette Funicello, who appeared in a whole series of movies with great titles like *Muscle Beach Party*, *Bikini Beach*, *Pyjama Party*, *Beach Blanket Bingo* and *How to Stuff a Wild Bikini*.

A little more music cred was shown in *C'mon Let's Live a Little*, with Jackie DeShannon, Bobby Vee, Eddy Hodges and a very young Kim Carnes.

Vincent Price teamed up with Frankie Avalon for *Dr Goldfoot and the Bikini Machine*, Sandra Dee laid claim to *Gidget* and Connie Francis began her string of hit movies with *Where the Boys Are*.

Straight surf action movies were also suddenly becoming very popular, and the music charts began a long affair with beach and surf music, notably from the Beach Boys, and Jan and Dean, and instrumental bands the Ventures and the Shadows.

IN WITH THE IN CROWD

THE WHOLE KIT AND CABOODLE

When the sixties began, clothes were still pretty much the conservative gear which had dominated throughout the fifties. Women in pretty waisted frocks and cardigans during the day, and overcoat, hat and gloves to go to the shops. Evening wear was somewhat more elegant, but dull, dull, dull. The men were even worse with drab brown and grey slacks, white or blue shirts and tweedy jackets. And most blokes wore braces to hold up their daks. Kids dressed like miniature versions of their parents, except boys wore shorts.

If someone from 1959 had been able to step into a time machine and wind it ahead six or seven years, their eyes would have popped clean out of their head.

In the very early part of the decade the bouffant look was still the go for women, where the top part was tight, and the skirt of the dress puffed out. In extreme cases, it was the stiff petticoat layers which caused the dress to puff out — it must have been hellishly awkward trying to sit down, with the front of your dress flying up and covering your face.

The French roll hairstyle of the fifties gradually gave way to the beehive look, where the living daylights was teased out of the hair, it was piled as high on your head as you could get it, then the outer layer was smoothed over and glued in place with the aerosol hairspray of choice. Popular brands were Gossamer and Alberto VO5.

Women's hair fashions were now beginning to be dictated by younger women and teenagers, who took their cues from the proliferation of female pop stars of the day. If Dusty Springfield, Cilla Black or Lulu sported a certain coiffure, you could bet your sweet bippy it would be in 'Janice's Hair Salon' in the main street of middle Australia within weeks.

The American girl groups had some influence too, but in the case of the Supremes, you couldn't help but think the hairstyles and wigs were only slavishly copying the Brit girls.

The particular sub-group you most identified with — bodgie, widgie, mod, rocker, surfie — pretty much dictated the style of clothes you might wear. The bodgies and widgies tended to stick to their fifties time warp as they got older. Uni students and Volkswagen drivers tended towards cord pants, duffle coats and desert boots; the rockers in what would pass as conservative bike gear today; and the mods in anything the Who or Dusty Springfield were wearing.

Right at the end of the sixties, the hippie look started to appear, but didn't really become widespread in Australia until the seventies.

Apart from an occasional renaissance of individual items of apparel, the only look which has survived essentially unchanged is the surfie. The Okanuis or baggy shorts are still with us, as are the loud shirts, in many variations, and even the baggy jumpers which used to be called 'sloppy joes'.

In Australia kids tended to adopt their favourite milk bar to hang out at, preferably one that made great milkshakes and thick shakes, and one which had a good jukebox with all the most up-to-date hits. It also helped if they made good hamburgers and steakburgers.

A hamburger had to have a meat patty, shredded lettuce, tomato, fried onion, cheese, beetroot, mayonnaise and sauce. Pickles arrived with Burger King. Some Burger King outlets in the sixties had covered parking bays, and when you pulled up, an attendant in a silly uniform would roller-skate out to you, take your order and then deliver it to you on a tray which clipped onto the window of your car. The show-bizzy glitz of it all was directly inverse to the quality of the food.

LA SPRINGFIELD

In the case of 'La Springfield', there was another feature to go with the truly big hair, and that was truly big mascara. Dusty had stolen the look from the French fashion models of the day and trowelled the mascara on, literally from eyelash to eyebrow. It must have been hell to remove at night (if, in fact, she *did*).

The Springfield look caught on, and for a couple of years in the early and mid-sixties, thousands of Australian girls were roaming around with impossibly high hair, pale pink lipstick and eyes that looked like they'd gone a couple of rounds with Sonny Liston.

I'm not sure how she did it, but Dusty somehow managed to keep one step ahead of everyday street wear. When she appeared on TV programs like *Hippodrome* or her own BBC show, she invariably wore a range of clothes, from day wear to evening gowns.

The empire-line gowns and baby-doll look that she championed soon started showing up on the dance floor at debutante balls and cabarets around Australia. When Dusty appeared on an American variety show singing 'Son of a Preacher Man' in a *pantsuit*, the dedicated followers of fashion slipped on the pants as well.

BODGIES AND WIDGIES

Another look was the beatnik, although in Australia these people were usually referred to as bodgies and widgies. The standard look was jeans for the blokes, often with a leather rectangular patch on the back pocket where they could burn their name, or the name of their girlfriend, with a hot soldering iron. A black leather jacket completed the look, and if the bodgie was really serious, black boots would top it off.

The widgie would wear really tight black stretchy pants, and a tight top with pointy bras underneath. On the feet they'd wear flat slipper-type shoes.

Bodgies and widgies always wore dark glasses, even at night-time, they chewed gum constantly and chain smoked. Middle-class kids were warned not to have anything to do with bodgies and widgies.

Even their cars were different, invariably hotted-up old Holdens which had been lowered and fitted with an extremely noisy exhaust system. Some people would cheat when 'lowering' their cars, and simply put bags of cement or spuds in the boot. One school of thought had it that in the case of the first model Holdens, you had to put weights in the boot to make it handle properly.

If your car had wheel covers over the back wheels, especially if they were white, and the rest of your car was a different colour, then you were definitely a bodgie.

And, if you work on the premise that the bodgies and widgies were probably at the lower end of the pecking order when it came to the old grey matter, it comes as no great surprise that one of their recreational pastimes was playing 'chicken'. This involved the highly intelligent act of racing their old Holdens or Zephyrs, which had been lowered and hotted-up and adorned with a fox-tail aerial, towards each other at breakneck speed to see which of the Einsteins would chicken out to avoid a collision. The constabulary were not amused.

'BEFORE I GET OLD'

Two other looks slavishly copied from the Brits were those of the mods and rockers. The rockers were really pretty much bodgies and widgies, with perhaps a sharper edge, and in the case of the blokes, slicked-back greasy hair.

The mods, on the other hand, were something really quite new. The Australian version of a mod varied from place to place, but the British roots were pretty evident. Although in the UK the mods were comprised mainly of kids from working-class families, they affected a somewhat stuck-up air, a sort of 'I'm better than you' attitude.

Mod boys dressed in suits or neat narrow trousers and jackets with very pointy shoes known as winklepickers The collarless suits that Pierre Cardin designed for the Beatles, with their pointy-toed Cuban-heeled boots, were pretty much a mod look.

Mod girls developed a sort of unisex look with shortish hair and lots of make-up.

Another part of mod paraphernalia was an Italian motor scooter. These were not nearly so common in Australia as they were in the UK, but if you wanted to look the part, a Vespa or Lambretta was pretty much de rigueur.

Mods preferred bands with a slightly less 'poppy' edge, those which were influenced more by the black American rhythm and blues sound, groups like the Small Faces, the

Kinks, the Who, the Yardbirds and the Rolling Stones.

The Who even dressed like mods, and sent their similarly dressed fans berserk with their slightly anarchic music. For example, 'My Generation': 'Hope I die before I get old.' On stage Pete Townsend would often smash his guitar to bits while Keith Moon would kick his drums over.

This sort of cool carry-on would unfortunately spill onto the streets, where the mods would search out some rockers to bash up or vice versa. Happily, the violent aspect of the gangs didn't really catch on in any big way in Australia, perhaps our weather was too good, or perhaps most of us were naturally laid-back.

I identified more with the mods, but didn't ever feel evenly remotely tempted to punch out a bodgie.

Television shows like *Ready Steady Go* were a showcase of mod culture. Along with the music and popular artists of the time miming outrageously, they'd feature the latest fashions and dance crazes, which the overwhelmingly mod studio audience would be performing in the background.

IT *IS* ME, BABE

There was another look which was a sort of morphing of the rockers and mods, and was adopted by a lot of university students and kids who wanted to look a bit alternative. This was the black duffel coat worn over jeans and a polo-neck jumper, with desert boots, or DBs as they were known, on the feet.

Even if you had perfect eyesight, the alternative look was completed with heavy black-rimmed glasses à la Buddy Holly, even though poor old Buddy had gone for the 'high jump' a few years before.

For those who were in the scene, the folkie thing was dead-set serious. For those who weren't it was all a bit laughable.

Coffee shops sprang up all over the place, where like-minded people could go and analyse Ginsberg and Kerouac endlessly. Pale and not very interesting spotty youths with lank hair and marginally grubby personal hygiene standards would strum their guitars and try to sound as tortured as Bob Dylan, their nasal voices pouring out stories of angst and tribulation.

The girls watched them adoringly, all of them being deeply intense, and desperately trying to look like Mary of Peter, Paul and Mary, or Jean Seberg in *Breathless*. And all trying to act like they 'did it' all the time — 'Sex is just not a hang up, man.' So predators who didn't have a sensitive soul in their bodies soon identified the joints to hang around for a quickie, even if you did have to endure the dreadful music and even more dreadful poetry.

The deeper and more obscure the poetry, the more admiration the poet attracted, when in fact ninety-nine point nine percent of what they were spouting was meaningless shit.

Of course, they all went to the '66 Dylan concert and sat quietly awestruck and respectful through the first half, and became a lynch mob in the electric half.

OP IN

British designer Mary Quant started her own fashion label in the mid-sixties, and suddenly miniskirts, coloured tights and vinyl-look clothes were all the rage.

The top model in the world, in the days before supermodels, was Jean Shrimpton. The Shrimp had been invited to come to Australia in 1965 for a two-week promotional visit, sponsored by the Victorian Racing Club, to appear at events up to and including the Melbourne Cup. To give you an idea of the popularity of the Shrimp, she was paid £2,000 for her appearance; the Beatles, just a year before, had been paid £1,500 for their tour.

When Jean appeared on Derby day to present the 'Fashion in the Field' prizes, conservative Melbourne was traumatised to the base of its whalebone corsets when she turned up at Flemington on a swelteringly hot Saturday dressed in a sleeveless white minidress with a hemline four inches above the knee, and two-toned low-heeled slingback shoes. Worse *still*, no hat, gloves *or* stockings.

The Melbourne matrons in twin-sets, hats, gloves and pearls were horrified. The British press described her appearance as 'like a petunia in an onion patch.'

Come Melbourne Cup day the following Tuesday, the Shrimp caved in to the pressure from the stodgy establishment and wore a conservative three-piece grey suit, hat, gloves, stockings and handbag.

Back in the UK, the fuss inspired Mary Quant to make even shorter dresses, and young girls all over Australia took to them like ducks to water.

Really trendy young guys started to wear suits which had mostly been copied from Italian designers. These were more tight fitting than suits had traditionally been. Single-breasted suits with jackets which had been tailored in at the back and with narrow lapels were worn with narrow-collared shirts and very thin ties, usually black, and sometimes even made of leather if you were really spivvy.

This look was pretty well established in the UK, with trendy suits common among the mod boys. With the change in attitude in the way guys dressed, the way was clear for men's fashion to accelerate in development for the rest of the decade.

Narrow pants became widespread, winklepicker shoes were common. Beatle haircuts gradually got longer and longer, crew cuts virtually disappeared (except in America, where they'll *never* disappear), and hair started to extend from the top of the head to the face, with sideboards slowly creeping downwards and forwards.

By the mid-sixties, with the short short miniskirts, op art became extremely popular, and fabric designers used optical illusions to create wild patterns of contrasting colours, often featuring bold distorted black and white checks.

Op art gear soon advanced into the psychedelic era — just as the music changed, so too did the clothes. Acid colours became popular, the brighter and more synthetic the better, and even blokes began to dress 'fancy' without much risk of being called poofs.

It was not uncommon for a young guy about town to hit

the nightspots with check flared trousers, à la The Beatles' *Yellow Submarine* look, a contrasting paisley shirt with exaggerated collar, strings of beads or a heavy metal medallion around the neck, and a scarf around increasingly lengthening hair. He wouldn't have stood out particularly, because more and more blokes were looking the same way.

The bird with him would no doubt be wearing the ubiquitous miniskirt with knee-high boots, perhaps a psychedelic jacket, beads, glasses in any colour other than dark or clear, and her hair, like his, beginning to lengthen as the teasing combs began to be used somewhat less than a few years previously.

HIPPIE, HIPPIE FAKES

By Woodstock, fashion had changed yet again. There had been, through 1967, a trend towards ethnic fashion. Suddenly, clothes some poor bloody peasant from behind the Iron Curtain, or from some impoverished African or Middle Eastern country, might wear by necessity, became fashionable in boutiques in more affluent societies, including Australia. Even the Nehru jacket from India and the Mao suit from China got a look in, however briefly.

The ethnic look quite naturally evolved into the hippie look, with boutiques flooded with piles of clothes made in Indian and South-East Asian sweatshops for next to nothing, then marked up a few thousand percent to adorn trendy young things in the West.

The more you spent on hippie clothes, the worse you could look, but no doubt because of the amount of 'weed' in the air, no one seemed to notice how bad that was.

Not everyone opted for the hippie movement, in fact in some quarters there was real disdain for this group of people who decided to opt out of a conforming society, and then immediately conformed to their own set of hippie rules — bathe minimally, become an environmental activist whilst travelling around the country in a clapped-out Volkswagen microbus polluting the atmosphere at a terrifying rate, work as little as possible, take up pottery and douse yourself in oil of patchouli, available from all good hippie shops and alternative markets.

'GIRLS WILL BE BOYS AND
BOYS WILL BE GIRLS'

The vast majority of kids who didn't head down the hippie trail ended up with an amalgam of gear from all the various fashions in their wardrobe, but as the sixties drew to a close, skirts began to lengthen (along with hair), floor-length dresses called 'maxis' became popular, and generally clothes began trending towards a more conservative look.

Hotpants appeared at the very end of the decade, but fortunately didn't strike a chord with the mainstream populace until Jane Fonda wore them in the movie, *Klute*, a couple of years later. But they quickly became something only a hooker would wear. Unfortunately, until then it seemed the appeal of hotpants was directly proportional to the size of the girl's bum, and it was not a good look.

By decade's end, girls looked more like blokes, and blokes looked more like girls, with much longer hair and wild ties in bright colours, which almost looked like bibs they were so wide. Paisley shirts with big flouncy sleeves were popular with the more daring. Also fashionable were Cossack shirts with fancy braiding, sprayed-on pants in bright purple and orange, some even made of velvet fabric, and to top off the whole look, collections of men's jewellery started coming into the shops — among the more popular items, heavy silver peace signs hanging on a chain.

Although some of the men's fashions at the extreme end might not have been out of place in a city nightclub, in the more conservative regional centres, no self-respecting young bloke would be seen dead in such gear.

Apart from anything else, the 1969 Peter Fonda, Dennis Hopper, Jack Nicholson movie *Easy Rider* and the redneck intolerance to difference that it portrayed might have been too close to home for some.

STOP YOUR JIVING, BABE

Non-contact dancing took off in a huge way in the sixties. For kids, the fifties had been dominated by rock-and-roll or jiving, yet the traditional dances were still popular.

It was not uncommon for many communities to have a fifty-fifty dance on a Friday or Saturday night, where a traditional dance band (piano, saxophone and drums) would cater for the mostly older patrons, then with the addition of an electric guitar or two, the band could suddenly switch to 'kids' music. This was usually done a bracket or two about, so that neither group got bored witless waiting their turn to dance.

When Chubby Checker released 'Let's Twist Again', the whole world was swept by the new dance craze. There were twisting competitions all over the country. Often these would be held during half-time at the pictures, right up there on the stage in front of the screen, with the judges helped by the 'applausometer' in the audience.

Chubby toured Australia with his Twist spectacular. Given the amount of touring he did, Chubby (or his managers) were smart enough to include place names in a number of his songs. For example, from 'Twistin' USA':

They're twistin' in Washington,
In Cincinnati, England, Europe,
They're twistin' in Asia, Africa, Australie (sic).

Other artists caught up on the twist craze. Joey Dee and the Starlighters had a hit with 'Peppermint Twist', Sam Cooke with 'Twistin' the Night Away', and the Isley Brothers with 'Twist and Shout', but The Beatles' version of the latter was the more popular in Australia.

Instructions on how to twist were sometimes included on the record cover, with one very accurate description instructing dancers to 'Imagine you're stubbing a cigarette out with both feet whilst drying your back with a towel.'

Although no other dance craze came even close to the twist, the sixties had a proliferation of new dances, and even the revival of some old ones, the hand jive and the charleston among them.

In alphabetical order, some of the hundreds of dance crazes were: the alley cat, the alligator, the banana split, the batman, the bird, the boney moronie, the boo ga loo, the boomerang, the bop, the bug, the bunny hop, the camel walk, the choo choo, the cinnamon cinder, the clam, the crawl, the dog, the drag, the duck, the Egyptian, the elephant walk, the fish, the flake, the fly, the frug, the funky jerk, the go-go, the guitar boogie, the gully, the Harlem shuffle, the hippy hippy shake, the hitchhike, the hokey pokey, the hop, the hucklebuck, the hully hully, the jerk, the jitterbug, the jive, the jump, the kangaroo, the limbo, the limbo rock, the locomotion, the lurch, the Madison, the Malibu, the march of the mods, the mash, the mashed potato, the Mexican hat dance, the monkey, the monster mash, the nitty gritty, the peppermint twist, the philly, the pogo, the pony, the Popeye, the pretzel, the push, the rebel walk, the shimmy, the shotgun boogie, the shout, the Simon says, the ska, the slosh, the slow jerk, the slow locomotion, the snake, the stomp, the stroll, the strut, the surfer stomp, the swim, the thing, the tiger walk, the trot, the turkey trot, the twist and the Watusi.

There were variations on all these dances wherever you were in the world. For instance, Sydney had its own version of the slosh called 'the Sydney slosh', which was very similar to the Madison.

The surf culture especially took to the stomp in a big way, with weekend stomps happening in surf clubs all over Australia.

GETTING INTO IT

At popular nightclubs, or discotheques as they became known, go-go girls would perform, often dancing in cages suspended above the dance floor. Parents by now had given up all hope of redemption for their teenagers, the rot had well and truly set in, and discotheques were just dens of iniquity where Lord only knows what went on. Mirror balls were particularly popular, as was black light — it suddenly became very trendy to wear white clothes to the disco, so that you became eerily luminescent in the violet glow.

The dance movements of the go-go dancers varied from girl to girl, but they were basically a hodgepodge of the popular dance crazes of the time. Typically the go-go dancers worked around a basic Watusi step. To begin:

Stand with your feet about a foot apart, knees slightly bent.

Hip action:
On the count of one, shift your weight to your right foot, swinging your hip out to the right.
On the count of two, shift your weight to the left foot, swinging that hip out.
Move from side to side with hips swinging right to left.

Arm action:

Hold your arms out in front of you as if you're gripping a golf club. Swing your hands to your right, then down in a half circle motion to your left, back to the right, then left and so on.

Get it together:

Do the hand and hip motions simultaneously from right to left.

(Not recommended for a particularly crowded dance floor, especially if one's movements are particularly vigorous.)

Special Cautionary Note

Readers who remember doing any of these dances at discos during the sixties are cautioned not to try them now. Dislocated hip joints and hernias are not fun! Anyone under twenty-one *go for it!*

SLIPPING BETWEEN THE SHEETS

And what were we trendy young groovers reading when we weren't tuned in to the tranny or hip to the beat at the disco?

Like many kids of my age, in my youth and into my teens I snapped up the books of Wilbur Smith and Alistair MacLean.

Between them, Smith and MacLean were very much in fashion and very prolific authors right through the sixties. In that period Wilbur Smith released *When the Lion Feeds*, *The Sound of Thunder* and *The Dark of the Sun*, and Alistair MacLean was a virtual bookselling 'hit factory' with *Ice Station Zebra*, *Night without End*, *Fear Is the Key*, *Force Ten from Navarone*, *The Dark Crusader*, *The Golden Rendezvous*, *The Satan Bug*, *Lawrence of Arabia*, *When Eight Bells Toll*, *Where Eagles Dare*, and *Puppet on a Chain*.

Like other reasonably avid readers, I joined a public library in the mid-sixties, and immediately the standard of what I was digesting lifted somewhat (with the occasional lapse). Among the books I read throughout the decade, the ones I found most memorable — apart from the ones I've already mentioned — were: *Hawaii* and *The Source* by James A Michener (I just loved the 'bigness' of his books, and the epic stories), *The Chapman Report* and *The Plot* by Irving Wallace (these were really a bit like Harold Robbins, but a slightly more upmarket), *To Kill a Mockingbird* by Harper

Lee (this was one I read at school, then read again a few years later I loved it so much), *The Rise and Fall of the Third Reich* by William L Shirer (Nazi Germany always held a morbid fascination for me, and this was *the* book. I also read *Mein Kampf* in the sixties but we all know that was written considerably before by you know who), *Tropic of Cancer* by Henry Miller (another supposedly naughty book, but I couldn't for the life of me see what all the fuss was about. Perhaps I'd become inured by the likes of Jackie Collins and Kyle Onstott), *Ring of Bright Water* by Gavin Maxwell (I read this in one night, I loved the story about Mij the Scottish otter), *The Shoes of the Fisherman* by Morris West (every Catholic kid practically had to read this. It wasn't as boring as I thought it would be, in fact I got really sucked in. Coming as it did soon after the death of the 'people's pope' John XXIII, this story was particularly moving. I also liked the fact the book was written by an Australian, and apart from kids' books, I hadn't read any books by an Australian author), *The Spy Who Came in from the Cold* by John Le Carre (this set me off on a spy-novel stage), *The Fixer* by Bernard Malamud (combined two fascinating themes, an exotic location in Russia and religion, which I always found intriguing. I first heard of *The Fixer* because it won a Pulitzer Prize, so I thought it had to be good. I soon discovered that winning a Pulitzer did not translate necessarily to being any good), *Airport* and *Hotel* by Arthur Hailey (these books provided a good bang for the buck because they were quite fat but exciting enough to rip through in a couple of days), *Myra Breckenridge* by Gore Vidal (I read this simply because it was so controversial, and of course there was a strong sexual content. I thought after I'd read it that I was probably unlikely for the rest of my life to ever be as disappointed with a book as I was with *Myra Breckenridge* — that was until years later when I was unfortunate enough to be given Norman Mailer's *Ancient Evenings* one Christmas), *Rosemary's Baby* by Ira Levin (I enjoyed this for the same reason I loved the movie: it scared the shit out of me. Having a somewhat vivid imagination, I found the book even scarier than the movie), *Couples* by John Updike (this was quite a sensual story, and this guy's attention to detail was something I found really appealing), *Listen to the Warm* by Rod McKuen (the hippie thing was at its peak when this came out, and lots of kids would sit around smoking a joint and reading stuff like this. I wasn't quite sure what I was when I was sixteen, but this book convinced me I certainly wasn't a hippie), *The Peter Principle* by Laurence J Peter and Raymond Hull (although I didn't realise it at the time, this little book was spot-on with its basic tenet 'In a hierarchy every employee tends to rise to his level of incompetency.'

I ploughed through plenty of other books too, but those are the few I recall most clearly from the sixties.

SIXTIES SPEAK

When it came to terms and language that were mainly used by kids in the sixties, we experienced something of an explosion of cool kid-speak. Some of these words had been around for decades and suddenly enjoyed a revival of popularity and therefore use, but many others were freshly coined to freak parents out, or so they wouldn't have the foggiest idea what you and your friends were going on about.

Some of the most common expressions widely used through the sixties were:

A gas — a lot of fun, 'It was a gas.'

Ape — to go ape, to go off your head, lose your temper.

Bag — as in 'What's your bag?' What are you up to? Where are you coming from? What are you interested in?

Bagged — took, stole, as in 'Who bagged my sunnies?'

Ball — party, good time, 'We had a ball.'

Blast — another good time, 'The party was a real blast.'

Blown — a car engine fitted with a supercharger, 'His blown Monaro went like a shower of shit.'

Blue flame — setting your fart alight.

Boss — something good, 'The Easybeats concert was boss.'

Bread — money, 'Can't go out Friday, I'm short of bread.'
Bummer — something bad or depressing.
Cat — a guy.
Chick — a girl or woman.
Chrome dome — a follically challenged person.
Cool — nice.
Crash — to go to bed, go to sleep.
Dag/daggy — stupid.
Deal — a quantity of marijuana.
Dibs — claim, as in 'I've got dibs on the front row at the pictures.'
Dig — to understand or appreciate, 'Can you dig it?'
Dope — marijuana, drugs.
Drag — to race another car over a short distance. Alternatively, something or someone who is dull and uninteresting, 'That kid is such a drag.'
Drives — drive-in pictures.
Far out — cool, excellent, very good.
Fink — a not very nice person, 'Stop being such a fink.'
Flake — a stupid or useless individual.
Flog — steal.
Flogging — masturbating.
Flower child — hippie.
Freak out — lose your cool over some upsetting event, 'When Dad told me I was grounded I freaked out.'
Funky — very cool.
Fuzz — the police.
Gone — cool, groovy, 'Man that cat is really gone.'
Groovy — nice, cool.
Grouse — good, pleasant, 'We had a grouse time at the drives.'

Hairy — out of control, frightening, 'The disco got a bit hairy.' Alternatively, huge, 'You should see the hairy motor he stuffed into his Hillman'.

Hang loose — relax.

Heat — cops.

Hep — with it, cool.

Hip — with it, cool.

Hook — to steal, 'I hooked the beach towel out of his car.'

Hunk — good-looking bloke.

Jacked off — to be cross at, 'I'm really jacked off at you.'

Kybosh — to put a stop to, 'Well the party was just starting and the old man came home and put the kybosh on it.'

Lay it on me — 'Tell me what it is you have to say'.

Lowered — to drop a car's suspension.

Moon — to bend over and show your bare bum, usually out the rear window of a car. 'You should have seen the look on that old bird's face when we mooned her at the stoplights.'

Neat — nice.

Old lady — Mum.

Old man — Dad.

Outta sight — very good, fantastic, 'The Kinks' new record is outta sight.'

Pad — where you live.

Passion pit — drive-in theatre.

Pig — cop.

Pig out — eat too much.

Pig pen — police station.

Pound — to belt someone, 'Man, I'm gunna pound you after school.'

Rags — clothes or, more vulgarly, sanitary pads.

Rap — talk, conversation, 'I was rappin' with the fuzz, can ya dig it?'

Rat fink — extreme fink.

Rave — monologue, talking incoherently. Alternatively, party.

Real gone cat — someone a bit 'out there'.

Right on — I agree totally.

Ripped off — to have something stolen, 'Someone ripped off the Singer Gazelle's hubcaps last night.'

Rule — to take ownership of.

Sad — a person who doesn't meet your approval, 'That bird is such a sad.'

Score — to obtain something you want, 'I scored The Beatles' new EP for my birthday.'

Shades — sunglasses.

Shaggin' wagon — panel van.

Skirt — a girl.

Skuzz — highly undesirable.

Skuzz bucket — a really ugly car, read Lightburn Zeta, any Skoda, Austin 1800, etc. etc.

So fine — really cool.

Souped-up — in cars, modified to go fast.

Spaz — a put-down for someone who is acting stupid.

Split — to leave.

Sponge — someone who is too mean to spend their own money and thus 'sponges' off others.

Square — not cool, 'He's so square, he doesn't have a single Rolling Stones record.'

Stacked — sizeable breasts, 'That bird is really stacked.' Alternatively, to crash, 'He stacked his Zephyr on Saturday night.'

Steady — current boyfriend or girlfriend.

Stoked — excited.

Stoned — out of it on drugs.

Stud — hunk.

The Bread — Dad.

The Cheese — Mum.

The most — something that is particularly good.

Three on the tree — a car with a three-speed manual transmission, with the gear lever fitted to the steering column.

Tooling — to drive around aimlessly, 'Oh I just spent the night tooling around the main street.'

Wipe out — to fall off your surfboard, to crash your car, etc.

It probably paid not to use a lot of these terms around your parents because it did truly unnerve them.

Also, different words meant different things depending upon location. For instance, someone in Melbourne might say they 'went for a drag in Lygon Street,' meaning they went for a drive. This could then be diminished to 'We did a few Lygons', or in Adelaide a few 'Wakefields', 'Pitts' in Sydney or 'Wellingtons' in Perth.

NICE SET OF WHEELS

THE PEOPLE GET WHEELS

The years following Second World War were prosperous ones for the vast majority of Australians. The country had become home to hundreds of thousands of 'New Australians' and they flocked to the bigger cities, and to wherever they could find work. Because most could speak no English, or very little, the jobs they could find were relatively low-skilled labouring jobs in the fishing industry, farming and forestry. They also provided valuable manpower for the fledgling car industry.

Holden's operations at Elizabeth, in South Australia, and Fisherman's Bend, in Victoria, Ford's factory at Geelong, and the Chrysler plant at Tonsley Park in Adelaide would provide the new generations of Australians with that most desirable of items — a new car. After the Australian dream of owning your own home, the new car wasn't far behind.

Up to and including the war years, you really had to be pretty well-off to afford a motor car in Australia. Since the inception of the automobile, there had been cars arriving in Australia, but never in vast quantities. A few were even built here. During the war lots of military vehicles were brought into Australia, and immediately following the war, these were sold off as army surplus, and many of them ended up as log trucks, or for hauling gear in the fishing industry. The four- and six-wheel-drives were particularly useful for these purposes.

The end of the war also marked an upsurge in popularity of American, or American-style, cars. Australians took to the roominess of the Buick, Chevrolet, Oldsmobile, Pontiac and Ford saloons. It came as no surprise then, that when Australia produced its 'own' car, it bore more than a passing resemblance to its larger American relatives.

The first Holden was sleek for its time, even if it does look a little bulbous in retrospect, and it even had some chrome bits and pieces.

Although Holdens had been produced since 1948, and had been immediate successes, Australian car design continued to remain rather conservative compared to some of the offerings from overseas. It was almost as if the Australian designers couldn't decide whether to go the glitzy over-the-top way of the Americans, or the dramatically more conservative three-piece-suit-and-bowler-hat styling of 'the mother country'.

What we ended up with was a kind of hybrid. Australian cars were neither fish nor foul, not as conservative as their British cousins, and certainly not nearly as gaudy as the American models. We did, however, owe more to Detroit than Luton in vehicle design. If we had fins on our cars they were almost rudimentary, as though they were slightly too self-conscious and embarrassed to be there. When it came to chrome trim, there might be a bit of flashing here and there, but definitely not in Yank proportions. Two-tone paintwork, or 'duco' as we called it, was about as wild and crazy as we got. But the sixties were about to change all that too.

The Poms were prolific producers of some pretty ordinary and downright ugly vehicles. Some said they were extremely reliable, although in my limited experience it seemed to me they were no more or less reliable than any other cars available.

One remarkable feature about so many of the British cars was the fact they seemed to rust out rather too rapidly, which was all the more remarkable when you consider the climate of their home turf. My dad's black Vanguard Spacemaster had an unnerving habit of conking out every time it was driven through a puddle. Mini drivers used half a plastic bucket cut lengthwise to cover the distributor to help keep it dry.

The Frogs made just plain weird cars, and the people who drove them could be described pretty much the same way, while the Dings made cars that in some cases went like a 'shower of shit' but rusted off their wheels in a couple of years — even faster than Pommy cars could achieve the same feat. Owners of Italian cars would speak in reverent terms about the 'engineering'. No doubt because you needed to be an engineer, or at least have one in the immediate family, to be able to keep your Italian thoroughbred on the road.

The Krauts were churning out Volkswagen Beetles which everyone called 'Hitler's revenge', but despite the sarcastic title they proved popular with Australians. Mercedes Benz were only driven by wealthy farmers, bankers or otherwise serious 'old' money, and the Japs were copying everyone, and then worked hard at making their cars slightly *more* ugly and weirder than everyone else's.

Until they imported some design and marketing people from the West, the Japanese had some serious teething problems with basic stuff like what to call new models of particular brands. Toyota chose the relatively safe route and stuck with royalty, or at least royal headgear. It gave us the Tiara, Corolla, Corona, Crown and Crown Royal. The Datsun/Nissan company was somewhat less conservative and presented us with memorable monikers like Sunny, Bluebird,

Gloria, and the big kahuna, the Cedric.

Meanwhile, the Yanks did what they do best, *excess.*

Because kids are pretty much into excess, it was the Yank tanks for me. At the height of their absurdity, I thought American cars were objects of great beauty and desirability, even the product of companies which were clearly going down the gurgler were fascinating to me, like the old Hudson Terraplane, which looked like it was coming and going at the same time, the Studebaker Hawk, which was so sleek looking, and even the Studebaker Lark, which was okay, even if it was as ugly as a hatful of snakes, though nothing compared to some of the brutes the Poms dished up. Besides, the American cops often drove Larks, probably because they had a V8 motor jammed into a body roughly the size of a Holden.

Although they were as scarce as hen's teeth in Australia, the most delicious Americana of all were the ones which were be-finned with as much chrome slapped on them as they could fit, with as many headlights, tail-lights and indicator lights as possible hanging off them.

Foremost among these were the very late fifties Chevies which had an acre of wraparound glass for the windscreen, a bonnet you could land a helicopter on, a boot you could smuggle eight kids into the drive-in with and, the pièce de résistance, the fins. These flared out from the back and centre of the boot and were finished with chrome flashing. Below the fins hung one chrome-encased tail-light, just above the main sideways elongated tail-light. The interior was finished in leather and plush carpet, with the bench seat wide enough to stretch out full-length to sleep on. And the dashboard was really something to behold. It was sort of Flash Gordon meets Joern Utzon, with space-age opera house-ish binnacles sweeping from the windscreen back into the cabin, in which were housed the speedometer and other instruments. Midway across the vast expanse of dashboard was the solid-state press-button radio, and further still across the metallic sweep, a glove box big enough to hold a lifetime supply of gloves. At the beginning of the sixties, some people still used glove boxes for gloves.

The Chevy was a thing of great beauty, or the ugliest pile of metal and upholstery ever bolted and spot-welded together, depending upon your point of view.

Other divisions of General Motors (US) produced a gem from time to time, among them Pontiac's Parisienne and Firebird, Oldsmobile's Toronado, Buick's Electra, and any Cadillac you want to name.

Though Chrysler was going through one of its dodgy patches financially, it produced some pretty serious metal. The Chrysler Royal was fairly popular in Australia, as were various models from its Dodge division. The Dodge Phoenix almost matched Chev's Belair and Impala models in terms of design excess.

By comparison, Ford tried hard, but even its aircraft-carrier sized Galaxies and Fairlanes of the early sixties couldn't quite outgross the other makers. But by the middle sixties, Ford hit pay dirt with its Mustang model. With its 'Coke-bottle hip', it was the coolest car around, but it decided not to sell it in Australia — just as it didn't sell the Thunderbird, one of the most drool-making cars ever built, I couldn't believe it! The best-looking car in the world and it wouldn't be coming here.

We had to content ourselves with the local Ford product, the Falcon — dull dull dull. And even when the local designers decided to give the Falcon a Coke-bottle hip, it was a puny half-hearted effort compared to what the Mustang had.

Another great car that Ford didn't bring to Australia was the Mercury. The Mercury was based on the Mustang, so it had the hip, and it also had ingenious turn indicators, in that the banks of tail-lights would illuminate in sequence to indicate the direction the vehicle intended to turn — gross but enthralling as far as I was concerned when I spotted a left-hand drive Mercury making a rare appearance on our streets.

When Chrysler decided to produce the Valiant in Australia, at last we had something away from the mundane. In the R series, with its fake tyre moulding on the boot, and space-age styling, we had a car that stood apart. The R and the succeeding S series, which were almost identical apart from the deletion of the 'tyre' on the boot lid, had a very cool automatic transmission called Torque Flite, the controls of which were push-buttons on the dash to the right of the steering wheel.

Chrysler in America had separate divisions just like General Motors. These divisions, notably Plymouth and Dodge, made some great-looking models with names like Barracuda, Duster, Dart and Fury. We ended up with Valiant, an okay name but why, when there were so many really cool names to choose from in the company stable?

The family of one of the kids I went to school with had a sloping-backed Valiant, others had HD Holdens with 'pedestrian slicers' framing the headlights, while one family had a Ford Galaxie, and yet another a Rambler Classic V8.

At the time, our family had recently traded in our respectable mid-fifties Ford Customline V8 which, despite the fact it was getting a bit long in the tooth, still went like the clappers, and had enough fin and chrome to make one want to be seen in it. And this was traded in for a brand new red and white Volkswagen microbus.

Okay, with our burgeoning family the Customline was no longer practical, and with eight kids and two more yet to come, the original people mover, with its three rows of seats, was the only practical solution. However, as one enters one's teenage years, one is intensely aware of what is cool, and what is not cool. A 1962 red and white Volkswagen microbus might be cool now — it was not cool in 1962. There was no end to my humiliation.

ACCESSORIES AFTER THE FACT

Even well into the sixties, unless you were buying an upmarket model most cars did not come fitted with a radio. Radios were 'optional extras'.

As an after market add-on, the Astor Diamond Dot was hugely popular. It cost an arm and a leg and came with a cradle that was bolted under the dashboard. The radio then slotted into the cradle and was locked into position by means of its carrying handle, which folded under the unit to form the locking mechanism.

The Diamond Dot was named for a tiny multi-faceted blueish light which illuminated when the radio was on.

The idea of being able to remove the radio from the car was not really a security consideration. At least where we lived, flogging other people's stuff was virtually unheard of. It was really a ploy to market the radio as versatile — you could have it in the car, take it into the house or office, or even to the beach.

Heaters, too, were often optional extras, and depending upon the vehicle they could be remarkably efficient or a means whereby you could gas yourself into unconsciousness in a matter of minutes. Air-cooled motors, like those in Volkswagens, seemed to drive incredibly efficient heaters, and simply by opening a vent you could have yourself doing a slow roast in no time. An electric element heater, which you could buy as an accessory for your standard Holden or Falcon, was somewhat less efficient, unless it came to draining the life out of the car's battery. At that, it was unsurpassed.

Among the many accessories which you could add to your pride and joy on wheels was a demister kit. Because many cars didn't have heaters, let alone demisters, these were essential, and for at least a couple of years the Christmas tree which didn't have a demister set wrapped up under it would have been rare indeed.

The demister must have been manufactured for about fifty cents, then marked up a thousand percent by the time it got to the shops. It was basically a strip of tin with a filament sheltered inside the curve of the tin. It had a plastic-coated wire attached to a plug thing which you shoved into the cigarette lighter socket. It seemed even the most basic model cars had cigarette lighters. When the electrical current was passed through the filament it would heat up, and the theory was the generated heat would warm the windscreen and make the condensation on the inside of the screen, caused by the difference in inside and outside temperatures, disappear. At least that was the theory. The demister strip would fit to the inside of the windscreen with rubber suction cups.

Add-on demisters were *not* a great success, thus their lack of longevity on the accessory market. You had an outside chance of clearing enough windscreen if you were driving something as small as a Mini or a VW Beetle although, to be perfectly frank, the wiring set-up in the Beetle was so dodgy, fitting a demister would probably have been foolhardy.

In reality, the demister might clear an area six or eight inches high by about a foot long at the bottom of the screen of a normal family-sized car. Another particular hazard with the demister was its use at the drive-in. Many a car had its battery flattened by that little filament clamped to the windscreen via the cigarette lighter.

Everyone had a favourite remedy for the problems of misted windows at the drive-in. For some people, misted windows were not a problem at all, but then we all knew what *they* were up to.

Some people reckoned metholated spirits on a cloth was just the trick to clear the windscreen, others swore that a wet baby's nappy did the job, and in this case we're talking a nappy that has been wet by the baby doing what comes naturally. I never actually got to experiment with that one, however I did try out the old half-a-spud routine.

Someone had come up with the scathingly brilliant idea that if you cut a spud in half, then rubbed the cut surface all over the windscreen, voila! the mist would vanish. This is perfectly correct, the mist would vanish, but only to be replaced by blurry smears which solidified into an opaque starch layer as they dried. Small but not insignificant issues such as these no doubt had a hand in the slow demise of the drive-in theatre.

Motoring innovation was hot, as were the sales of motoring magazines like *Wheels* and *Modern Motor*.

Wheels had its prestigious Car of the Year Awards, which caused much discussion and argument between the various motoring camps, and a list of the award recipients from the sixties makes some interesting reading, especially with the advantage of hindsight.

Wheels first Car of the Year (COTY) Award was made in 1963. The award was restricted to cars either built or assembled in Australia and was an attempt by the magazine to improve the quality of cars on Australian roads. Our local products might have had a reasonable reputation for reliability, but often the design quality came in for a bit of a caning from the motoring journos.

Full imports were excluded, but seeing that everyone from Renault to Mercedes Benz either built or assembled cars in Australia, there was no shortage of candidates to choose from. Most of us still thought that the only 'real' Australian cars were Holdens, Fords and, to a lesser extent, because the early models were so radical, the Chrysler Valiant.

Imagine what a poke in the eye it was then when the inaugural COTY was the Renault 8. Sheesh! I couldn't believe it, a funny-looking Froggy car with its motor in the back and boot in the front as the 'Australian' Car of the Year.

This was about the time I decided that all motoring journalists were duffle-coated, beret-wearing, Gitane-smoking wankers who wouldn't know a twin headlight from a Lukey muffler.

Insult was added to injury when, the following year, the winner was the Morris 1100. Even though financial necessity forced me into one of these brutes in the late sixties, there's no way on God's earth it should ever have been Car of the Year. These cars ate velocity joints faster than I could eat a hamburger, as I sadly learned, and it was a financial imperative that I quit the 1100 before it sent me to the cleaners. The 1100 was traded on a clapped-out Daihatsu Compagno Spider convertible, and *no* I was *not* on drugs. Just goes to show the *Wheels* writers were not the only ones who wouldn't know a twin headlight from a Lukey muffler.

Some cred was restored in 1965 when Falcon won with the XP, and repeated the success in 1966 with the XR. Don't get me wrong, the Falcons weren't exactly state-of-the-art, and no doubt they were based on the design of one of the most conservative-looking vehicles made in the US, but at least they were an advance on the Morris 1100, even if they were just as boxy looking.

In 1967 we saw the Chrysler VE Valiant get the nod. It too was a bit of a box — perhaps that's what the judges were looking for.

Then, in 1968, either *Wheels* got a new batch of motoring writers or the old ones binned their duffle coats and desert boots, because a *real* car, the Holden HK Monaro, won. The Monaro was a thing of great beauty. You could get the wimpy church-on-Sunday variety with plain colours and six-cylinder engine, or the 'brute', the GTS. It came with an optional Chevy 327 V8 fire-breather of a motor, and cost $3790 brand new in 1968.

The sixties saw the birth of the Ford/Holden rivalry in Australia, and once you were in one camp or the other you stayed there. I was firmly a GMH boy, so as far as I was concerned the decade ended on a high note when the Holden LC Torana won the *Wheels* Car of the Year Award in 1969. I was a fan of *Wheels* for life! The magazine stated at the time that the award was to 'encourage local outfits to design better cars and then build them better' — it worked.

POMMY BRICKS

The Mini, it has to be said, was one of the sure-fire hit vehicles to come out of the UK during the sixties. Australians took to it immediately. Though we were a nation rapidly going down the bigger-is-better road with the increasing Americanisation of our most popular family cars, the 'flying brick' struck a chord, and that chord resonated across the generational divide.

Wrinklies liked it for its economy and practicality, kids liked it because it was 'different' and 'cool' — it was swinging-sixties London at its groovy-baby best.

But everything about the Mini (at least on paper) suggested it would be a dud. The motor was put in sideways; the suspension was funny; you sat on the road, or damn near it; the starter button was on the floor beside the driver's seat, almost like an ejector seat button; and it did look like a brick. For its day though, it had plenty of zip, and the ingenious layout of its little motor, and the fact it was front-wheel drive, meant there was no transmission hump running through the cabin, giving the little car an amazingly roomy interior, with pockets and crannies dotted around the cabin to store stuff. It transported two adults and two kids with great ease, and for a car with such diminutive exterior dimensions, even the boot was quite generous.

The Mini gained even more cred with kids when the

Cooper and Cooper S versions arrived, setting Mt Panorama at Bathurst ablaze with excitement when it competed there in the Bathurst 500 with great success.

There were competitions, mainly by university students with nothing better to do, to see how many kids you could squeeze into a Mini, there were Carnaby Street Minis and psychedelic Minis — they were indeed *the* car for the swinging sixties, at least as far as the UK and a big legion of devotees in Australia were concerned.

BMC, the company which developed the Mini from Alex Issigonis's brilliant design, was markedly less successful with much of its other product. The Mini was of the Morris family, which had developed a sound reputation in Australia through the fifties mainly due to the popularity of the Morris Minor, its larger brother the Morris Major, and close relatives, the Austin family of cars.

Apart from the MGB sports car, there was precious little else of an even remotely funky nature coming out of BMC. In Australia we got the Morris 1100, 1300 and 1500, all of which shared much of the Mini's innovative engineering, but somehow they just didn't come together so well, and the cars were plagued with niggling engineering and design problems.

BMC, later to become Leyland, had a real interest in setting up a successful operation in Australia. Their Australian adventure produced some of the ugliest looking cars ever (that is if you preclude anything which came from behind the Iron Curtain, where they took ugly tin to the level of an artform, but fortunately didn't inflict any of their automotive treats on Australia, even at the height of the cold war).

The Australian experiment for BMC/Leyland culminated in the locally built and ill-fated (but still revered in some quarters, and achieving a kind of ironic cult status in others) Leyland P76. The P76 was supposed to take on the big three, Holden, Ford and Chrysler.

Certainly the car was big enough in dimension — some people thought it looked quite nice, others thought it looked downright ugly. Part of its peculiar design was a heavy-looking rear end. Word got around that this was because part of the design pitch was that farmers should be able to fit a forty-four-gallon drum in the boot. This you could certainly do, the boot was enormous, so were the fuel bills with all that metal to drag around. (Hence the need for a forty-four-gallon drum of petrol in the boot, I guess.)

Many people still have a kind word to say about various Austins, especially the largest 1800 model, also made by BMC, but apart from remarkable interior space, they were not one of the prettiest cars ever bolted together. When I first saw one I seriously thought about studying car design — if this was the best they could come up with, I'd surely have a rosy career ahead of me.

As for the Morris Marina, the less said the better. American consumer advocate Ralph Nader reckoned the Chevrolet Corvair was 'unsafe at any speed' — he clearly hadn't driven a Marina! The people who were to become my in-laws owned a Morris Marina; it handled a bit like a dinghy with outboard motor, but without a rudder.

When the 1800 reached the end of its run, BMC produced a car called the Tasman, and the more upmarket Kimberley. These were supposed to take on the Ford-Holden-Chrysler trio, but were so hopelessly bland they were doomed for failure before they even started rolling off the production line.

ROOTY—TOOTS

The British company Rootes was affiliated with Chrysler and they produced a number of vehicles which were reasonably popular with Australians, including the top-of-the-line Humber Super Snipe (a sort of lounge room on wheels — it had lots of leather and timber trim). The Humber even gave a (very brief) nod in the direction of trendy American design when it incorporated a very discreet Coke-bottle hip and twin headlights, however it was mainly driven by old blokes who wore hats, tweed jackets and smoked pipes.

The Rootes people, having seen the incredible success of the Mini, decided to do their own version of a mini vehicle. It was to be the Hillman Imp. It was almost as quirky as the Morris Mini, but it had a tall 'glasshouse'-type cabin and a motor in the back, à la the Beetle and other more oddball European cars. It, too, apparently handled like a dinghy with an outboard motor, but that was only hearsay, and at least in Australia it was not all that popular except with those people who wanted to be seen tootling about in a vehicle which looked as though it was straight off the set of the *Jetsons* TV series.

The bigger Hillmans, like the Minx, and later the Arrow and Hunter, were somewhat more popular.

The Rootes company built several of other vehicles which

sold in varying quantities in Australia, among them the Singer Gazelle, which was basically a rebadged and slightly modified Minx, much along the lines of what the BMC company used to do, to provide very similar models across the Morris and Austin brand names.

The Sunbeam sports car also came from the Rootes stable. For some reason the company had a massive racing and rally department, which had considerable success in the sixties.

One of its products which I try to block out of my mind is the Hillman Hunter — one of these won the London to Sydney marathon in 1968 and, in doing so, beat a couple of blokes from Oz in a Holden Monaro.

The London to Sydney, as it was commonly called, really caught the imagination of the Australian public. Months and months of planning and publicity culminated in what for many of us was something of an anticlimax when the Hillman won. How could this happen?

When the cars arrived in Australia by ship at Fremantle, thousands of people turned out from all over the country to greet them. They were displayed at Gloucester Park trotting track before continuing the final leg of the rally across Australia to Sydney.

So how come a Hillman beat our Holden Monaro? Many excuses have been offered, but from what I can ascertain from other seriously warped revheads, it was simply a case of the Monaro team's being unable to match the 'service assistance' (read money) which had been provided by the giant Rootes Group to its team in the Hunter. The result of the London to Sydney Marathon is one motoring fact of the sixties which is really best left without further mention.

YANKEE BULLDOGS

The British division of General Motors was called Vauxhall, and though they were the Pommy Holdens, they were still brought into Australia in considerable numbers, from the small Viva, grading upwards to the Victor and the race-winning Velox and Cresta. There was even a model called Wyvern. God only knows where it dreamed up its model names.

The rapidly improving quality and reputation for reliability of Australia's Holden models soon saw the demise of the Vauxhall in Australia.

The Ford Motor Company in Britain was at least called Ford, so there was no confusion on that front, the confusion came in when you looked at the cars. They just didn't look anything like what you expected a Ford to look. The Prefect and Consul were old-fashioned boxy-looking things, without even a passing nod to design trends of the sixties.

The Zephyr was slightly trendier with tiny fins that got (slightly) larger with each facelift of the model. At least the Zephyr had a bit of grunt, and had a bit of cool cred after it appeared as 'Z Victor One', the car in the opening titles of the popular British police TV drama, *Z Cars*.

There were also the highly successful small cars including Cortinas, which enjoyed so much racetrack success in their 'hot' form. The Cortina pretty much replaced the Anglia, a reliable but strange-looking thing with its inwardly sloping rear window.

How could a motor company have models on one side of the Atlantic with such exciting names as Mainline, Skyliner, Thunderbird, Fairlane, Galaxie and Mustang, and on the other side produce such dull-sounding models as Prefect, Consul, Zephyr and Cortina?

Australia's home-grown (via the USA) Ford, the Falcon, soon spelt the demise of the Zephyr, in much the same way as the Holden saw off the Vauxhall.

TRUE BLUES

The sixties saw big changes for General Motors–Holden with the model range expanding dramatically. The small car which replaced the Vauxhall Viva was called the Torana and came in basic through to plush models, and eventually evolved into a fire-breathing rocket which tore up Bathurst for a period.

The family saloon evolved from the fin era and became a staid-looking box design with the EJ. Minor design changes led to the EH, which was widely regarded as one of the best Holdens ever, and at last offered some real performance with a couple of engine choices.

The much-loved EH was replaced by the completely new design HD, with the controversial pedestrian-impaling fins protruding around the side of the headlights.

Newspapers were full of huge advertisements featuring the new HD Holden. The images weren't actual photographs but rather artist's impressions, which always made cars look sleeker and larger than they were in real life.

Depending on the section of the market they were trying to appeal to, a station wagon could be featured with a happy family packing fifteen tons of luggage and the family dog into the back before embarking on a happy holiday.

If it was a sportier model, some lucky groover would have

birds with tight pants and lots of hair drooling over him and his car.

The accompanying blurb when the HD was first released went:

You don't need a crystal ball to predict the shape of things to come — just take a look at the new Holden. Those sleek curves are a mark of advanced design the world over. Performance? Crackerjack! Your choice of three engines up to the 140hp. In the fiery new X2. New braking power from 30 percent bigger self adjusting brakes, or new optional power-assisted discs. Other cars have a lot of catching up to do.

I'm not at all convinced that there was any hard evidence to back the assertions up, but a consistent and prolonged whispering campaign suggested all manner of unfortunate injuries had befallen unsuspecting pedestrians who might have come into contact with the HD's fins. The designers went back to the drawing board, blunted down the fins, and voila! another highly popular model, the HR, was born.

From the very beginning of the sixties, the tried and true Holden model names were gradually changing. The standard name just became plain Holden, then we had the Special, and the top of the line Premier. There was even a hotted-up motor called the X2, and later the 186S. Racing legend Jack Brabham gave his name to a hot Torana called the Brabham Torana. This actually evolved from a hot Vauxhall Viva, but the less said about that the better.

Any hint of the Holdens of old, and their familial resemblance to British GM (read Vauxhall) products ended with the arrival of the HK. The HK saw the introduction of the Belmont as the base model, then came the incredibly popular and now legendary Kingswood. The Premier name was retained for the luxury model, and a new model with a stretched-out rear cabin and boot, the Brougham, was introduced. The Premier and the Brougham stood apart from the more humble models, with an altered rear roof line which increased interior space, and the inclusion of twin headlights on both models.

The Brougham featured luxurious-looking brocade upholstery which snagged women's stockings, itched like buggery on the back of kids' bare legs and frayed hopelessly within a couple of years.

A problem with the HK Premier was the fake tail-light, a red strip which connected the real tail-lights to give the impression the light went right across the entire rear end of the car. The fake bit soon faded in the Aussie sun — this was not a good look.

The Monaro *was* a good look. Basically a Kingswood with two doors taken out and a sleek sloping roof line, it was revhead heaven. There were basic models, but why would you when there was the GTS with a 327 cubic inch V8, which came with off-centre racing stripes that swept across the length of the car? It looked hot and it was hot.

Ford Australia, in the meantime, was not sitting on its hands. Having failed to bite the bullet with the Mustang, the Falcon honchos, following the brute design of their Yankee cousin more closely, launched the Falcon GT, a worthy opponent to the Monaro. Even if it didn't look as good as the Holden, it had balls and went like the clappers

— thus begun the legendary Ford–Holden rivalry in Australian motor sport.

Although they never enjoyed quite the success of the souped-up Monaros and Ford GTs, Chrysler produced a couple of drool items for the revheads with the Valiant Charger and the somewhat more sedate Pacer. In the Charger there was an unforgettable three-on-the-floor shift, complete with chrome handle. The Pacer was pretty much a Valiant with two doors instead of four and some rather wild paintwork. Despite the paint, the Pacer always looked to me like a bit of a half-hearted effort.

One of the most remarkable (for remarkable, read extremely odd) Australian 'cars' of the sixties was a strange thing made at the Lightburn washing machine factory in Adelaide. Lightburn had a good reputation as manufacturers of washing machines, however their foray into vehicle production wasn't quite as successful — although in its own way it was memorable.

The Lightburn car was called the Zeta and it was dubbed 'Australia's second car', presumably Holden being the 'first' car. It had a two-cylinder motor and an ingenious mode of reversing.

To reverse, you turned off the motor then turned the key the other way and bingo! — suddenly the motor was running the other way, and you could proceed to work your way through the gears in reverse. Meaning, the car had the capability of travelling at the same speed forwards or backwards.

I'm not sure if anyone ever managed to get the Zeta going flat chat in reverse, but given the car's modest top speed, it probably wasn't as hair-raising as it sounds.

It has to be reiterated though, that Lightburn *did* make very good washing machines — perhaps it should have stayed in the laundry.

THEY ALSO RAN, MOSTLY

Unlike the marketing of Australian cars, some companies took a more conservative line. The very British Humber Super Snipe relied heavily on the traditional factor: leather seats, plush carpets, woodgrain dash, etc. The '65 model sold for £2,149, while the 'baby' Humber Vogue was a snip at £1,349, mind you it was small and bloody ugly to boot.

Among the cheapest cars on the market was the Daihatsu Compagno saloon. Daihatsu was a new player in the Australian market in 1965, and their entry model was £799.

Mercedes Benz were not really what you'd call stylish vehicles in the sixties. You either loved them, in which case you bought one or saved up for ten years dreaming of buying one, or sneered dislike because you wouldn't want one anyway.

They all seemed to be black, white or cream, and to this untrained eye, I couldn't quite see what the fuss was about. The Merc styling was inoffensive, not flashy like the yank tanks, and not nearly so ugly as the Pommy cars, they were just sort of there in their own timeless way. The headlights might change a bit every few years, but nothing much else seemed to.

Unless they had a clapped-out very old one, you knew that people who drove Mercedes cars didn't have to worry about how much it cost to 'put a tiger in your tank'.

The other Kraut was much more accessible. The VW Beetle had been around all through the fifties with only aficionados being able to pick the subtle design changes over the years. To me it seemed that with the sixties the windows got bigger, the tail-lights got bigger and the headlights got buggier. If unkind (or jealous) people called the Beetle 'Hitler's revenge', those more kindly disposed called it the 'pregnant pasty'.

Well-off students drove old Beetles, teachers and university lecturers drove new Beetles. All Beetle drivers tended to wear polo-neck jumpers, corduroy pants and Buddy Holly-style black-rimmed glasses.

The best thing about Beetles was the lack of a back shelf. Where the shelf would be in a conventional car, there was a deep compartment, large enough to smuggle a medium-sized kid into the drive-in. Not the economy of scale of an American tank boot, but a handy innovation nonetheless.

A good mate in the motor industry told me a really interesting story about the VW Beetle. Around 1928, the Rover motor company in the UK, manufacturers of middle-class cars for doctors and bank managers etc., decided to cash in on the market for cars for plebs. In 1929 they produced a small four-seater, air-cooled rear-engined car called the Scarab. Unfortunately 1929 was not a good year for bank managers or anyone else, so of course the car failed. A total of 630 were built.

The story goes that at some time in the early 1930s, a Dr Ferdinand Porsche visited England and was a guest of one of Rover's board members. On a visit to the Rover plant, the good doctor was very taken with the Scarab and, in a gesture of generosity, the board member crated one of the little cars up and sent it to the doctor in Germany as a gift. Some time later when the Volkswagen appeared, those with knowledge of its roots, nicknamed it the Beetle in honour of the Scarab.

A number of really strange 'niche' cars came out of Germany as well as the big sellers, among them the NSU Prinz and some DKW ... things — although rather than vehicles these probably fell more into the category of Mixmasters on wheels.

The French have never made anything but quirky cars, and somehow manage to convince people all around the world to buy them in their thousands. I've long had the view that Frog engineers take a close look at everything the Germans and Brits are doing, then do the opposite. This, I suppose, could be described as Gallic perversity, or perhaps it's the rest of the world who are perverse.

French cars were buggers of things to service because nothing is where the mechanics expect it to be. Costly hours can be spent just looking for the battery in some French cars. Renault, Peugeot and Citroën all produced cars that looked like no other, at least you had to hand that to them.

To the untrained eye, French cars stood out like dog's balls, and no other country, with the possible exception of the Soviet Union, had cars that unique. (In the case of the Soviets, it was because their cars looked like, and probably had been built from, recycled Panzers.)

From the cute and perky to the Spartan, from the sumptuous to the ridiculous, French car manufacturers provided something for everyone.

Peugeot gained quite a reputation for reliability and ruggedness through the sixties, even if they weren't very exciting to look at. The Peugeot brand name was always well represented at the many rallies and trials which were so popular throughout the sixties. A Redex around-Australia trial back in the fifties wouldn't have been the same without Peugeots.

Renault with its rear-engined 10 series was affordable and just different enough for those people who would normally be inclined to get behind the wheel of a VW Beetle but wanted to show they weren't going along with the herd.

Citroën could not be pigeonholed anywhere. The Diane and Pallas models looked like giant slaters. The Citroëns had appeal just because they *were* genuinely different. They had a suspension system you could alter from inside the cabin, so you could adjust the ride of the vehicle from ground-hugging sleek, to tall and gangly for driving across a rocky paddock. For this reason the big Citroëns were more popular with farmers than they might otherwise have been. You could also adjust the tilt of the headlights from within the car, and the turn indicators at the rear were moulded into the back of the guttering on the roof.

Even if they didn't go like the clappers, they *looked* like they did, and to certain people, looks are everything.

It was a real shame that Citroën didn't release its cute little Deux Chevaux or 2CV in Australia, because I'm sure it would have had an appeal far in excess of its curiosity value.

The 'Ugly Duckling', as it was dubbed, was hugely popular in other parts of the world, and was really the French version of a 'people's' car. In some ways it even looked like a Volkswagen Beetle, although by comparison the VeeDub was positively luxurious, so that will give you an indication of how basic the 2CV really was.

Originally the 2CV came with canvas seats stretched over

a bent metal frame, and a two-horsepower motor, from which it derived its name. With bug eyes for headlights, its styling was also reminiscent of the Beetle, but it was even more slab-sided.

The Italians were doing their own thing, not as quirky as the French, but still a bit odd to the Australian eye. Fortunately for the 'eyetie' car makers, more and more Italian migrants in Australia were finding themselves in a more prosperous position, and able to consider buying a new car, thus families were getting behind the wheels of Fiats, while the slightly more sporty types were into Lancias, and the even sportier car buffs into Alfa Romeos. Alfa Romeos, particularly, seemed to be predominantly red.

A friend of mine had a Fiat Bambino. The Bambino was so small it made a Mini look like a full-size sedan, and a Volkswagen Beetle or Citroën 2CV like a stretch-limo. It was powered by a two-cylinder motor, and could not be recommended for anyone over five feet tall.

Whether it was deserved or not, Italian cars suffered from a reputation that they rusted. Some car dealers even went to the extent of advertising that their vehicles had special underbody sealant to adapt them to Australian conditions.

Cobble together the features of all the cars mentioned so far and we begin to get a rough idea of where the Japanese car industry was coming from in the sixties. They were sucking up engineering designs and technology like a blotter sucks up ink. The sometimes novel vehicles, which they'd produced in the fifteen years after the war, were rapidly giving way to a more structured marketing program. The once strange-looking vehicles were beginning to look more mainstream, initially with an overwhelmingly British and European influence, and later a smattering of Americana.

The first really nice-looking Japanese car was the Mazda sedan designed by the Bertone studio in Italy. It really heralded the arrival of the quirky Japanese manufacturers into the mainstream.

Among the makers from Japan jockeying for a position in the Australian market in the sixties were Toyota, Nissan, Honda, Mazda, Subaru, Mitsubishi, Isuzu, Suzuki, Daihatsu and Hino.

Language was something of a barrier, and many a belly laugh was had from reading the instruction books that came with new Japanese cars. One of my brothers had an early sixties Datsun Bluebird and the instruction manual was a hoot. It must have been written by an engineer who perhaps had English as a third or fourth language. Once you could work your way around a bit of French, with a little German thrown in for good measure, you might be able to work out how to operate the jack to change a flat tyre.

MEATY BEATY
BIG AND BOUNCY

THE SPORT OF KINGS AND SPIVS

When the Melbourne Cup was first held in 1861, legend has it that the winner, Archer, had walked all the way from Nowra to Flemington, a distance of 850 kilometres. Since that first race, the Cup had built a legend of romance, spectacle, heroism, tragedy and fashion.

Australians took to the event in their droves, and although it has been suggested that the inaugural crowd numbers were down because of the news of the deaths of explorers Burke and Wills, the race was still attended by four thousand people.

When the Melbourne Cup was run for the first time, prize money for the winner was £170, and a trophy of a hand-beaten gold watch. By 1960, the Cup itself was worth £750.

When American writer Mark Twain visited Australia in the late 1800s he wrote of the Melbourne Cup: 'Nowhere in the world have I encountered a festival of people that has such a magnificent appeal to the whole nation. The Cup astonishes me.' It's an observation which has remained true throughout the long and illustrious history of the Cup.

By the sixties, the Melbourne Cup had one hundred years of tradition behind it, and the Jean Shrimpton miniskirt 'scandal' in 1965 ensured that the sixties would always be featured in any in-depth discussion about Melbourne Cup highlights.

Quite apart from Jean Shrimpton, horses too were the stars of the Cup through the sixties. The winners for the period were:

1960   Hi Jinx
1961   Lord Fury
1962   Even Stevens
1963   Gatum Gatum
1964   Polo Prince
1965   Light Fingers

(In this year some relatives of mine travelled from South Australia for the Cup. Having parked in the car park, they were heading to the course when they remembered they'd left their binoculars on the back shelf of the car. In the minutes it took them to return to the vehicle, the binoculars had disappeared. The car hadn't been broken into, you just didn't bother to lock up in the sixties. Naturally the theft was an omen, so they chose Light Fingers when placing a bet. An unfortunate start to Cup day ended very happily.)

1966   Galilee
1967   Red Handed
1968   Rain Lover
1969   Rain Lover

REVHEADS

The Great Race as it soon became known in Australia, began as the Armstrong 500 at Phillip Island in Victoria in 1960. It was originally over 130 laps and a distance of five hundred miles (805 kilometres), and was supposed to be the ultimate endurance test of everyday production cars. Unlike other forms of motor racing where the vehicles on the track resembled a family car about as closely as a banana resembles a watermelon, people could get to see the sort of cars that many of them drove in their day-to-day lives hurtling around the track.

The first races were separated into classes according to the cost of the car on the showroom floor. Some modifications were allowed, otherwise it might have been as exciting as watching a snail race, because the stock-standard vehicles sold out of the showrooms would hardly set the world alight in performance terms.

The inaugural race was won by a Vauxhall Cresta (is there no end to the shame?). The Vauxhall Cresta was a lumbering clunker of a thing, which must have really had some work done on it. A Peugeot 403 came in second, with a Simca Aronde third. To be brutally frank, although not uncommon, these cars were not all that representative of the cars increasingly clogging the highways and by-ways of Australia at the time.

As if this inaugural result weren't insult enough for any serious revhead, the indignity was compounded when the class 'A' race at Phillip Island was won by an NSU Prinz. The Prinz was a peculiar little thing. It was supposedly a four-seater, however back-seat passengers would have to have relatives in Lilliput, and it was powered by a two-cylinder four-stroke motor. This was one serious 'buzz box' — one can only imagine what it was competing against, perhaps a Gogomobil or a Lightburn Zeta?

In 1961 Bob Jane and Harry Firth were overall winners in a Mercedes 220SE, with David McKay and Brian Foley second in a Studebaker Lark, and in third place, Frank Croad and John Roxburgh in a (shudder) Vauxhall Velox.

The Velox was not quite as clunky as the Cresta model which had won the year before, but it still wasn't quite the 'excitement machine' either.

The Armstrong 500 was held at Phillip Island for the last time in 1962, with Bob Jane and Harry Firth taking the honours in a Falcon XL, Bill Graetz and Fred Sutherland in a Studebaker Lark second, and another Falcon XL, driven by Ken Harper, John Reaburn and Syd Fisher, third.

At last, with the possible exception of the Studebaker, the cars enjoying success and growing legions of fans were those appearing in increasing numbers on our roads. The car manufacturers had already picked up on the fact that to win the Armstrong 500 meant more activity in terms of interest and sales from the dealers' showrooms, and before long a phrase commonly bandied about was 'Win on Sunday, sell on Monday'.

When the Phillip Island track needed resurfacing, the motor racing authorities decided to move the race to Mt Panorama, at Bathurst, in New South Wales.

It was originally thought that the Mt Panorama track was best suited to small cars because the bigger and more powerful beasts would battle with excessive wear on tyres and brakes. This was proved true when in 1963 Bob Jane and Harry Firth won again, but this time in a far cry from the Falcon — they steered a Cortina GT to the checkered flag, the small Ford making it a trifecta with Frank Morgan and Ralph Sach second, and Bruce McPhee and George Ryan third.

The Cortinas made a clean sweep again in 1964, this time, in order, Bob Jane and George Reynolds, Barry Seton and Herb Taylor, and Harry Firth and John Reaburn.

Then suddenly the Mini Cooper S was the flavour of the month, and it came with a real sting in its tail. A swarm of them competed at Bathurst in 1965, but still the Cortinas held sway with Barry Seton and Midge Bosworth first, and Bruce McPhee and Barry Mulholland second, then, ominously, Brian Foley and Peter Manton in their Cooper S third. Five of the next six places were taken by the flying bricks.

The stunning performance of little cars was a portent of things to come, with the 1966 'Gallaher 500' featuring the Minis in the first nine places, with Rauno Altonen and Bob Holden first, Bill Stanley and Fred Gibson second, and Bruce McPhee and Barry Mulholland third.

The Cooper S reign was short-lived, though, because 1966 was the last time a normally aspirated four-cylinder vehicle took outright honours at Bathurst. With changing technology, braking systems were improving rapidly, and the weight of the lumbering but enormously high-powered 'supercars' was no longer the limiting issue it had been around the tough circuit at Mt Panorama.

The fire-breathing Falcon XR GT of Harry Firth and Fred Gibson took the flag in 1967, followed by Leo and Ian Geoghegan in their Falcon, with the Alfa Romeo GTV of Doug Chivas and Max Stewart third.

1968 saw the 'lion' roar on Mt Panorama when the *Wheels* Car of the Year, 'sex on wheels', Holden Monaro HK GTS of Bruce McPhee and Barry Mulholland won, with two more of the beasties coming in second and third, driven by Jim Palmer and Phil West, and Tony Roberts and Bob Watson respectively.

And '68 saw yet another name change when the Great Race became the 'Hardie-Ferodo 500'.

The decade closed on Mt Panorama with another win for Holden, this time the Monaro was driven by Colin Bond and Tony Roberts. The Ford Falcon XW GTHO Phase 1 of Bruce McPhee and Barry Mulholland came second, and Des West and Peter Brock in a Monaro third.

The era of the supercars and Peter Brock had well and truly arrived, with nine of the top ten places taken by the big Fords and Holdens, the exception being an Alfa Romeo GTV in eighth place.

FASTER THAN THE ROADRUNNER

In the fifties, Donald Campbell received worldwide fame with his attempts on speed records. He held the water speed record of 260.35 miles per hour (419.16 km/h), which he'd set on Coniston Water, in the Lake District of England, late in the decade, and wanted to have a go at the land speed record. The attempt was at the Bonneville Salt Flats in the United States, but ended with his car, Bluebird, veering off the course and crashing at 360 miles per hour (579.6 km/h). Campbell was quite badly injured, but while he was recuperating in hospital, he told the press he was going to have another go.

With a new Bluebird, Donald Campbell and his team arrived at Lake Eyre in South Australia in 1963. The smooth dry bed of the lake should have been ideal for the attempt on the record but, bugger it, shortly after they arrived it began pissing down with rain (something which hadn't happened in yonks) and the course was destroyed.

The following year Campbell returned to Lake Eyre for another attempt, and on 17 July he set a new world land speed record of 403.1 miles per hour (648.99 km/h).

After setting the new world land speed record, Campbell set his sights on the West. On New Year's Eve 1964, he set a new water speed record of 276.30 miles per hour (444.84 km/h) on Lake Dumbleyung, in Western Australia. He had succeeded in setting new land and water speed records within the same calendar year (just).

On 4 January 1967, Donald Campbell returned to Coniston Water to have a crack at breaking 300 miles per hour (483 km/h) on water. On his first run, he clocked 297 miles per hour (478.17 km/h), so near and yet so far. On his return run down the lake at a reported speed of 328 miles per hour (528.08 km/h), the boat gently lifted nose first out of the water, flipped over backwards and plunged straight down into the lake, killing Campbell instantly.

THE ADORATION OF THE BOOT

Geographical location in Australia determines what you might call 'football'. In Victoria, Western Australia, South Australia, Tasmania, the Northern Territory and (perhaps) Queensland, it's Aussie Rules. In New South Wales and (perhaps) Queensland it's Rugby League. To 'dagoes' it's soccer; to college boys and other assorted poo-bahs, it's Rugby Union. So it's all rather confusing, and always has been, although it was slightly less so in the sixties than it perhaps is now because Aussie Rules had yet to begin its expansion across the nation into a national league, with a team in both Sydney and Brisbane.

By far the most elite Aussie Rules competition was in Victoria, with the Victorian Football League sides feeding off the smaller states' football talent like a vampire on a victim's neck. Mostly the talent was happy to be exploited because the VFL was the big league, and it could pay better.

In the sixties the VFL had twelve teams: Essendon, Hawthorn, Collingwood, Fitzroy, South Melbourne, St Kilda, Melbourne, North Melbourne, Footscray, Geelong, Carlton and Richmond. Premiers for the sixties were:

1960	Melbourne
1961	Hawthorn
1962	Essendon

1963   Geelong
1964   Melbourne
1965   Essendon
1966   St Kilda
1967   Richmond
1968   Carlton
1969   Richmond

Our family began following the Geelong club, simply because a cousin of mine, Doug Long, played seventy-three games with them between 1957 and 1961. These days most footy followers wouldn't touch Geelong with a barge pole, except if the only other option was Collingwood.

In South Australia, Sturt won four premierships in the sixties and Port Adelaide three. In Western Australia the decade was also dominated by two teams, Perth and Swan Districts, each winning three premierships.

In New South Wales Rugby League, St George dominated the sixties, winning the premiership each year from 1960 to 1966 inclusive. Souths won in '67 and '68, and Balmain in '69. In the Brisbane Rugby League, Norths dominated the sixties, winning seven out of the ten premierships.

RUNNING, JUMPING AND EVERYTHING BUT STANDING STILL

Australians covered themselves in sporting glory and a swag of medals at the Olympic games throughout the sixties — at Rome in 1960, Tokyo in 1964 and Mexico in 1968. Many of the stars of these Olympics have gone on to become national heroes.

At Rome in 1960 gold medals were won by:

Herb Elliot — 1500m, athletics.
Laurie Morgan — three-day event, individual, equestrian.
Australian team (Neale Lavis, Laurie Morgan, Bill
      Roycroft) — three-day event, teams, equestrian.
John Devitt — 100m freestyle, swimming.
Murray Rose — 400m freestyle, swimming.
John Konrads — 1500m freestyle, swimming.
David Theile — 100m backstroke, swimming.
Dawn Fraser — 100m freestyle, swimming.

Silver medals went to:

Noel Freeman — 20km walk, athletics.
Brenda Jones — 800m, athletics.
Neale Lavis — three-day event, individual, equestrian.
Murray Rose — 1500m freestyle, swimming.
Neville Hayes — 200m butterfly, swimming.

Australian team (Terry Gathercole, Neville Hayes, David
    Theile, Geoff Shipton) — men's 4x100m medley
    relay, swimming.
Australian team (Alva Colquhoun, Lorraine Crapp, Dawn
    Fraser, Ilsa Konrads) — women's 4x100m freestyle
    relay, swimming.
Australian team (Jan Andrew, Dawn Fraser, Rosemary
    Lassig, Marilyn Wilson) — women's 4x100m medley
    relay, swimming.

Bronze medals:

Dave Power — 10,000m, athletics.
Ollie Taylor — bantamweight, boxing.
Tony Madigan — light heavyweight, boxing.
John Konrads — 400m freestyle, swimming.
Australian team (John Devitt, David Dickson, John
    Konrads, Murray Rose) — 4x200m freestyle relay,
    swimming.
Jan Andrew —100m butterfly, swimming.

At Tokyo in 1964, as well as pinching a flag, 'Our Dawnie'
grabbed some medals. Gold medals were won by:

Betty Cuthbert — 400m, athletics.
Bob Windle — 1500m freestyle, swimming.
Kevin Berry — 200m butterfly, swimming.
Ian O'Brien — 200m breaststroke, swimming.
Dawn Fraser — 100m freestyle, swimming.
Australian crew (Bill Northam, Peter 'Pod' O'Donnell,
    James 'Dick' Sargeant) — 5.5m class, yachting.

Silver:

Michelle Mason-Brown — high jump, athletics.
Australian team (Lyn Bell, Dawn Fraser, Jan Murphy,
        Robyn Thorn) — women's 4x100m freestyle relay,
        swimming.

Bronze:

Judy Amoore — 400m, athletics.
Marilyn Black — 200m, athletics.
Ron Clarke — 1000m, athletics.
Australian team (Merv Crossman, Paul Dearing, Raymond
        Evans, Brian Glencross, Robin Hodder, John
        McBryde, Donald McWatters, Pat Nilan, Eric Pearce,
        Julian Pearce, Desmond Piper, Donald Smart,
        Anthony Waters, Graham Wood) — hockey.
Ted Boronovkis — open class, judo.
Allan Wood — 400m freestyle, swimming.
Allan Wood — 1500m freestyle, swimming.
Australian team (David Dickson, Peter Doak, John Ryan,
        Bob Windle) — 4x100m freestyle relay, swimming.
Australian team (Peter Reynolds, Ian O'Brien, Kevin Berry,
        David Dickson) — 4x100m medley relay, swimming.

The Tokyo Olympics highlight was the remarkable
comeback of Betty Cuthbert after her triumph in Melbourne
in 1956, but Australia's efforts were overshadowed by Dawn
Fraser's suspension, along with some of her team-mates, for
alleged misconduct. It brought her fabulous career to an end.

The Mexico City Olympic Games were held against a
backdrop of world strife, and there was civil unrest in Mexico

itself. The Soviet army had brutally invaded Czechoslovakia to slap down its reformist government, and the US was torn with increasing opposition to the Vietnam War and race riots flaring up everywhere.

Added to this was the problem with the location. With Mexico City sitting at 2,240 metres above sea level, the rarefied atmosphere would cause problems for most athletes who normally performed at or near sea level, thus giving a distinct advantage to athletes from other high-altitude countries, like Ethiopia.

Nevertheless, Australians performed well, with a respectable tally of medals.

Gold:

Ralph Doubel — 100m, athletics.
Maureen Caird — 80m hurdles, athletics.
Mike Wenden — 100m freestyle, swimming.
Mike Wenden — 200m freestyle, swimming.
Lyn McClements — 100m butterfly, swimming.

Silver:

Peter Norman — 200m, athletics.
Raelene Boyle — 200m, athletics.
Pam Kilborn — 80m hurdles, athletics.
Australian team (Paul Dearing, Raymond Evans, Brian
        Glencross, Robert Haigh, Donald Martin, James
        Mason, Pat Nilan, Eric Pearce, Gordon Pearce,
        Julian Pearce, Desmond Piper, Frederick Quinn,
        Ron Riley, Donald Smart) — hockey.
Australian crew (Peter Dickson, David Douglas, Alfred
        Duval, Joseph Fazio, Alan Grover, Michael Morgan,

Gary Pearce, John Ranch, Robert Shirlaw) — rowing
eights.
Australian team (Greg Rogers, Mike Wenden, Graham
White, Bob Windle) — men's 4x200m freestyle relay,
swimming.
Australian team (Lyn McClements, Judy Playfair, Jenny
Steinbeck, Lynne Watson) women's — 4x100m
medley relay, swimming.

Bronze:

Jenny Lamy — 200m athletics.
Australian team (Bill Roycroft, Wayne Roycroft, Brian
Cobcroft) — three-day event, teams, equestrian.
Greg Brough — 1500m freestyle, swimming.
Australian team (Robert Cusack, Greg Rogers, Mike
Wenden, Bob Windle) — 4x100m freestyle relay,
swimming.
Karen Moras — 400m freestyle, swimming.

At the Melbourne Olympics in 1956, long-distance runner
Ron Clarke got to carry the Olympic torch into the stadium,
but his best was yet to come. In a period of five years,
beginning in 1963, Clarke set seventeen world records for
distances from two to twelve miles, and he wasn't even slightly
black! On 22 February 1964, Ron Clarke smashed the world
three-mile indoor record when he covered the distance in 13
minutes 18.4 seconds at an athletics event in New York.

FLANNELLED FOOLS

Cricket was still cricket in the sixties, the almighty dollar hadn't taken over; 'pyjama' one-day cricket would have been considered sacrilegious, and competition didn't change names to suit the sponsor.

In the national Sheffield Shield competition, New South Wales was going through a purple patch, winning the Shield on five occasions, 1959/60, 1960/61, 1961/62, 1964/65 and 1965/66. Victoria won in 1962/63 and 1969/70, South Australia in 1963/64 and 1968/69, and Western Australia in 1967/68.

Australia played sixty-seven Test matches in the sixties, winning twenty-three of them, losing fourteen, and drawing twenty-nine to became the first team — with the West Indies — to tie a test match.

It was not until the 498th Test match of all time that the result was a tie. Between 9 and 14 December, in the first Test of the 1960/61 series against the West Indies, Australia went into the second innings requiring 233 runs to win. With three of their last four wickets falling to run-outs (Davidson, Grout and Meckiff), Australia lost its last wicket (Meckiff) with the scores tied and the first Test in the history of Test cricket tied. During that Test match, Alan Davidson became the first player in the history of Test cricket to achieve the double of a hundred runs and ten wickets in a single Test match — with a broken finger!

Australia retained the Ashes throughout the sixties, either winning or drawing the four series played.

During the sixties, Australia had a total of six Test captains, Richie Benaud, Neil Harvey, Bob Simpson, Brian Booth, Bill Lawry and Barry Jarman.

Thirty-two Australians made their Test debuts during the decade, bringing the number of players to represent Australia to 247 by the end of it. Bill Lawry, Graham McKenzie, Ian Redpath, Ian Chappell, Doug Walters, Keith Stackpole, John Inverarity and Ashley Mallet were among the better-known cricketers to make their debuts, the full list was:

J W Martin v West Indies, Melbourne, 1960/61
F M Misson v West Indies, Melbourne, 1960/61
D E Hoare v West Indies, Adelaide, 1960/61
W M Lawry v England, Birmingham, 1961
G D McKenzie v England, Lords, 1961
BC Booth v England, Manchester, 1961
C E J Guest v England, Sydney, 1962/63
B K Shepherd v England, Sydney, 1962/63
N J N Hawke v England, Sydney, 1962/63
A N Connolly v South Africa, Brisbane, 1963/64
T R Veivers v South Africa, Brisbane, 1963/64
I R Redpath v South Africa, Melbourne, 1963/64
G E Corling v England, Nottingham, 1964
R M Cowper v England, Leeds, 1964
R H D Sellers v India, Kolkata, 1964/65
I M Chappell v Pakistan, Melbourne, 1964/65
D J Sincock v Pakistan, Melbourne, 1964/65

L C Mayne v West Indies, Kingston, 1964/65
P I Philpott v West Indies, Kingston, 1964/65
G Thomas v West Indies, Kingston, 1964/65
P J Allan v England, Brisbane, 1965/66
K D Walters v England, Brisbane, 1965/66
K R Stackpole v England, Adelaide, 1965/66
D A Renneberg v South Africa, Johannesburg, 1966/67
H B Taber v South Africa, Johannesburg, 1966/67
G D Watson v South Africa, Cape Town, 1966/67
J W Gleeson v India, Adelaide, 1967/68
A P Sheahan v India, Adelaide, 1967/68
E W Freeman v India, Brisbane, 1967/68
L R Joslin v India, Sydney, 1967/68
R J Inverarity v England, Leeds, 1968
A A Mallett v England, The Oval, 1968

South Africa played Test cricket through to 1970 and then, because of the sanctions imposed against the apartheid regime, had to wait two decades before playing another Test.

Wisden Cricketers of the Year from Australia included:

1962 — R Benaud, A K Davidson, W M Lawry, N C O'Neill
1965 — P J P Burge, G D McKenzie, R B Simpson

Players who were 12th men and who never played a Test match were:

I M McLachlan, SA, v England, Adelaide, 4th Test, 1962/63

I W Quick, Vic, v England, Manchester, 4th Test, 1961

J Potter, Vic, v South Africa, Melbourne, 2nd Test, 1963/64

              v England, Nottingham, 1st Test, 1964

              v England, Leeds, 3rd Test, 1964

S C Trimble, Qld, v West Indies, Port-of-Spain, 5th Test, 1964/65

G R Davies, NSW, v West Indies, Brisbane, 1st Test, 1968/69

Many years later I was to sit alongside I M (Ian) McLachlan in Australia's federal parliament.

BIFFO

Throughout the sixties, Lionel Rose and Johnny Famechon were Australian boxing heroes.

Lionel's story was something of a fairytale. Born in rural Victoria, he grew up to become one of Australia's most successful boxers. While he was growing up, Lionel would watch his dad, who was also a boxer, and he thought that boxing might be his way out of crippling poverty in the country. He won his first amateur title at fifteen, and went on to cap his career with a world title.

He won the bantamweight title in 1968 from Masahito 'Fighting' Harada from Japan. A popular story that did the rounds said Harada had been told if you hit an Aborigine in the legs, he'd collapse immediately. He clearly didn't heed the advice, and Lionel was triumphant.

In his professional career, he fought fifty-three bouts, winning forty-two and losing eleven, with a total of twelve knockouts. And, in 1970, Lionel Rose had one more big hit, this time it was a recording of a song written by Johnny Young called 'I Thank You'.

Johnny Famechon was also popular with boxing fans, and he sure gave them plenty to cheer about. With his career also spanning the sixties, he fought sixty-seven bouts, won fifty-six with twenty knockouts, lost only five, and drew six. He became Australian Featherweight Champion in 1964,

Commonwealth Featherweight Champion in 1967 and World Featherweight Champion in 1969. He is the only World Featherweight Champion never to have been knocked out.

Johnny Famechon retired in 1970.

Cassius Clay first caught the eye of boxing fans when he won the gold medal in the light heavyweight division at the 1960 Rome Olympics. He quickly turned professional and earned a (well-deserved) reputation as a shameless self-promoter and loudmouth.

Clay gained headlines by making up appalling poems about what he was going to do to his opponent in a forthcoming bout. 'The Louisville Lip', as he was dubbed, thrived on press conferences and was always good for a quotable quote or instant headline.

As the cameras whirred away and press photographers snapped away, the Lip would loudly sing his own praises with sayings like 'I'm young, I'm pretty, and I can't possibly be beat,' 'Float like a butterfly, sting like a bee,' and 'I am the greatest.'

After turning professional, success came immediately and, in 1964, Cassius Clay fought the heavyweight champion Sonny Liston. Clay won, and in the return bout the following year, he won again.

With his success came controversy and notoriety. After joining a group called The Nation of Islam, he changed his name to Muhammad Ali, and refused to serve in the US army during the Vietnam War saying 'No Vietnamese ever called me a nigger.' Ali had his championship belt taken from him, as well as his licence to box, and didn't get his career back on the rails again until the seventies.

Muhammad Ali had millions of fans, but I wasn't one of them. I could never quite see the point of two blokes punching each other senseless, and his carry-on on TV, I thought, just made him look as though he was incredibly thick.

WHACKING BALLS

The sixties was a golden era for Aussie tennis, with some of the greatest players of all time making their mark. Margaret Smith (Court) achieved some amazing successes on the court. She was the Australian singles champion ten times, 1960–66 and 1969–71. She won Wimbledon in '63, '65 and '70, the French singles title four times, and the American title six times. In 1970 she won the Grand Slam.

'Rocket' Rod Laver came to international tennis stardom in the sixties, and during his magnificent career won twenty major titles in singles and doubles. He contributed to Australian Davis Cup victories, won Wimbledon in '61 and '62, and again as a professional in '68 and '69. In 1962 he won nineteen singles tournaments with a match record of 134–15, and in 1969 seventeen singles tournaments with a record of 106–16.

When Rocket turned professional in 1963, there was resistance by tournament operators to paying professionals, so he didn't play at Wimbledon or in any of the other great championships for five years.

The so-called 'open' era of tennis began in 1968 and, despite the fact his career was nearing its end, Rod Laver was the first tennis player to pass the $1 million mark in prize money. Who knows what his record might have looked like had he been able to play during that five-year period when he was at his peak.

Ken Rosewall was a champ of the fifties who turned professional in 1958, but still managed to win the French singles title for a second time in 1968. Roy Emerson was Australian champion six times: 1961 and 1963–67. He won the US title twice, in '63 and '67, and the doubles four times, the French singles in '63 and '67, and doubles six times consecutively from 1960, Wimbledon singles twice in '64 and '65, and the doubles twice.

John Newcombe, who went on to have an outstanding career into the seventies, announced his arrival at the end of the sixties, beginning with both the Wimbledon and US Open titles in '67. He ended up winning twenty-five Grand Slam titles in singles, doubles and mixed doubles. And he and Rod Laver were the only players to win both the US and Wimbledon titles as both amateurs and professionals.

(MOSTLY) UNSUNG

For a nation which prides itself on its sporting prowess, Australians mostly pay only passing attention to what are known as the 'minor' sports. However, the achievements of the following athletes, who were prominent in the sixties, were anything but minor.

Heather McKay dominated international squash for two decades. Among her extraordinary achievements in tournaments throughout the world were winning the Australian Amateur Squash Championship 14 times (1960–73) and the British Amateur Squash Championship 16 times (1962–77). She was beaten only twice in her 20-year career, once in a NSW State championship in 1959 and once in the final of the Scottish Championship in 1960.

Heather McKay also represented Australia in hockey in the late fifties and had taken up squash to improve her fitness for hockey.

Jack Brabham was a champion motor car racing driver through the fifties and the sixties, winning the World Championship three times (1959, '60, '66). His 1966 victory was in a self-designed car. He was selected as Australian of the Year in 1966. He retired in 1971

Australians have figured quite prominently in the world of golf for many years, and the sixties had a couple of real champs when it came to impressive stroke play.

Kel Nagle won 55 major golfing tournaments between 1938 and 1978, and was perhaps at his peak through the sixties. He won the Australian PGA six times, the New Zealand Open and the New Zealand PGA nine times each, the British Open (1960), and the World Series twice in the early seventies

Peter Thomson was also a dominant figure in golf through the sixties. He won 57 major tournaments between 1949 and 1979. He won the British Open five times, the Australian Open twice, the New Zealand Open nine times and the Canada Cup (now called the World Cup), with Kel Nagle, twice.

At the beginning of the sixties, surfing was a minority sport in Australia, with a small band of enthusiastic die-hards, but there were a couple of Australians who really put our country on the map as a surfing mecca, and lifted the profile of the sport enormously through the sixties. Our first champs of the waves were Bernard 'Midget' Farrelly and Robert 'Nat' Young.

Midget Farrelly began it all by winning the Makaha International Surfing Championship in Hawaii in 1963. This prompted Ampol Petroleum to sponsor the first official World Surfboard Championship in 1964, at Manly, NSW, which Midget Farrelly then proceeded to win.

Nat Young won the World Surfboard Championship in San Diego in 1966. He was the first person to win the title who was not a resident of the host country.

Bill Northam took up sailing at the age of forty-seven, and won the 5.5m Olympic gold medal in 1964 in *Barrenjoey*, becoming the oldest person (at 59) to win a gold medal.

Bill Roycroft (equestrian) competed in five Olympic games from 1960, where he won a gold medal in the three-day event. He won Olympic bronze medals in the same event in 1968 and '72

'STOP, HEY, WHAT'S THAT
SOUND? EVERYBODY LOOK,
WHAT'S GOIN' DOWN'

WHAT A WONDERFUL WORLD!

In our schools in the sixties we were constantly being exhorted to look outward. Geography had a lot of importance placed on it as a subject, and by Grade six or seven, a kid might be expected to be able to point out the location of most countries of the world, many of which had different names in the sixties from those they're known by today.

Every classroom had a map of the world on the wall, the flasher ones could be pulled down for the class, then retracted, much like a holland blind. On that map of the world, the countries which made up the British Empire were coloured in red. There was a lot of red.

As well as knowing where the countries were, we'd be trained like parrots to rattle off their capital cities and political leaders. As a result most kids who spent at least a few years in a sixties classroom would be familiar with world leaders Mao Zedong, the Chinese Chairman, even though over the years his name was spelt a dozen different ways, and pronounced even more; Chiang Kai-shek (Taiwan, or Formosa as we used to call it); Nasser (Egypt), Charles de Gaulle (France); Nehru, Shastri and Indira Ghandi (India); Ben-Gurion (Israel); Hirohito (Japan); Pope John XXIII and Paul VI (Vatican); Khruschev and Brezhnev (USSR); Harold Macmillan and Harold Wilson (UK); presidents Eisenhower,

Kennedy and Johnson (United States) and chancellors Adenauer, Erhard and Kiesinger (West Germany).

As if the Russians weren't scaring the living daylights out of us enough, the secretive Chinese government was providing plenty of fodder for news of the world. In 1966 the Chinese leader, Mao Zedong, launched his Cultural Revolution. For years Mao encouraged so-called revolutionary committees with their brigades of Red Guards to take power from the authorities of the state. As a result, over a period of about three years until 1969, many Chinese citizens were killed and millions were imprisoned.

The Little Red Book or the thoughts of Chairman Mao was carted around by his Red Guard thugs as justification of their persecution of the so-called intellectuals. *The Little Red Book* was extremely popular with the 'champagne socialists' in Australia's universities.

Although I never got anywhere within cooee of university, I did manage to get my hands on a copy of *The Little Red Book*, but after wading through stuff like 'Every Communist must grasp the truth, political power grows out of the barrel of a gun,' and 'If there is to be revolution, there must be a revolutionary party. Without a revolutionary party, without a party built on the Marxist-Leninist revolutionary theory and in the Marxist-Leninist revolutionary style, it is impossible to lead the working class and the broad masses of the people to defeat imperialism and its running dogs,' and 'All reactionaries are paper tigers,' I decided a better title for Chairman Mao's *Little Red Book* might be 'The Little Brown Book', because it was totally full of shit!

HOT AND COLD RUNNING WARS
THE SIXTIES IN A FLASH

As the sixties began, the West was not alone in its fear and suspicion of the Soviet Union. The commies were falling out between themselves.

Peking was highly critical of the somewhat more pragmatic approach Kruschev was taking to world events, and communist neighbours could not agree on their border demarcation, so from time to time they'd slug it out with skirmishes along their frontiers. We only got limited reporting about this because Soviet and Chinese societies were virtually sealed off from the West.

Gradually, more and more countries were gaining their independence, with the updated atlases of the world becoming decidedly less red, as the British Empire shrank, along with the other European empires.

In Africa, Niger, French Congo, Belgian Congo, Mali, Chad, Mauritania and Madagascar all threw off their shackles to rather quickly slide into varying forms of chaos.

In the lead-up to the ceremony to mark Nigerian independence, an announcer on the BBC in London was reading the introduction for a live cross to Lagos, the Nigerian capital at the time, and he read 'We now take you to Her Majesty Queen Elizabeth the Second in the land of the Nigger.' Intentional it was not, but it earned the announcer some weeks' suspension.

The United States was hideously embarrassed when the Russians managed to shoot down an American U2 spy plane. The U2 was supposed to be able to fly fast enough and high enough to go undetected — clearly it didn't. As if relations between the US and Soviets weren't bad enough, the U2 scandal dominated the news for weeks with claim and counterclaim, and speculation about how the Russians would torture Gary Powers, the U2 pilot, to get him to speak.

Because of world tensions, the arms race was going full tilt and, in 1960, the Americans successfully fired a Polaris missile from a submarine. This meant that US nuclear weapons were not all land based in future, and therefore, safe from a Soviet 'first strike'. The US also launched its first nuclear-powered aircraft carrier, the *Enterprise*. Now they were capable of roaming the oceans of the world without refuelling.

The start of the decade also witnessed the beginning of the 40 year US blockade of Cuba and the Rome Olympics.

In 1961 John F Kennedy was elected president of the United States. We followed his every move on TV because compared to the rather grey and uninteresting presidents who'd immediately preceded him, Kennedy was young, photogenic, and had an extremely beautiful wife with whom the press was in love.

Women were influenced by the clothes Jackie Kennedy wore, and magazines were full of articles about how Jackie was changing the White House, about the food the Kennedys ate, and about her pregnancies and children. Even her miscarriage was big news.

With the Kennedy family wealth, and their luxurious holiday compound at Hyannis Port in Massachusetts, it seemed the Kennedys had it all. Small wonder this period of their lives got dubbed 'Camelot'. It was not to last for long.

With all the propaganda surrounding the arms race, and the enormous leaps being made in weapon technology, many of us got lulled into a false sense of security because the Yanks were on our side. This confidence took a bit of a hiding when the American-supported Bay of Pigs invasion of Cuba was a complete balls-up. The CIA had supported the invasion by Cuban rebels, but Fidel Castro's troops took care of them in very short order. Kennedy took full responsibility for the mess, and the stage was set for the Cuban missile crisis the following year. We knew we were living in dangerous times.

The Cuban missile crisis was certainly one of 1962's biggest stories, and people all over the world were terrified that it would all escalate into nuclear war. We all knew that a nuclear war would be the end of us all.

There was renewed interest in nuclear shelters, and *Popular Mechanics* magazine had an article on how to build a nuclear shelter in your own backyard.

The tensions of the Cuban missile crisis were defused a little when the Yanks and the Russkies at least started talking about banning the testing of nuclear weapons, and actually reached consensus on the testing of such weapons above ground when they were banned after an agreement in 1963.

In 1962 the space race was competing with the arms race for headlines. The first international satellite broadcast of TV took place, and immediately TV news was transformed. No longer did viewers have to wait for newsreels to be flown from around the world to be shown, in many cases two or three days after the news had occurred. Although the first TV satellite images were a bit ghosty, they soon sharpened up with new and evolving technology.

Telstar was the name given to that first TV satellite, and the name conjured up visions of everything that was modern, sixties and cool.

The British instrumental group the Tornados had a big hit single which went to number one around the world called 'Telstar'. It featured spacy sound effects — even though there is no sound in space that was a minor concern, at least 'Telstar' was what we imagined space might sound like.

Trumped in 1961 by the USSR's Yuri Gargarin to get the first man in space, the Americans managed, at last, in 1962, when Alan Shephard became the first American in space. Even if the flight only lasted fifteen minutes, at least they'd done it, and the Americans seemed to be taking it all very seriously after President Kennedy earlier that year declared that America intended to put a man on the moon before the decade was out — and they did!

1962 also saw the death of well-known Kennedy associate, Marilyn Munroe.

The trial of Adolf Eichmann came around at last. After the Second World War, Eichmann, who had been in charge of the 'Jewish' department of Hitler's Gestapo, had fled to South America like so many other Nazis. Secret service agents from Israel had spent years hunting him down, and finally managed to catch and smuggle him out of Argentina in 1960.

Eichmann's trial seemed to go on forever, and the TV images of him in the courtroom in a specially made bulletproof glass box were common on our TV screens. After the long drawn-out trial, with weekly revelations of unthinkable Nazi atrocities against the Jewish people and others, Eichmann was convicted and sentenced to death for crimes against humanity.

Such was the media interest in his trial and execution that even the fact that he refused his last meal and instead requested a bottle of red wine, which he half consumed before going to the gallows, was reported in the press. Adolf Eichmann was hanged on 31 May 1962. (I hope they didn't waste that other half of the bottle of red!)

Back closer to home, our South-East Asian neighbours were beginning to get themselves organised as the red-shaded countries in the atlas continued to shrink. Agreement was finally reached on the establishment of a Malaysian Federation, comprising Malaysia, Singapore, Sarawak, Brunei and British Borneo.

The agreement was to go into effect on 16 September 1963. Singapore didn't stick around in the federation for long, and after some race-based political upheaval, its leader, Lee Kwan Yew, took the tiny island state to independence.

America's CIA was up to its old tricks and in South Vietnam things were going from bad to worse. The Vietnamese military, with the backing of the CIA, overthrew the government of Ngo Dinh Diem. It was thought Diem was not pursuing the war with the communists with enough vigour.

In 1962 Diem had pleaded with the US and its allies for assistance in sorting out the communists. Australia initially sent thirty 'advisers', known as the Australian Army Training Team Vietnam. This was our first tentative 'toe dip' into what was to turn out to be a quagmire, and a war which would divide Australia down the middle.

And at home, 1962 saw Aboriginal Australians given the right to vote.

The British Empire diminished further in 1963 with Kenya opting out, but remaining within the Commonwealth. Their first leader was an imposing fellow called Jomo Kenyatta. As kids growing up in the fifties we'd heard plenty of lurid and grisly tales about a gang of thugs in Kenya called the Mau Mau. As well as featuring in news bulletins, the Mau Mau provided plenty of fodder for filmmakers wanting to flesh out their African epics with a bit of blood and gore.

And back in Blighty herself, 1963 saw two infamous events: the Profumo Affair — starring a government minister and call girls, Christine Keeler and Mandy Rice Davies — and the Great Train Robbery — starring Ronnie Biggs.

On top of their problems in the wider world, domestically the Americans were also having a bumpy ride. In Alabama, Governor George Wallace threatened to block the admission of the first two black students to the University of Alabama. President Kennedy ordered the National Guard to ensure their admittance was facilitated.

In Washington, two hundred thousand people participated in the biggest peaceful demonstration ever held to support civil rights, and this was where Dr Martin Luther King made his famous speech which included the immortal lines, 'I have a dream that one day this nation will rise up and live out the true meaning of its creed: "We hold these truths to be self-evident, that all men are created equal".'

It must have been a year for memorable speeches, because this was the year President Kennedy made his famous Berlin

Wall speech on a trip where he was greeted like a pop star. In West Germany, as well as the country of his ancestry, Ireland, and in Rome where he visited the Pope, adoring fans turned out in their thousands. Less than six months later, the object of their adoration was shot dead in Dallas.

China added to the woes of the world in 1964 when they exploded their first nuclear bomb. The other nuclear powers at the time were the US, the Soviet Union, Great Britain and France. The concerns of the world weren't allayed much when China declared it would not be the first to use nuclear weapons.

Other events of 1964 were that Tanganyika and Zanzibar decided they'd be better off as one country, so they amalgamated as Tanzania. The Beatles appeared on the *Ed Sullivan Show* in February 1964, and by the first week in April held the top five spots on the American charts. In June they began their only Australian tour. In South Africa, Nelson Mandela was sentenced to life inprisonment, whilst the Civil Rights bill was finally passed in the US, and Dr Martin Luther King was awarded the Nobel Peace Prize. The Warren Commission concluded that Lee Harvey Oswald had acted alone in the assassination of President John F Kennedy, and debate over this still continues. Lyndon Johnson won the presidency over rival Barry Goldwater, who didn't stand much of a chance anyway, what with the incumbent enjoying something of a sympathy vote, and Goldwater wanting to 'nuke' Vietnam.

In Australia in 1964, conscription was introduced for overseas military service, and HMAS *Voyager* sank after a collision with HMAS *Melbourne*.

After another African nation, Gambia, gained its independence in 1965, Rhodesia decided to get itself in on the act and unilaterally declared independence in open defiance of the British government. Its government, led by Ian Smith, was all white in an overwhelmingly black country. Immediately sanctions were applied to the Smith regime, supported by the United Nations.

In Britian 1965 saw the death of old war-warrior, Sir Winston Churchill.

Racial violence escalated markedly in the US and in 1965, in Selma, Alabama, six hundred civil rights marchers were attacked by state troopers on 'Bloody Sunday', and in the Watts area of Los Angeles, riots broke out resulting in thirty-four deaths and over a thousand injuries.

1965 also saw the first commercial satellite launched, beginning a boom in the telecommunications services industry.

Harold Holt became prime minister of Australia in January 1966 upon the retirement of Australia's longest-serving prime minister, Sir Robert Menzies.

Menzies had first been PM between 1939 and 1941, and then was again elected to the position in 1949. Menzies, in hindsight, has been criticised for not doing much while prime minister for such a long period, but the fact he had such a stranglehold on the job would suggest the Australian people must have thought he was doing something right.

During his time at the helm, he established the CSIRO, helped set up the Colombo Plan and the ANZUS Treaty, pushed through the Australia–Japan Trade Agreement, greatly expanded the education system and introduced medical and hospital benefits. Australia prospered, and the standard of living of its people increased throughout the Menzies era.

Because Menzies had such an enormous presence, and the fact he'd been leader for so many years, the prime ministers who followed him in the sixties seemed somewhat weak and ineffectual by comparison.

Harold Holt was a strong supporter of the United States and their involvement in the Vietnam War. It was Harold Holt who made the statement that Australia would go 'All the way with LBJ' to indicate support for the then president, Lyndon Johnson.

In 1966 Holt pulled off an astounding election win on a pro-Vietnam War platform. When President Johnson visited Australia that year, Victorian police estimated that more than three-quarters of a million people turned out to see him during his whirlwind visit to Melbourne.

Johnson had security people freaking out as he repeatedly jumped out of his car to greet the crowds, at one stage the president grabbed an 'All the way with LBJ' placard from one of the cheering crowd, and waved it above his head.

Harold Holt is probably best remembered for the fact that he disappeared while swimming off Cheviot Beach, near Portsea, in Victoria, in December 1967. His body was never found and the police concluded that 'There has been no indication that the disappearance of the late Mr Holt was anything other than accidental.' The rumour mill ground into action, and stories started to do the rounds that the PM had been taken by frogmen from another country, that he'd been bumped off by our own secret service, and the most popular theory of all, that Holt had secretly been a spy for the Chinese and he'd arranged to be picked up by a Chinese submarine submerged offshore at Portsea ready to take him to safety in China, where he'd live happily ever after.

In the confusion following the disappearance of Prime

Minister Holt, the deputy PM, 'Black Jack' John McEwen, stepped in to fill the void until a new leader could be elected. McEwen was prime minister from 19 December 1967 until the Liberals elected a new leader on 10 January 1968. They chose John Gorton.

Gorton had served in the RAAF as a pilot during the Second World War. He was discharged in 1944 having been severely wounded during air operations. His face had been badly disfigured, and even after extensive plastic surgery, the extent of his wounds was obvious.

When he first became prime minister, Gorton was quite well liked because of his easygoing style, but he had a few enemies within the public service, and in his own party. His detractors reckoned he played favourites, and that he appointed his cronies to his 'cocktail cabinet'. He brawled with the Americans over not keeping him informed as to what they were up to in Vietnam, he managed to get his state Liberal leaders offside over state's rights issues, and he got in trouble with women.

The most notorious example of Gorton's women worries was his young private secretary Ainslie Gotto, who some thought wielded far too much power. When Gorton sacked one of his ministers, Dudley Irwin, in 1969, Irwin told the media he had no doubt who was to blame — 'It's shapely, it wiggles and its name is Ainslie Gotto.'

Without apparent rhyme or reason, 1966 also saw Australia's only assassination attempt when Labor leader Arthur Calwell was shot by Peter Kocan, who later became a poet.

1966 saw India and Pakistan 'at it' over Kashmir, and they've been at it ever since. In Africa, the former Bechuanaland

Protectorate became Botswana, the British colony of Basutoland became Lesotho, and Nigeria slipped into civil war, with the governor of eastern Nigeria declaring the new Republic of Biafra.

A glance at my old stamp album from 1966 is quite enlightening with places like Abyssinia, Aden, Aitutaki, Bahawalpur, Bamra, Basutoland, Bechuanaland, Belgian Congo, Bhopal, Bohemia, British Guiana, British Honduras, Bussahir, Cape Juby, Cape of Good Hope, Chamba-Charkari, Cochin, French Congo, Cyrenaica, Dahomey, Diego-Suarez, Dutch Indies, Funchal, Gwalior, Hyderabad, Indore, Jaipur, Labuan, Levant, Lourenzo Marquez, Madeira, Mayotte, Moheli, Nyassaland, Orcha, Oubangui-Chari-Tchad, Patiala, Persia, Rhodesia, Saar, Sirmoor, Somaliland, Toga, Trans Jordan, Transvaal, Travancore, Trieste, Union of South Africa, Wadham, West Germany and Zanzibar now no longer appearing in atlases as separate entities.

1966 saw the first use of direct-dial phones. Up until then, all international calls required assistance from operators. Suddenly a swag more jobs went down the gurgler.

Since the inception of the State of Israel in 1948, there had been simmering unrest with its Arab neighbours, which often flared into skirmishes and outright hostility. In the latter part of 1966 there had been a marked increase in terrorist attacks against the Jewish state, with Syria and Jordan accused of harbouring the terrorists. The attacks and counterattacks, the claims and counterclaims escalated until May, when the Egyptians told UN forces, who had been peacekeeping on the Israeli-Egyptian border in the Sinai desert since a flare-up in the mid-50s, to get out. The secretary-general, U Thant withdrew the troops, and the Egyptians blockaded the Straits of Tiran, cutting off access to Eilat, Israel's port on the Red Sea.

Day by day it became obvious that sooner or later the shit was going to hit the fan. The Arabs were all ganging together, negotiating mutual defence agreements and setting the stage for a combined attack on Israel.

On 5 June, the Israeli Air Force launched a pre-emptive strike against the Arab allies' airfields, and effectively caught them napping, wiping out each of their air forces, taking out more than four hundred planes. On the ground, the Israelis attacked and surrounded Egyptian forces in the Sinai, and within forty-eight hours had swept through to the Suez Canal, capturing the whole Sinai Peninsula. On the TV news, we were shown abandoned Egyptian tanks and artillery, and there were reports of Egyptian infantry taking off their boots so that they could run faster in retreat.

King Hussein of Jordan had been warned to keep out of the fray, but artillery from Jordan began shelling west Jerusalem, and troops from Jordan grabbed the UN headquarters and Government House in Jerusalem. When the Israelis counterattacked, they captured the Old City and reunited Jerusalem for the first time since it had been carved up in 1948. Israel then turned its attention to Syria, and attacked the Golan Heights, defeating the Syrian army.

In six days the war was over, and the festering sore that is the Middle East continued to fester, with no old wounds healed, and fresh wounds opened.

Communist pin-up boy Che Guevara assumed idol status by getting himself killed in 1967 by Bolivian troops hunting down rebels in their country. Guevara was a shadowy figure who rose to a certain prominence as an offsider to Fidel

Castro, the Cuban communist revolutionary. With Castro's backing, Guevara was attempting to take the revolution to all of South America.

After his killing, Guevara's image became a popular T-shirt design, with the trademark close-clipped beard, black beret and red star, and he was the pin-up boy for left-leaning uni students all over the world, and Australia was no exception. The more affluent the suburb, the more likely your chances of spotting Che gazing at you from someone's chest.

In 1967, Britian's Francis Chichester became the first person to complete a solo circumnavigation of the world, calling in on Australia on his way.

Meanwhile, in Australia the big event was the successful national referendum which resulted in Aboriginal people gaining full citizenship rights.

South Africa hit the headlines in a really big way in 1968. This time it was for all the right reasons, and rather than stories of sanctions or further apartheid atrocities, it was a medical breakthrough. At the Groote Schuur hospital, in Cape Town, Dr Christiaan Barnard and his team performed the world's first heart transplant. Louis Washkansky, the recipient, lived for just eighteen days, but at least Barnard had proved the operation could be done.

In America, Dr Rene Favalero performed the world's first heart bypass operation that same year.

Anti-Vietnam War protests gained more and more intensity through 1966–68. Common pictures coming out of America showed young guys openly defying their government by burning draft cards in the street, accompanied by the loud approval of thousands of onlookers.

In 1968, students were restless the world over, and were taking to the streets in large numbers to protest.

At Columbia University, in New York, students barricaded themselves inside a number of significant buildings on campus, protesting about a variety of issues, predominantly the Vietnam War and race relations. After days of intense media coverage, the authorities broke into the buildings and violently put down the unrest, arresting more than seven hundred people in the process.

Soon after, in Paris, thousands upon thousands of students brought the city to a grinding halt as they demonstrated in support of workers on a general strike over poor wages. With the French economy in fine shape, it seemed a large section of society was missing out, and fully half the workforce walked off the job.

For several weeks there were no mail deliveries, no banking, no public transport and no fuel, and food supplies were becoming perilously low. As the protest wore on, with nightly news footage of students being bludgeoned and cars and buildings being torched, public sentiment moved to the side of the students and workers, and hardened against the once impregnable government of Charles de Gaulle, whom many had assumed would be president for life.

The protest ended as fast as it began when the workers negotiated a generous thirty-five percent pay rise. The students were left to protest on their own, but because it coincided with the beginning of their summer holidays, everyone lost interest.

A year later de Gaulle called a referendum seeking a vote of confidence from the French people. By a very narrow margin they voted against him, and he quit.

Not to be left out of the changes sweeping the globe, the Czechoslovakian leader, Alexander Dubcek, announced sweeping reforms under the banner of 'Communism with a Human Approach'. His reforms allowed for freedom of speech and freedom of the press, something almost unheard of behind the Iron Curtain.

The reforms were greeted warmly by the Czech people, and the short time they lasted became known popularly as the 'Prague Spring'. It was a short season, and came to an abrupt halt when Soviet troops promptly invaded Czechoslovakia and arrested Dubcek and his government.

The Cold War dropped a degree or two when an American spy ship the, USS *Pueblo*, was captured by the North Koreans. The communists said it was spying on them, the Americans said it wasn't. The crew was eventually released, but not the ship itself.

Amid the social struggles going on in the US, on 4 April 1968 human rights activist Dr Martin Luther King was assassinated on the balcony of a motel in Memphis. James Earl Ray was later convicted of his killing. When news of King's death was reported in the media, rioting broke out in dozens of cities across America.

Just two months later, while the country was still reeling from the death of Martin Luther King, Bobby Kennedy, who had just won the Democratic primary for the presidency, was killed by a lone nutter, Sirhan Sirhan.

When Richard Millhouse Nixon won the Republican nomination for president of the United States, he said in his acceptance speech, 'When the strongest nation in the world can be tied down for four years in a war in Vietnam with no end in sight, when the richest nation in the world cannot manage its economy, when the nation with the greatest tradition of the rule of law is plagued by unprecedented racial violence, when the president of the United States cannot travel abroad, or to any major city at home, then it's time for new leadership for the United States.' He was elected president later that year — and it would all end in tears.

In February 1969, the first test flight of a Boeing 747 'Jumbo' jet was made. At more than seventy metres long, and weighing over 322 tons (328 tonnes), the giant aircraft was hailed as a modern marvel. The following month the supersonic Concorde made its maiden flight. The plane had been on the drawing boards since the fifties.

The 'troubles' continued in Northern Ireland, and over a three-day period of rioting and violence in 1969, eight people were killed and more than two hundred wounded. The British sent in the army in an attempt to restore some semblance of order. The troops were to be there for a very long time.

In July there was much happier news when Neil Armstrong, Michael Collins and Edwin Aldrin journeyed to the moon. On 20 July, the *Eagle* lunar module separated from *Columbia,* the command ship. Despite alarm bells going off constantly, and the surface of the moon being boulder strewn, Neil Armstrong was able to report back to Earth that 'The *Eagle* has landed' at a site in the Sea of Tranquillity.

Six-and-a-half hours later, Armstrong became the first man to set foot on the lunar surface. After spending less than a day on the moon, Armstrong fired the *Eagle*'s engines to return him to the *Columbia.*

The three astronauts returned to Earth heroes on 24 July.

NASHOS AND 'NAM

In 1964 the Australian Air Force began its military involvement in the war in Vietnam with a flight of Caribou transport planes sent to South Vietnam.

By the mid-sixties it was pretty obvious the South Vietnamese couldn't hold out against the communist insurgents, and the Australian Government sent the 1st Battalion Royal Australian Regiment to serve alongside the Americans in Bien Hoa.

The escalation was rapid, and in 1966 the government announced the 1st RAR would be replaced by two battalions and a squadron of helicopters, to be based at Nui Dat in Phouc Tuy province, where they were to have their own area of operations.

The Australian troops included conscripts ('nashos') who had been called up under the National Service Scheme.

The scheme began in 1964 and was based on a birth-date ballot of twenty-year-old blokes. If you were called up, you had to serve two years in the army, followed by a further three years in the army reserves.

From its inception, the nasho scheme was highly controversial. Conscientious objectors were harshly dealt with, and by law objectors had to prove an objection to *all* wars, not just the Vietnam conflict.

I was pretty ambivalent about being called up for the

nashos. Being young and stupid, I thought it might be a bit of fun. However, when you see what Vietnam did to so many poor buggers who were called up, that's one ballot I'm glad I didn't win. In reality, by the time I turned twenty in 1971, the National Service Scheme was all but finished.

At the height of Australia's involvement in the Vietnam War, Australia's commitment numbered around eight-and-a-half thousand troops, with further contributions from the RAAF and the Royal Australian Navy.

One of Australia's fiercest battles of the Vietnam War was the battle of Long Tan. In more than three hours of full-on fighting, in which a company of 6 RAR seemed sure to be annihilated by an overwhelmingly stronger enemy force, the Viet Cong suddenly withdrew, leaving behind 245 dead, and carting away many more dead and wounded. Eighteen Australians were killed in the battle, with twenty-four wounded.

As the sixties wore on, the war in Vietnam became more and more bogged down. After the 'Tet' offensive in the 1968 rainy season, it became pretty clear this was a war that could never be won, and more and more people began asking what the hell we were doing there anyway.

More and more disturbing images were coming out of Vietnam, like the massacre of villagers at My Lai, and the picture which more than any other traumatised the world — the distraught little girl running naked down the road, her clothes having been burnt off her in a napalm attack. That was the day I decided we shouldn't be in Vietnam, and my heart bled for all the young nashos who were still there.

The Vietnam War moratorium marches, which rapidly grew in size through the latter half of the sixties, saw thousands upon thousands of people taking to the streets all over Australia to protest our involvement in the war.

Of the combatants in the Vietnam War, the deaths were as follows:

Taiwan — 0
Spain — 0
New Zealand — 35
Thailand — 350
Australia — 520
South Korea — 4,407
United States — 57,702
South Vietnam — 185,528
North Vietnam and Viet Cong — 924,048

NOT HAVING A BRA OF IT

The middle sixties saw the blossoming of the women's liberation movement in Australia. For women who wanted to be liberated this was the beginning of something wonderful. To others, it was something quite scary, with the emergence of outspoken, bra-burning 'lezzos'. There was considerable hostility among more conservative sections of society towards these women who, they believed, 'wanted to be blokes'.

The modern women's movement really began in the United States when Betty Friedman published her book, *The Feminine Mystique*, in 1963.

With the arrival of the contraceptive pill, women discovered, too, that they didn't necessarily have to spend their reproductive lives chained to children and the sink. The pill provoked enormous and heated debate right through society, with the Catholic church leading the charge against its introduction. The battle was futile, and by the end of the sixties many women had discarded other methods of contraception and were on the pill.

Despite the battle being over, propaganda surrounding use of the pill was intense with all sorts of rumours circulating about what side effects it would have. These stories gained more credence from the fact that Australia was still reeling from the thalidomide tragedy.

The drug thalidomide had been prescribed to pregnant women to help alleviate the discomfort of morning sickness. Unfortunately the drug resulted in horrific birth defects in thousands of babies around the world in the late fifties and early sixties. These children became known as 'thalidomide babies'.

But in the sixties, more and more women certainly began to discover they had a plethora of new career and educational options opening up before them with their new freedom.

I formed a view that the ringleaders of the feminist movement were all so bloody ugly that no bloke would want them anyway. Betty Friedman, who was often arguing the cause on our TV screens was living proof that all feminists had been hit with the ugly stick, but then along came Gloria Steinem. Gloria was an intellectual and rapidly became the new face of feminism, she was drop-dead gorgeous, a fact not lost on some of her more strident and radical 'sisters', who didn't think that make-up and perfect grooming equated with their view of the newly liberated woman.

Australia established itself as a focus of the feminist movement at the end of the decade after Germaine Greer published *The Female Eunuch* in 1970.

BLUE PERIL

The sixties saw a shift in Australia from the outright banning of certain books and films to a system of 'classification'. Censors were much more preoccupied with sex than violence and so for years D H Lawrence's novel, *Lady Chatterley's Lover* was prohibited because the powers that be considered it to be little more than a corrupting 'bonkathon', however well written it might have been.

The censorship debate got some real heat in it with the prosecution of the editors of *Oz* magazine. *Oz* was an underground magazine originally published in Sydney between 1963 and 1966. Its second and more famous incarnation was published in London between 1967 and 1973.

The original editorial team included Australian university students Richard Neville, Richard Walsh and Martin Sharp, with early contributions from future *Time* magazine critic and art historian Robert Hughes.

The final straw for authorities was the 1970 *Schoolkids* edition, featuring a very adult Rupert Bear cartoon, which resulted in prosecution and, ultimately, the end of the magazine.

Despite the protestations of those involved in the attacks on *Oz* throughout its life, it was really little more than a relatively harmless, slightly subversive, smutty but often funny 'rag'.

Far more worrying for the wowsers here in Australia were Kenneth Tynan's 1969 stage production *Oh! Calcutta!*, and Philip Roth's novel, *Portnoy's Complaint. Oh! Calcutta!* was the first production to feature nudity and upset everyone, mostly those who hadn't seen it. A movie version was also widely banned, however by 1976 all had changed and a new Broadway production ran for thirteen years.

Portnoy's Complaint was banned and became a prohibited import, and state governments across the country prosecuted local publishers and retailers. This in spite of the fact *Portnoy's Complaint* was among the biggest selling books of 1969 internationally.

If a book were banned, that meant you simply *had* to read it. I read *Lady Chatterley's Lover* in the early sixties as I was going through puberty. I think every other boy in our school did too, as the copy I read had seen better days, with particular pages clearly coming in for special attention.

Portnoy's Complaint was deliciously funny because although the main character was a Jewish kid in New York, there were startling parallels, although I never developed an attachment to a piece of liver, except to eat it.

Anything by the Marquis De Sade was also a no-no, but the good old Marquis was a bit 'out there', even for me.

Although I was a voracious book reader all through the sixties, I went through a stage, just like all the other kids my age, of devouring the smutty ones, and there were plenty of them. Books would be handed around with instructions as to what pages or chapters to go to for the 'good' bits, if you didn't want to have to wade through all the waffle that separated the 'action'.

Jacqueline Sussan provided *The Valley of the Dolls* and *The Love Machine*, Harold Robbins *The Carpetbaggers*, *The*

Adventurers and *The Inheritors,* Jackie Collins *The World is Full of Married Men* and *The Stud,* and perhaps the most lurid of all, Kyle Onstott's *Mandingo* stories, which featured interracial 'pesterin' and a pleasurin" in the slave plantations of the Deep South. In between the bonking, there was plenty of whipping thrown in for good measure.

A CHANGE OF NOTE(S)

One of the defining moments of the sixties in Australia was the introduction of decimal currency. In 1959, the government had set up a committee to investigate the pros and cons of a decimal currency for Australia. The committee presented its report in 1960, and in 1963 the government announced that a system of decimal currency was to be introduced into Australia, and a tentative changeover date was set for 14 February 1966.

The new system was to be based on a major unit which turned out to be the dollar. Prime Minister Bob Menzies wanted the unit of currency to be called the 'royal', which is hardly surprising given his hardline royalist background. The minor unit, which was subsequently named the cent, would be valued at one hundredth of the major unit, and therefore would be equal to about tuppence in the old system.

The government also announced it would pay 'reasonable' compensation to owners of large numbers of monetary machines, like cash registers, calculators etc, so that they could more easily convert to the machines required for the decimal system.

In schools across the country, classes were indoctrinated with the details of the conversion and the conversion tables. A massive education campaign began well before the proposed introduction date for decimal currency, and covered radio, TV, newspapers and direct mail-outs of decimal currency packages.

The most effective part of the campaign, at least as far as I was concerned, was the character, Dollar Bill. Dollar Bill was an animated one-dollar note who would explain the new currency. He also sang a song which was repeated over and over on radio and TV. The Dollar Bill song was sung to the tune of 'Click Go the Shears', with the lyrics:

In come the dollars and in come the cents,
To replace the pounds and the shillings and the pence,
Be prepared to change when the coins begin to mix
On the fourteenth of February nineteen sixty-six.

Chorus
Clink go the coins, clink, clink, clink,
Change over day is closer than you think,
Learn the value of the coins and the way that they appear,
And things will be much smoother when the decimal point is
*   here.*

In come the dollars and in come the cents,
To replace the pounds and the shillings and the pence,
Be prepared, folks, when the coins begin to mix,
On the fourteenth of February nineteen sixty-six.

Decimal currency day came and went with hardly a hitch, with most of us keen to get a look at the new currency 'in the flesh'. The new notes were designed to approximate their old counterparts, at least in colour, thus the one-dollar note was brown like the ten-shilling note it was to replace, and the two-dollar green, like the one-pound note it replaced.

Some people, especially much older people, were quite amazed when the world didn't end on 14 February 1966. Some people vowed to, and perhaps did, stash away some old money in the tea caddy or under their mattress just in case the new stuff went bad.

Initially in co-circulation with the new decimal money, the old currency was gradually phased out by the banks, and soon vanished altogether.

I rarely saw notes of a higher denomination than one, two and five dollar notes, but I thought they looked good, even if they took some getting used to because for a start they looked like 'play' money.

ICON SAILS IN CHOPPY WATER

Although the Sydney Opera House was conceived well before the sixties, and wasn't opened until 1973, it was never far from the headlines as controversy raged over the years.

Pressure for an appropriate concert facility for Sydney had been mounting since the 1940s and, in 1955, the New South Wales government announced an international competition to design an opera house.

Danish architect Joern Utzon won, with a complex design of interlocking concrete shells which reflected the billowing sails on the adjacent Sydney Harbour. Problem was, Utzon might have won the competition, but his design was impossible to build with late fifties engineering capabilities. But, by 1961, Utzon had figured out how to build the distinguishing 'sails' of the Opera House roof.

Costs on the project blew out continually, and increasingly the public was coming to the view the whole thing was a massive white elephant. Utzon received constant criticism from politicians, the media and the general public about the costs and the exterior and interior design.

In 1966 the shit really hit the fan and, tired of continually brawling with the government over spiralling costs and the building's design, Utzon walked out and returned to Denmark, leaving the building to be completed by others.

The Opera House Lottery had been set up in 1957 to

fund the cost of the building. The first lottery tickets cost five pounds, and the first prize was £100,000. The final cost of the Opera House was $102,000,000, and the lottery raised four times that amount. No surprises for guessing where the surplus of the Opera House Lottery went.

THE HITS AND MISSES
OF THE SIXTIES

MY TOP 40 HIT SONGS

The list of the best forty songs of the sixties is fairly difficult to compile, given the massive amount of new music and the number of new artists who swamped the charts. Any list like this has to be highly subjective, and this one surely is. At any gathering of baby boomers, pose the question 'What was the best song of the sixties?' and there's a good chance you'll have no two answers alike. These are in no particular order, because if I did that, I'd have to keep changing them every day as my mood changed.

1. **'Hey Jude' — The Beatles.**
   Just because these guys stood astride the sixties and towered over (and influenced) everyone. 'Jude', like so much of their best stuff, was so different from anything heard before. At just over seven minutes long, it was more than twice the length of most pop songs of the day. Even more remarkable is the fact about two-thirds of the song is taken up with the repetitive chorus 'na na na na na na na, na na na na, hey Jude'. For the disc jockeys, the saving grace was the opportunity to fade the song out without too many people noticing if they were a bit pressed for time.

2. **'Friday on My Mind' — The Easybeats.**
   A perfect pop song tells a story, and is well produced and

edgy. 'Friday on My Mind' set up the Easybeats as a world-class act, and Harry Vanda and George Young as first-class contemporary songwriters.

3.   **'I Heard it through the Grapevine' — Marvin Gaye.**
This song introduced Australians to a different style of black American music. Until this, our perceptions had been influenced almost entirely by the Tamla Motown sound coming out of Detroit, pop songs which had been deliberately crafted to appeal to a wide audience. Marvin Gaye pushed the envelope very successfully with 'Grapevine'.

4.   **'Running Scared' — Roy Orbison.**
This was Roy at his best: dramatic vocals and a story told entirely within a less-than-three-minute pop song. The guy thinks he's lost his love to a rival, 'Then all at once he was standing there, so sure of himself, his head in the air. My heart was breaking which one would it be … you turned around and walked away with me.'

5.   **'Spicks and Specks' — The Bee Gees.**
Their first big hit, while they were still just kids. It was reported on the radio that the Bee Gees had been on their way to England to have a crack at the big time when they were told on board ship that 'Spicks and Specks' was a massive hit back home in Australia. The rest is history.

6.   **'Elenore' — The Turtles.**
The Turtles were never as big in Australia as they were in their native US, but this song is an example of their brilliant harmonies and ability to perfectly craft and present a pop song. Sort of somewhere between the Beatles and the Beach Boys.

7.   **'The Loved One' — The Loved Ones.**
These guys from Melbourne flashed across the charts like

a shooting star, but for a brief moment excited us with very different sounding music from the regular fare in 1966. (Their LP *Magic Box* remains a must-have in any Aussie music collection.)

8. **'Ruby Tuesday'/'Let's Spend the Night Together' — The Rolling Stones.**

    It borders on sacrilege to say it, but I was never a huge Stones fan. It was either the Beatles or the Stones, and for me it was the former. This double-sided hit, though, proved the versatility and songwriting capabilities of the boys. The fact I wasn't a big fan appears not to have stunted their career in any way.

9. **'Lodi' — Creedence Clearwater Revival.**

    Everyone had a copy of the album, *Cosmos Factory*, and despite the songs having a certain sameness about them, 'Lodi' stood out for me because of the story it told of a muso on the road who was down on his luck: 'Things got bad and things got worse, I guess you know the tune.' The fact that every pub band in Australia could do a pretty good impression of Creedence no doubt kicked their record sales along.

10. **'Good Vibrations' — The Beach Boys.**

    What kid wasn't gobsmacked the first time they heard this? Up until now we all loved the Beach Boys but their music was hardly high art, consisting mainly of very accessible catchy songs with terrific harmonies and their distinctive beach sound. Then came 'Good Vibrations', and we all looked a bit closer and recognised there was a bit of genius happening at the beach.

11. **'Something in the Air' — Thunderclap Newman.**

    This trio was put together as something for Pete Townsend of the Who to work on in his spare time. It consisted of John 'Speedy' Keen on lead vocal, drums and rhythm guitar, Andy 'Thunderclap' Newman on keyboards, and sixteen-year-old Jimmy McCulloch on lead guitar (Jimmy later went on to play with Stone the Crows and Paul McCartney's Wings). 'Something in the Air' was an important-sounding song, though God knows what it was about: 'Call out the instigators because there's something in the air, we've got to get together sooner or later, because the revolution's here, and you know it's right ...'

12. **'Light My Fire' — The Doors.**
From the opening note of Ray Manzarek's keyboard, this song had hit written all over it. Add Jim Morrison's incredible vocals and the frenetic nature of the song. 'Light My Fire' was the epitome of a sixties song, it had flair, it was rebellious and it was 'ours'.

13. **'The Sound of Silence' — Simon and Garfunkel.**
What unlikely pop heroes these two were — a short pudgy dude and a skinny red-headed bloke with an afro. It just so happened the short pudgy bloke was a brilliant poet and songwriter, and the redhead had the voice of an angel. Together they traversed the folk/pop/ballad/protest genres effortlessly. What other act could release songs like 'Scarborough Fair', '59th Street Bridge Song (Feelin' Groovy)', 'Bridge over Troubled Water' and 'Silent Night/7 O'Clock News' and still retain any kind of cred? Simon and Garfunkel did, no doubt aided by intelligent lyrics: 'Hello darkness my old friend, I've come to talk with you again. Because a vision softly creeping, left its seeds while I was sleeping, and the vision that was planted in my brain still remains, within the sound of silence.'

14. **'You Really Got Me' — The Kinks.**
    This is the song that launched the Kinks. Pete
    Townsend admitted that the Who were heavily
    influenced by the Kinks, and that when rock gurus were
    suggesting the big three British bands were the Beatles,
    the Rolling Stones and the Who, the Kinks should have
    been in place of the Who. After 'You Really Got Me',
    the Kinks ripped themselves off with 'All Day and all of
    the Night'. Ray Davies, the front man and chief
    songwriter, went on to pen classics like 'Sunny
    Afternoon', 'Well Respected Man', 'Waterloo Sunset'
    and 'Lola'.

15. **'Reach Out — I'll be There' — The Four Tops.**
    One of Motown's finest songs and performances. The
    black roots are evident, with a melodic and catchy hook.
    The song had just enough edge to hold it back from
    slipping into pap. A white band could never have done
    this song justice.

16. **'Tar and Cement' — Verdelle Smith.**
    This lady with her beautiful voice had a huge smash hit
    in Australia with this song, although it didn't do much in
    her native US, only just managing to scrape in at the
    lower end of the Top 40. The song was originally a hit
    for an Italian artist, and then for the French singer
    Françoise Hardy (of 'Only You Can Do It' fame), before
    some American lyricists wrote some English words and
    called it 'Tar and Cement'. Part of the appeal of the song
    was the theme of isolation and alienation, big issues for
    the average teenager: 'And every night I'd sit alone and
    learn what loneliness meant, up in my rented room
    above the world of tar and cement.' After this song
    Verdelle disappeared without trace.

17. **'Summer in the City' — The Lovin' Spoonful.**
    This song was so energetic it just *had* to be a hit.
    Perfectly crafted, it had the lot — catchy hook, city
    sound effects and a story told completely in three
    minutes with John Sebastian's lyrics: 'Hot town, summer
    in the city, back of my neck getting dirty and gritty, been
    down, isn't it a pity, doesn't seem to be a shadow in the
    city ...'

18. **'Something Tells Me I'm into Something Good' —
    Herman's Hermits.**
    A cute young lead singer in Peter Noone, and an
    optimistic, jaunty little pop song. This couldn't miss.
    Even starring in an appalling movie called *Hold On*
    didn't damage the career of Herman's Hermits. Although
    they were considered pretty lightweight, the group were
    enormously successful all over the world.

19. **'I Got You Babe' — Sonny and Cher.**
    These guys knew how to package themselves and did so
    brilliantly. They adopted the 'hippy meets Hollywood'
    look and for a while made it all their own. Cher had a
    distinctive voice, and the fact that Sonny couldn't sing at
    all didn't hold this duo back.

20. **'Keep on Running' — The Spencer Davis Group.**
    Despite the fact Stevie Winwood was barely into his
    teens, his amazingly mature and soulful voice really
    powered the Spencer Davis Group along. 'Keep on
    Running' was quickly followed by two more powerhouse
    performances in 'I'm a Man' and 'Gimme Some Lovin''.

21. **'Stop·in the Name of Love' — The Supremes.**
    So representative of the trio. Although they had a
    number of personnel changes, and persistent rumours
    that Diana Ross was pretty unbearable to work with, the

Supremes were able to capitalise on all that was marvellous coming out of the Detroit studios.

22. **'A Whiter Shade of Pale' — Procul Harum.**
This is a prime example of a group's first hit being just too good to follow up. It was a massive hit for the group with the weird name that fans could speculate about endlessly. There was lots of speculation, too, as to what the song is about: 'And so it was that later as the miller told his tale, that her face at first just ghostly, turned a whiter shade of pale.' If a pub band could emulate the organ intro to this, they were on a winner.

23. **'Jesamine' — The Casuals.**
This little-known British band had been knocking around Europe in the mid-sixties before getting their big break by appearing on the Pommy TV show, *Opportunity Knocks*. In 1968, they had a massive hit with 'Jesamine': 'What am I supposed to do with a girl like Jesamiiiiiiiiiiiiiine.' Although they are generally considered one-hit wonders, the Casuals did follow up 'Jesamine' with a minor hit called 'Toy'.

24. **'The Real Thing' — Russell Morris.**
What a sensation this song caused, convincing parents all over Australia that yes, the worst had happened, every kid across the country was on drugs. How else could you possibly get into something like this? Released as a double-sider, 'The Real Thing Parts 1 and 2', the record was amazing in more ways that one. The psychedelic marathon was written by none other than Johnny Young, who up until that time was best known for the saccharine-sweet 'Step Back'/'Cara Lyn', and his incredibly schmaltzy slow version of the Beatles' 'All My Lovin''. The production by Ian 'Molly' Meldrum

set a benchmark for future Australian recordings.

25. **'In the Year 2525 (Exordium and Terminus)' — Zager and Evans.**

   A massive international hit for Denny Zager and Richard Evans, who were *genuine* one-hit wonders. This protest song (of sorts) predicted a grim future: 'In the year 2525 if man is still alive, if woman can survive they may find …'

26. **'Suspicious Minds' — Elvis Presley.**

   How to choose from the massive body of work that Elvis churned out? This song marked a departure from from frothy movie-driven hits and sentimental ballads which had become a mainstay of Elvis's repertoire. Despite the change of style, the fans remained loyal and Elvis picked up even more devotees with his new more 'now' style.

27. **'Where Do You Go to My Lovely?' — Peter Sarstedt.**

   This epic waltz caused much speculation as to who the jetsetter was he was singing about: 'Your name it is heard in high places, you know the Aga Khan, he sent you a racehorse for Christmas, and you keep it just for fun, for a laugh ha ha ha ha.' Some thought it might have been Sophia Loren, but that didn't fit, because the subject of the song appeared to be French.

28. **'Space Oddity' — David Bowie.**

   From the opening line, 'Ground control to Major Tom', this had to be a hit, after all, this was the year man walked on the moon, so anything with a space theme had to have an advantage. Coupled with David Bowie's spaced-out look. Although 'Space Oddity' wasn't a number one hit around the world, it established Bowie, and is a genuine sixties classic.

29. **'My Generation' — The Who.**

From the moment 'People try to put us down' explodes out of the speakers, you know you have an anthem of the sixties. This is the band the mods followed around slavishly, and it wasn't all a one-way street. Pete Townsend said, 'We learnt, by watching our audience, how to be innovators … in a secret society. A secret society of clothes, a secret society of music appreciation and peculiar kinds of chauvinism.' From Roger Daltrey's affected stutter to the line 'Hope I die before I get old', 'My Generation' *was* the sixties.

30. **'Like a Rolling Stone' — Bob Dylan.**

For a bloke whose voice is not the best in the world, Bob Dylan did all right for himself. We all read so much into his lyrics, much of which wasn't there, but we could dream, couldn't we? 'Once upon a time you dressed so fine, you threw the bum a dime in your prime, didn't you? People call, say, "Beware doll, you're bound to fall"…' Bob's songs were treated much more commercially by other artists, but this one stood out because of the almost chanted lyrics, the wailing organ, and the fact it went for over six minutes.

31. **'You Never Can Tell' — Chuck Berry.**

For all the influence bands like the Beatles might have had on other artists of the day, here was the man who influenced the Beatles, the Rolling Stones and most other rhythm and blues outfits. All through the fifties Chuck Berry was producing classic songs like 'Maybelline', 'Rock and Roll Music', 'Sweet Little Sixteen', 'Johnny B Goode' and 'Little Queenie'. Then in the sixties the classics like 'Promised Land' and, in 1964, 'You Never Can Tell' showcased his special talent as a gifted lyricist: 'It was a teenage wedding and the old folks wished them well, you could see that Pierre did truly love the mademoiselle …' With the rocking honky-tonk piano and sax riffs, 'You Never Can Tell' is a timeless rock classic.

32. **'San Francisco' — Scott McKenzie.**
Hippie turned freebie (what the hell did that mean?), Scott McKenzie had the right song at the right time. 'San Francisco (Be Sure to Wear Some Flowers in Your Hair)' was written by John Phillips, of the Mamas and the Papas, and was released in the lead-up to the heavily promoted Monterey pop festival. It worked as a fabulous advertisement for the festival: 'For those who go to San Francisco, summertime will be a love-in there.'

33. **'Brooklyn Roads' — Neil Diamond.**
Although not one of his best-known songs, 'Brooklyn Roads' was a pointer to the man's genius as a songwriter and storyteller. With its autobiographical content, the song struck a chord, at least with me, and led to a lifelong appreciation of Neil's more introspective work: 'If I close my eyes, I can almost hear my mother, callin', "Neil go find your brother, Daddy's home and it's time for supper, hurry on." And I see two boys, racin' up two flights of staircase, squirmin' into Papa's embrace, and the whiskers warm on their face, where's it gone?'

34. **'I Only Want to Be with You' — Dusty Springfield.**
After leaving the Springfields, the hugely popular folk/pop trio consisting of Dusty, her brother Tom (Dion O'Brien) and Tim Field, critics were waiting for Dusty to fall on her face — she didn't. Her first release, 'I Only Want to Be with You' was a huge departure musically for her and owed much more to rhythm and

blues than folk. It laid the bedrock for the career of the woman who is arguably lauded as Britain's finest ever female pop vocalist.

35. **'Georgy Girl' — The Seekers.**

    The Seekers were the big beneficiaries of the break-up of the Springfields. The Seekers arrived in the UK from Australia to 'test the water' just as the Springfields were disintegrating. Tom Springfield directed his creative energies toward the Seekers and provided them with instantaneous hits like 'I'll Never Find Another You', 'A World of Our Own', 'The Carnival is Over' and 'Georgy Girl', all of which he wrote and produced. 'Georgy Girl' was from the soundtrack of a movie of the same title, and was never intended to be released as a single. But the Americans picked it up where it displaced the Monkees' 'I'm a Believer' at number one. It got to number two in both Britain and Australia.

36. **'Just Like a Woman' — Manfred Mann.**

    Another classic example of a Dylan song made accessible. The Manfred Mann group had a certain affinity with Bob Dylan's compositions, having success with 'If You Gotta Go, Go Now' and 'Mighty Quinn'. Despite the fact their albums were full of esoteric crap, Manfred Mann managed to string together an impressive number of single hits through the sixties.

37. **'Eloise' — Barry Ryan.**

    This gets a guernsey because it's so over-the-top. Starting at a dramatic rush, 'Every night I'm there, I'm always there, she knows I'm there, and heaven knows, I hope she goes,' 'Eloise' builds crescendo upon crescendo to end in a thundering blaze of rock orchestra and hysterical vocals. A bit like 'A Whiter Shade of Pale' for

Procol Harum, 'Eloise' proved a hard act for Barry Ryan to follow.

38. **'Black Pearl' — Sonny Charles and the Checkmates Ltd.**

Although not a massive hit, 'Black Pearl' in the last year of the sixties brought together so many of the contrasting styles which made the decade. A black vocalist, a sweeping orchestral arrangement, and legendary producer Phil Spector with his trademark 'wall of sound'.

39. **'Big Girls Don't Cry' — The Four Seasons.**

With Frankie Valli's distinctive falsetto, the Four Seasons were a hit machine, churning out smash after smash including 'Sherry', 'Let's Hang On', 'Rag Doll' and 'Big Girls Don't Cry', all beautifully crafted and presented pop songs.

40. **'Bus Stop' — The Hollies.**

Of all the thousands of hit songs of the sixties, this one strikes me as the most clever use of sparse lyrics. Songwriter Graham Gouldman (who later went on to form 10CC), had already carved out a successful career as a songwriter in his teens, having written 'For Your Love' and 'Heart Full of Soul' for the Yardbirds. Graham wrote 'Look Through Any Window' for the Hollies, and was asked to provide them with a follow-up hit. The follow-up was 'Bus Stop', and the tight lyrics virtually tell the story of the song in the first verse: 'Bus stop, wet day, she's there, I say please share my umbrella. Bus stop, bus goes, she stays, love grows, under my umbrella. All that summer we enjoyed it, wind and rain and shine. That umbrella we employed it, by August she was mine.'

MY WORST 20 HIT SONGS

These twenty dreadful songs from the sixties are by no means the worst of what made it onto our charts, but I have confined myself to just those atrocities that not only made it onto the charts, but also made it to the top — that actually reached into the Top 20. I have also tried to represent each of the various genres: bubblegum, ballads, novelties, tearjerkers, etc.

1. **'Tie Me Kangaroo Down, Sport' — Rolf Harris.**
   This song deserves pride of place, because it embarrassed Australia in the eyes of the world, even if we didn't know it at the time. The Poms loved it, and Rolf's career was made. The totally politically incorrect lyric, 'Let me Abos go loose, Lou', wouldn't see the light of day today, and the wobbleboard got its first airing, further reasons to despise this song. Rolf also inadvertently encouraged the likes of Charlie Drake to have a go at Australiana, which led to our next atrocity ...

2. **'My Boomerang Won't Come Back' — Charlie Drake.**
   Charlie Drake was a British comedian who had a novelty hit record in 1962 with a bizarre little ditty called 'My Boomerang Won't Come Back'. The lyric writer clearly had no idea about Australia or Australian expressions, because the song opens with the lines 'In

the bad, bad lands of Australia many years ago, the Aborigine tribes were meeting, having a big powwow'. Until Charlie's effort, I'd never heard the Aussie outback described as 'bad lands' or a corroboree as a 'powwow'. This enormously popular release also featured a quasi-African chant in the background.

3.   **'Honey' — Bobby Goldsboro.**
This guy managed to pack onto a 45 a story of pathos and misery about a bloke whose young wife is taken from him far too young: 'One day while I was not at home, while she was there and all alone, the angels came. Now all I have is memories of Honey and I wake up nights and call her name.' The girls loved it. This was a sort of late sixties version of the 'tragedy' songs which had been popular a few years before, like 'Teen Angel' and 'Tell Laura I Love Her'.

4.   **'Asia Minor' — Kokomo.**
Because instrumental hits were regularly appearing on the charts, a bright spark called Jimmy Wisner, working under the name Kokomo, decided to work over a classical piece. He chose Grieg's Piano Concerto in A Minor, thus the 'Asia Minor' of the title. He played it in a frenetic honky-tonk piano style, and it was a smash hit. It also sent classical music lovers up the wall. (Mm, maybe it had something going for it after all.)

5.   **'The Cha Cha Cha' — Bobby Rydell.**
Rydell was one of those artists who survived on energy, good looks, pompadour hair and reasonable production values. He got away with 'Swingin' School', but didn't get away with 'The Cha Cha Cha'. How could he with lines like 'Somethin's missin' when were

twistin', let's start kissin' do the cha cha cha' …? It was dire.

6. **'Star Crossed Lovers' — Neil Sedaka.**
    This guy had talent oozing out his pores, problem was he was short, fat and sounded like a girl. Sedaka, with songwriting partner Howard Greenfield, churned out scores of hits for other artists and one or two for himself in the early sixties: 'Oh Carol', 'Happy Birthday, Sweet Sixteen', etc. 'Star Crossed Lovers' came late in the decade, and it seems Neil used every device imaginable to make it a hit. Syrupy lyrics, huge production, tubular bells and what sounded like the Mormon Tabernacle choir, with enough sugar piled on top to turn the world diabetic. It worked, 'Star Crossed Lovers' topped the charts for weeks.

7. **'Love Child' — Diana Ross and the Supremes.**
    This song came not too long before Diana left the Supremes, and was a reworking of everything they'd done before, with edgy lyrics about an illegitimate kid. It was one of the few Supremes songs you couldn't dance to.

8. **'You're Everything' — Don Lane.**
    Because he was a big TV star, Don somehow got it into his head that he could sing. He couldn't.

9. **'Aquarius'/'Let the Sunshine In' — The 5th Dimension.**
    This was from 'the American tribal love rock musical *Hair*'. The most memorable thing about *Hair* was just that, hair — mostly pubic hair, and lots of it. The music was awful, apart from a couple of songs, 'Aquarius' and 'Good Morning Starshine'. Unfortunately, on this 5th Dimension outing, someone

decided to tack 'Let the Sunshine In' onto the end of 'Aquarius'. Most sensible DJs faded it out before the crappy bit started.

10. **'A Little Bit Me, a Little Bit You' — The Monkees.**
These guys were largely written off as a studio group, but were actually quite talented. This song was written by Neil Diamond. The Monkees should have left it to him.

11. **'Picking up Pebbles' — Matt Flinders.**
This guy had a smooth voice, sort of like a poor man's Matt Monro, and the song was given heaps of lush strings and a big production, unusual for an Australian artist at the time. The lyrics were awful, and Matt went down with the ship, disappearing without trace.

12. **'Step Back'/'Cara Lyn' — Johnny Young.**
This double-sider was a massive hit. It stayed five weeks in the number one position on the Australian charts, but nothing can forgive 'Pretty as a picture, isn't she a mixture, she's got everything I need, satisfaction guaranteed'.

13. **'Penny Arcade' — Roy Orbison.**
The Big O never put a foot wrong, except for this. He'd gone through a bit of a dry spell on the charts, and this 'poppy' number at least brought him back, but compared to his earlier work, it was dross.

14. **'Act Naturally' — The Beatles.**
Here's another act you'd not expect to see on a list of worse songs (unless you single out John Lennon after he went silly or Paul McCartney at his most excessive) but the Beatles should never have let Ringo anywhere near a lead vocal. They got away with it on 'Yellow Submarine' but not with this atrocity. If 'Act Naturally' had been

released under any other name than the Beatles, it wouldn't have come within cooee of the charts.

15. **'Hey Paula' — Paul and Paula.**
    Everyone loved this smoochy-woochy love song, with the vocalists wooing each other separately and together. It would make you dry-retch now.

16. **'My Old Man's a Dustman' — Lonnie Donegan.**
    A novelty song relying heavily on Pomminess. Perhaps it was all the British migrants who had settled in Australia who bought this for sentimental reasons. I think we even had a copy of this at home, I don't know how that happened.

17. **'What a Mouth' — Tommy Steele.**
    (See 'My Old Man's a Dustman'.)

18. **'Hitch Hiker' — Bobby and Laurie.**
    This really wasn't a half-bad song, written by Roger Miller. When Bobby and Laurie put the spoken bit in the middle of it, with an appalling American-ish accent, I can't imagine what they were thinking. The groaning guitar effect didn't help either.

19. **'Build Me Up Buttercup' — The Foundations.**
    This song possibly doesn't deserve to be here, but with the attrition of time and its merciless exploitation in commercials over the years, the memory treats it somewhat less kindly.

20. **'Little Arrows' — Leapy Lee.**
    Leapy survived his entire career basically on the strength of this one song. It was catchy, too catchy, you couldn't get the damn thing out of your head — and, damn; it's just happened again: 'There's a boy a little boy, shooting arrows in the blue, and he's aiming them at someone, but the question is at who …'

MY TOP 30 FLICKS

My Top 30 flicks of the sixties, in no particular order, were:

Midnight Cowboy — Dustin Hoffman as Ratso Rizzo was just brilliant, and the scene at the end where he pisses himself on the bus while the soundtrack has Nilsson singing 'Everybody's Talkin'', is absolutely gut-wrenching.

Breakfast at Tiffanys — Audrey Hepburn was at her elegant peak as the party girl, Holly Golightly. Among the memorable lines: 'I don't want to own anything until I find a place where me and things go together. I'm not sure where that is, but I know what it feels like. It's like Tiffany's.'

The Guns of Navarone — Every young (and not so young) bloke in the sixties was a fan of Alistair MacLean. This movie was based on one of his popular books, and was worth seeing for the incredible rollcall of stars appearing in it, *and* for the 'guns'.

West Side Story — I didn't quite get this movie at the time, but have appreciated it since. I thought it was a sort of bodgies and widgies musical, which I suppose it was.

Lawrence of Arabia — Peter O'Toole had the girls drooling and the guys all wanting to be him. The desert and battle scenes were awesome, and the motorbike crash at the start of the film really set it all up.

To Kill a Mockingbird — Just a really fine movie based on Harper Lee's really fine book, with really fine acting from Gregory Peck as Atticus Finch.

Whatever Happened to Baby Jane? — Despite the sixties not being particularly kind to Bette Davis's career, she camps it up to buggery in this, and the scene where she shoves Joan Crawford down the stairs is priceless.

The Birds — Alfred Hitchcock at his manipulative best. This scared the crap out of me and even feeding our chooks became traumatic for a while.

The Great Escape — Another epic war movie with a cast of thousands. Made while there was still plenty of World War Two equipment lying about the place. For a revhead, Steve McQueen's leap on the motorbike alone was worth the admission price.

My Fair Lady — Everything about this was classy. It had a big budget, Audrey Hepburn and Rex Harrison in ideal roles, and great music to boot.

Doctor Zhivago — How gorgeous was Julie Christie? How gorgeous was Omar Sharif? And how gorgeous was Russia in winter? Pity about the sixties make-up and hairstyles.

The Sound of Music — Every schoolkid got to see this because there wasn't a single suss scene. The Von Trapp kids were a bit uncool, but there were great music and Julie Andrews to make up for them.

Born Free — This film was soooo popular, no doubt because it was helped along by having a huge hit song, sung by Matt Monro, as its theme. And working with animals didn't do any harm to the careers of Virginia McKenna and Bill Travers.

Bonnie and Clyde — This was the first time I was aware of Warren Beatty and Faye Dunaway, and they looked nothing like the real Bonnie Parker and Clyde Barrow, who were as ugly as a hatful of snakes. But there was lots of action, culminating in the shocking machine-gunning scene at the end, which meant lots of kids weren't allowed to see it.

Wait Until Dark — One of the scariest movies ever made. Audrey Hepburn was just fantastic, and if you didn't jump out of your seat half-a-dozen times during this, you must have been sedated.

The Lion in Winter — Two of the world's best actors, Katharine Hepburn and Peter O'Toole, trading insults in some of the wittiest dialogue ever written.

Oliver! — Dickens brought alive with wonderful music. I reckoned Jack Wild stole the show as the Artful Dodger.

Planet of the Apes — This was a ripper story starring Charlton Heston, and it didn't matter one bit that he couldn't act. He was more than made up for by Roddy McDowell and Kim Hunter as apes.

Rosemary's Baby — Coming from a Catholic background, I had a healthy respect for the devil, and he got Mia Farrow into diabolical trouble in this.

The Prime of Miss Jean Brodie — The first time I was aware of Maggie Smith, she was brilliant. The movie had a hit song as its theme 'Jean' by Oliver.

The Dirty Dozen — This was sort of *The Great Escape* all over again, heaps of top actors and heaps of action.

Zulu — Another sixties epic. This features a really scary scene where for ages before they become visible, you can hear the Zulu army banging their spears on their shields. I could never work out why the British army in Africa wore red jackets, it made them stick out like dog's balls.

Goldfinger — Not the first Bond film, but the one I liked best. Connery, gadgets and girls. What more could a lad ask for?

The Sundowners — This was something of a novelty, because it was a *big* movie, and it was set in Australia. The stars were all from elsewhere but Chips Rafferty was in it, as he needed to be because he was the only Australian actor I'd ever heard of. Chips was a dreadful actor.

Mutiny on the Bounty — Tall ships and trouble and strife. A bit of overacting, but who cared?

A Man for All Seasons — This was really something for the parents, with Paul Scofield leading a cast of really classy actors in his role as Sir Thomas More.

Psycho — The shower scene was reason enough to see this.

Guess Who's Coming to Dinner — Towards the end of their careers, Hepburn and Tracy still had what it took, and the racial element with Sidney Poitier was a controversial twist.

To Sir with Love — A movie which appealed to adults *and* kids. Lulu, who had a hit with the theme song, was surprisingly good as the schoolgirl, Babs. And Judy Geeson was also very serious perv material for schoolboys everywhere.

The Trouble with Angels — As schoolgirl Mary Clancy, Hayley Mills is always coming up with 'the most scathingly brilliant ideas'. Rosalind Russell was terrific as Mother Superior.

MY WORST 10 FLICKS

When it comes to a list of the worst movies of the sixties, it's a case of where to begin? Many of the Hammer Horrors could easily feature, but leaving those aside, the Top (if that's the word) 10 worst movies, again in no particular order, might be:

Santa Claus Conquers the Martians — The title pretty much says all that has to be said about this gem.

One Million Years BC — Okay, so it did have Raquel Welch running around in next to nothing, but there was not a single other redeeming feature.

Captain Nemo and the Underwater City — Normally the B-grade Captain Nemo stories were bearable, but with this one they tried too hard to make it something it wasn't — a serious underwater adventure.

The Earth Dies Screaming — 'nuff said!

Beach Blanket Bingo — Or any other movie with beach in its title.

Any Japanese horror or science fiction movie — These were

all indescribably bad, with appalling special effects. The Japanese moviegoers loved them.

Carry On Screaming — Although many of the *Carry On* movies could slot nicely into this category, some of them were actually funny, at least they were in the sixties.

Barbarella — Again, almost saved by a semi-naked Jane Fonda, but deserving to feature here because it inspired the Austin Powers movies.

The Beach Girls and the Monster — For having both 'beach' and 'monster' in the title.

Cleopatra — So it cost a fortune. It was turgid, the original release ran for four hours and three minutes — Rome wasn't built in a day, but this movie seemed to take a day to see.

EPILOGUE AND CLOSE

BORN TO RUN, BABE

The sixties provided the world with a wide variety of new arrivals, many of whom have gone on to leave an indelible mark, some good, others not so good, and yet others downright dreadful. Among those who arrived during the decade were:

Michael Stipe (Muso, REM)
Nigella Lawson (Delectable British foodie)
Michael Hutchence (Ill-fated lead singer, INXS)
Nastassja Kinski (Actress)
Prince Andrew (Served in the Falklands war, married
        Fergie and that's about the extent of it)
Ivan Lendl (Tennis champ)
Adam Clayton (Muso, U2)
Ayrton Senna (Brazilian racing champion, killed on the
        track)
Hugo Weaving (Australian actor)
Roger Taylor (Muso, Duran Duran)
Bono (Modest lead singer of U2)
Yannick Noah (Dreadlocked tennis champ)
Mick Hucknall (Once dreadlocked muso, Simply Red)
Jeffrey Dahmer (Serial killer with cannibalistic tendencies)
David Duchovny (Actor, *The X Files*)
Antonio Banderas (Latin hunk, acts occasionally)

Hugh Grant (Pommy hunk, acts and occasionally loiters a bit)

Daniel Baldwin (Actor with a lot of brothers)

Diego Maradona (Very good soccer player, lacks self-discipline)

John F Kennedy, Jr (Son of President John F Kennedy and Jackie, unfortunately copped the family curse in spades)

Amy Grant (God-bothering pop singer)

Glynis Nunn (Very fit Aussie athlete)

Kenneth Branagh (Serious British actor, silly enough to let Emma Thompson slip through his fingers)

Julia Louis-Dreyfus (Elaine in *Seinfeld*)

Henry Rollins (Very intense rocker)

Camryn Manheim (Very intense and substantial actress)

Fabio (Model and cover boy for a billion 'bodice rippers')

Eddie Murphy (Funny actor)

Joan Chen (Not so funny actress)

George Clooney (Actor, Rosemary's nephew)

Dennis Rodman (Basketball player and sometime actor who is seriously in touch with his feminine side)

Enya (Irish singer and songwriter of unintelligible but pretty songs)

Melissa Etheridge (American singer and songwriter of hard-edged but not particularly pretty songs)

Diana (Princess of Wales, RIP)

Carl Lewis (Very, very fast American)

The Edge (Muso, U2)

Scott Baio (Eternally youthful actor, *Happy Days*, *Joanie Loves Chachi*, etc. etc.)

Heather Locklear (Actress, lots of hair)

k.d. lang (Singer, not much hair)

Meg Ryan (Actress, time to change her hair)

Mariel Hemingway (Actress, related to Ernest)

Ben Johnson (Very fast Canadian, he's no stranger to speed)

Jim Carrey (Very funny Canadian actor, not sure how fast he is)

Clint Black (Country music star, big hat — don't they all?)

Jennifer Jason Leigh (Actress)

AXL Rose (Muso, Guns 'n Roses)

Garth Brooks (Another big-hatted country music star)

Sheryl Crow (Singer)

Lou Diamond Phillips (Actor)

Steve Irwin (Father of the Year who combines it with crocodile feeding)

Jon Bon Jovi (Singer and actor)

Jackie Joyner Kersee (Athlete)

Terence Trent D'Arby (Singer)

Matthew Broderick (Actor)

Rosie O'Donnell (Talk show host, actress, and all-round fine stamp of a girl)

M C Hammer (Rapper who should be hammered)

Emilio Estevez (Actor, one of Martin Sheen's boys)

Ally Sheedy (Actress and weightwatcher)

Paula Abdul (Pint-sized pop star)

Tom Cruise (Actor and ex of Mimi and Nicole.)

Wesley Snipes (Actor)

Rebecca DeMornay (Actress)

Baz Luhrmann (Talented Aussie director)

Melissa Sue Anderson (*Little House on the Prairie*)

Kelly Preston (John Travolta's missus)

Joan Cusack (Actress)

Flea (Muso, Red Hot Chili Peppers)

Evander Holyfield (Boxer)

Courtney Walsh (Cricketer)

Demi Moore (Actress, not to be trusted to babysit post-pubescent boys)

Jodie Foster (Child star who became a grown-up star and award-winning director)

Andrew McCarthy (Actor, can't quite remember which one he is, 'cos he looks like a lot of the others)

Matt Dillon (Actor, I think he looks like Andrew McCarthy and the others)

Tracy Austin (Tennis champion)

Ralph Fiennes (Actor and member of a family too talented for their own good)

Michael Jordan (Very handy on a basketball court)

Seal (Singer)

William Baldwin (Actor, yep, another of the Baldwin mob)

Vijay Singh (Very handy on a golf course)

Vanessa Williams (Singer who was once Miss America)

Quentin Tarantino (Trendy director)

Gary Kasparov (Very handy at a chess board)

Jet Li (Actor, very handy on the set on any martial arts film)

Natasha Richardson (Actress, one of the Redgrave dynasty)

Mike Myers (Austin Powers, Yeahh Baby)

Johnny Depp (Actor, seriously cool despite some seriously dodgy roles)

George Michael (Singer and occasional Cottager)

Phoebe Cates (Actress)

Lisa Kudrow (Actress and Friend)

John Stamos (Actor and occasional drummer with the Beach Boys)

Natalie Merchant (Singer-songwriter)

Benjamin Bratt (Actor)

Brad Pitt (Actor, bared his six-pack in *Thelma and Louise*, and the rest, as they say, is history.)

Nicholas Cage (Actor, once married to Lisa Marie Presley)

Lisa Marie Presley (Singer, once married to Nicholas Cage, *and* Michael Jackson, but we don't want to talk about that)

Bridget Fonda (Actress, one of Henry's grandies)

Juliette Binoche (An actress as tasty as the pastries her surname sounds like)

Prince Edward (Prince and maker of some fairly ordinary documentaries about his relatives)

Rob Lowe (Actor who rescued his career after starring in a quite remarkable home movie)

Irene Cara (Singer, 'Fame', 'I'm gonna live forever')

Elle McPherson (Supermodel, 'The Body', Mimi's sister)

Tracy Chapman (Singer-Songwriter-Anthropologist, show-off)

Russell Crowe (Actor-party animal-musician?-dad-Academy Award-winner-born in New Zealand-lives in Australia)

Hank Azaria (Actor, voices *The Simpsons*)

Melissa Gilbert (Actress, Laura Ingalls, *Little House on the Prairie*)

Lenny Kravitz (Rocker, serious dreadlocks)

Jeff Fenech (Aussie Boxer, 'I luvs yas all')

Wynonna Judd (Singer, The Judds)

Courtney Cox Arquette (Actress)

Sandra Bullock (Actress)

Keanu Reeves (Actor and coolish dude)
Calista Flockhart (Actress and slimmer's pin-up girl)
Eddy Vedder (Singer, Pearl Jam)
Sophie Rhys-Jones (Prince Edward's missus)
Brandon Lee (Actor and martial arts aficionado)
Sarah Jessica Parker (Actress)
Robert Downey Jr (Sometimes troubled actor)
Brooke Shields (Actress famous for being famous)
Mick Doohan (Aussie motorcycle champion)
Elizabeth Hurley (Actress and girlfriend of Hugh Grant
     until he went a kerb too far)
J K Rowling (Writer who sent the whole world 'Potty')
Shania Twain (Seriously sexy country pop artiste)
Moby (Muso — the other Moby, the aquatic variety, was
     born well before the sixties)
Ben Stiller (Actor)
Katarina Witt (Rather clever ice-skater)
Cindy Crawford (Supermodel)
Billy Zane (Actor, the baddy in *Titanic*)
Tone-Loc (Rapper, should be locked up)
Prince Fred of Denmark (Married to Princess Mary of
     Australia)
Edie Brickell (Singer)
John Daly (Large-ish golfer)
Stephen Baldwin (Actor, yep another Baldwin boy)
Janet Jackson (Singer, Michael's sister)
Eric Cantona (Very handy on the soccer field)
Helena Bonham Carter (Actress, appeared in every
     Merchant Ivory production ever made)
Mike Tyson (Boxer and Rhodes Scholar … NOT)
Halle Berry (Actress)
Adam Sandler (Actor and comedian)

Kiefer Sutherland (Actor, Donald's boy)
Sophie Marceau (Actress, the window-dressing in *Braveheart*)
Jeff Buckley (Muso, died far too young)
Dave Matthews (Muso)
Kurt Cobain (Muso, also died too young)
Evan Dando (Muso, Lemonheads)
Matt LeBlanc (Actor and Friend)
Harry Connick Jr. (Actor and extremely cool singer)
Michael Johnson (Very handy on a racetrack)
Julia Roberts (Actress and front-page material for every gossip magazine in the entire universe)
Lisa Bonet (Actress, *The Cosby Show*)
Boris Becker (Tennis Champion, not to be trusted near broom closets)
Anna Nicole Smith (Clearly smarter than she seems, extraordinarily massive hooters)
Sarah McLachlan (Singer with the voice of an angel)
Ed Burns (Actor)
Gary Coleman (Actor, quite severely vertically challenged)
Patsy Kensit (Actress, silly enough to get involved with that awful Liam Gallagher from Oasis)
Lisa Loeb (Singer)
Lucy Lawless (Actress and gay icon)
Celine Dion (Singer and gay icon)
Patricia Arquette (Actress)
Ashley Judd (Actress and Wynonna's sister)
Traci Lords (Actress, porn queen)
Kylie Minogue (The singing budgie)
Eric Bana (Aussie actor and comedian)
Mohammad Atta (Hijacker, terrorist, mass murderer and all round nice guy)

Will Smith (Rapper, with the redeeming feature he can act)

James Caviezel (Actor who copped a very grim time playing the lead role in Mel Gibson's *The Passion of the Christ*)

Tony Braxton (Singer)

Hugh Jackman (Actor and 'Boy From Oz')

Michael Schumacher (Over-achieving racing car driver)

Marilyn Manson (Thing)

Bobby Brown (Singer and naughty husband of Whitney Houston)

Jennifer Aniston (Actress and Friend)

Renee Zellweger (Actress and Bridget Jones)

Cate Blanchett (Top Australian actress)

Steffi Graf (Very handy on the tennis court)

Edward Norton (Actor, Ted to his friends)

Christian Slater (Actor, Chris to his friends)

Matthew Perry (Actor, Matt to his Friends)

Dweezil Zappa (Muso and son of Frank — Dweez to his friends)

Shane Warne (Very handy on a cricket field, not so handy near a mobile phone or a packet of Nicorettes)

Hansie Cronje (Disgraced South African cricketer, RIP)

Catherine Zeta-Jones (Actress and Michael Douglas's handbag)

Ernie Els (Golfer)

Trey Parker (Part of the *South Park* brains trust and 'out there' dude)

Matthew McConaughey (Actor)

THE DEARLY DEPARTING

Although the sixties saw the arrival of so many remarkable and variously talented people, they also marked the dead end for some of the great names of our time, even some of the greatest names in history. Among others, the decade saw the following go through the check out:

Neville Shute (Writer, *On the Beach*, *A Town Like Alice*, *The Far Country*)

Tunku Abdul Rahman (Malaysian leader)

Mack Sennett (Pioneer movie producer and director)

Dashiell Hammett (Writer, *The Maltese Falcon*, *The Thin Man*)

Patrice Lumumba (Prime minister of the Congo)

Gary Cooper (Actor and Hollywood legend)

Dag Hammerskjold (Secretary-General of the United Nations)

Chico Marx (Actor, comedian, one of the Marx Brothers)

Earl Paige (Eleventh prime minister of Australia)

Adolf Eichmann (Nazi, executed for war crimes committed during the Second World War)

Lucky Luciano (Notorious American gangster)

William Faulkner (Writer, *Requiem for a Nun*, *The Reivers*, *Sound and the Fury*).

Marilyn Monroe (Actress and Hollywood legend)

Herman Hesse (Writer, *Steppenwolf*)

Eleanor Roosevelt (Former first lady of the United States)

Queen Wilhelmina (Of the Netherlands)

Charles Laughton (Actor, director and Hollywood legend)

Frances Poulenc (Composer)

Sylvia Plath (Poet/Writer, *The Bell Jar*)

Patsy Cline (Singer and country music legend, 'I Fall to Pieces', 'Crazy', 'Sweet Dreams')

Pope John XXIII

Edith Piaf (Singer and massive French star, 'Milord', 'La Vie En Rose', Je ne Regrette Rien')

Jean Cocteau (Writer, *Indiscretions*, *The Difficulty of Being*)

Diem (President of South Vietnam)

John F Kennedy (Thirty-fifth president of the United States)

Aldous Huxley (Writer, *Brave New World*)

C S Lewis (Writer, *The Lion, the Witch and the Wardrobe*)

Alan Ladd (Actor and Hollywood legend)

Peter Lorre (Actor)

Douglas MacArthur (Former US general)

Nancy Astor (British parliamentarian)

Nehru (Indian leader)

Harpo Marx (Another of the Marx Brothers)

Cole Porter (Songwriting genius, 'I Get a Kick out of You', 'Begin the Beguine', 'I've Got You under My Skin', 'Night and Day', and hundreds of others.)

Herbert Hoover (Thirty-first president of the United States)

T S Eliot (Poet)

Jeanette MacDonald (Actress and singer)

Alan Freed (Disc jockey who coined the term 'rock-and-roll')

Winston Churchill (British prime minister)

Nat King Cole (Singer)

Malcolm X (American black activist)

Stan Laurel (Actor and comedian, Laurel and Hardy)

King Farouk (Of Egypt)

Buster Keaton (American silent movie star)

Hedda Hopper (Hollywood gossip columnist, famous for her incredible collection of hats)

Billy Rose (Bandleader, 'The Stripper')

Maxfield Parrish (Artist)

C S Forester (Writer, *The African Queen*, the 'Hornblower' series)

Battista Pininfarina (Car designer responsible for the design of many beautiful vehicles, and unfortunately, the Austin 1800)

Evelyn Waugh (Writer, *Sword of Honour*, *Brideshead Revisited*)

Montgomery Clift (Actor)

Nendrik Verwoerd (Prime minister of South Africa)

Elizabeth Arden (Beautician)

Walt Disney (cartoonist and Hollywood legend)

Jack Ruby (The bloke who 'offed' Lee Harvey Oswald)

Donald Campbell (Very fast car and boat driver, who went a little too fast on Coniston Water in the Lake District of northern England)

Edward White, Gus Grissom and Roger Chaffee (Astronauts who died in a flash fire on board *Apollo 1* on the launch pad at the Kennedy Space Centre)

J Robert Oppenheimer (Scientist, leader of the 'Manhattan' atomic bomb project)

Nelson Eddy (Actor and singer)

Konrad Adenauer (German Chancellor)

Vivien Leigh (Actress)

John Coltrane (Jazz muso)
Joe Orton (Playwright)
Stanley Bruce (Eighth prime minister of Australia)
Brian Epstein (Beatles manager)
Woodie Guthrie (Muso and Arlo's dad, 'This Land is Your Land')
Clement Attlee (British Prime Minister)
Che Guevara (Revolutionary commo)
Pu Yi (Last Emperor of China)
Otis Redding (Muso, 'Sittin' on the Dock of the Bay')
Harold Holt (Seventeenth prime minister of Australia)
Paul Whiteman (Bandleader)
Frankie Lymon (Singer, 'Why Do Fools Fall in Love')
Yuri Gagarin (Cosmonaut, first man in space)
Dr Martin Luther King Jnr. (Black civil rights activist and minister)
Helen Keller (Deaf and blind woman who had an extraordinary career)
Robert F Kennedy (Brother of JFK, and another to fall victim to the Kennedy curse when he was gunned down in a hotel in Los Angeles)
Tallulah Bankhead (Actress and Hollywood legend)
John Steinbeck (Writer, *The Grapes of Wrath*, *East of Eden*, *Cannery Row*, *Of Mice and Men*)
Dwight D Eisenhower (Thirty-fourth president of the United States)
Mary Jo Kopechne (That old Kennedy curse again)
Sharon Tate (Actress and victim of the Manson mob)
Rocky Marciano (Boxer)
Judy Garland (Dorothy from Kansas, Liza's mum)
Ho Chi Minh (North Vietnamese president)
Sonja Henie (Ice-skater and actress)

Jack Kerouac (Writer, *On the Road*)
Princess Alice (Phil the Greek's mum)
Maude Matilda Harrap (The author's grandmother)

ROLLING INTO THE WORLD
Memoirs of a Ratbag Child

Eoin Cameron

Eoin Cameron has written a completely natural and highly readable book ... what keeps the reader interested is the sheer ratbaggery of this heathen altar boy and his nine siblings ... this means tiger snakes, experiments with ether and the boys' deliberate attempt to electrocute and kill their father. All washed down with lashings of rainbow cake and Passiona. But not even a guardian angel on penalty rates can save Eoin as the Marist Brothers enter [his] story. Chapter 12 is titled, simply, 'Bastards in Black'. Yet one of the most joyous images provided by Cameron is that of his teacher, the Josephite nun Sister Andrina Foreman, dancing the tarantella to illustrate Hilaire Belloc's poem.

Kathy Hunt, *The Bulletin*

ISBN 1920731067

First published 2004 by
FREMANTLE ARTS CENTRE PRESS
25 Quarry Street, Fremantle
(PO Box 158, North Fremantle 6159)
Western Australia.
www.facp.iinet.net.au

Consultant Editor Ray Coffey
Production Vanessa Bradley
Cover and logo design Caitlin Moffatt
Printed by Griffin Press.

National Library of Australia
Cataloguing-in-publication data

Cameron, Eoin, 1951- .
The sixties : an irreverent guide.

ISBN 1 920731 52 0.

1. Nineteen sixties. 2. Popular culture - History - 20th century.
3. Counterculture - History - 20th century.
4. Civilization, Modern - 20th century. I. Title.

909.826